Will Cuppy, American Satirist

Will Cuppy, American Satirist

A Biography

WES D. GEHRING

Foreword by Mark H. Massé

McFarland & Company, Inc., Publishers
Jefferson, North Carolina, and London

ALSO BY WES D. GEHRING AND FROM MCFARLAND:
Forties Film Funnymen: The Decade's Great Comedians at Work in the Shadow of War (2010); *Film Clowns of the Depression: Twelve Defining Comic Performances* (2007); *Joe E. Brown: Film Comedian and Baseball Buffoon* (2006); *Mr. Deeds Goes to Yankee Stadium: Baseball Films in the Capra Tradition* (2004)

All photographs are from the author's collection.

LIBRARY OF CONGRESS CATALOGUING-IN-PUBLICATION DATA

Gehring, Wes D.
    Will Cuppy, American satirist : a biography / Wes D. Gehring ; foreword by Mark H. Mass.
       p.   cm.
    Includes bibliographical references and index.

    ISBN 978-0-7864-6961-1
    softcover : acid free paper ∞

    1. Cuppy, Will, 1884–1949. 2. Authors, American—20th century—Biography. 3. Critics—United States—Biography. 4. Humorists, American—20th century—Biography. I. Title.

PS3505.U47Z68 2013   818'.5209—dc23   [B]   2013032002

BRITISH LIBRARY CATALOGUING DATA ARE AVAILABLE

© 2013 Wes D. Gehring. All rights reserved

No part of this book may be reproduced or transmitted in any form or by any means, electronic or mechanical, including photocopying or recording, or by any information storage and retrieval system, without permission in writing from the publisher.

Front cover: "Will Cuppy and Friends"—a publicity photograph for *How to Tell Your Friends from the Apes*, 1931 (author's collection)

Manufactured in the United States of America

McFarland & Company, Inc., Publishers
  Box 611, Jefferson, North Carolina 28640
    www.mcfarlandpub.com

For my grandson,
Michael David Long

Table of Contents

Foreword by Mark H. Massé	1
Preface and Acknowledgments	5
ONE: Hoosier Childhood, 1884–1902	9
TWO: University of Chicago Years, 1902–1914	23
THREE: A Wannabe Playwright and His Humor Mentor: Isabel Paterson	38
FOUR: Writing *How to Be a Hermit*	53
FIVE: Early Greenwich Village Years, Groucho Marx, and *How to Tell Your Friends from the Apes*	75
SIX: Easing Into the 1930s, and Two More Important Friendships	89
SEVEN: Cuppy's Multifaceted 1930s	103
EIGHT: Here Come Cuppy's Mystery Anthologies of the 1940s	123
NINE: The Years Leading to Suicide—Literally, *How to Become Extinct*, and Still *Attract the Wombat*	140
TEN: Enhancing a Legacy by Way of Posthumous Publications	158
Afterword: Comparing Cuppy to Some of His Comic Contemporaries	174
Chapter Notes	185
Bibliography	198
Index	211

Foreword by Mark Massé

> The paradox of writing a biography is that your subject becomes an almost friend ... and yet there remains a sense of an enigma.
> — Wes D. Gehring

Who was Will Cuppy and why should today's readers care about him? Film scholar and biographer Wes Gehring is quick to explain that Cuppy was a prolific author and humorist in the first half of the 20th century. Gehring notes that Cuppy had a distinctive satirical, darkly comedic writing style that mirrored better-known contemporaries Robert Benchley and Groucho Marx.

Although Cuppy is largely forgotten in today's frenetic pop culture, 61-year-old Gehring considers him a kindred spirit. He says writing this book about a reclusive, curmudgeonly Midwestern writer connected with him. He identifies with Cuppy's writer's work ethic, erudite insights and sarcastic view of human nature. Wes feels that "while the typical individual is so unfocused s/he is practically blurry, Cuppy remained productively driven ... though ultimately at a great cost."

"This subject sucked me in," says Gehring, author of more than 30 texts on noted American comedic talents, including Charlie Chaplin, W. C. Fields, the Marx Brothers, Laurel & Hardy, Joe E. Brown and Red Skelton. Gehring has also written books on such film legends as James Dean, Steve McQueen and Robert Wise. Since 1978, Wes Gehring, an Iowa native, has been a professor of film in the telecommunications department at Ball State University (Muncie, Indiana).

As associate mass media editor of *USA Today Magazine*, for which he also writes the column "Reel World," Gehring punningly described Will Cuppy in a 2011 feature article as a "Cuppy-ful of Laughter — and Sorrow," a title meant to suggest the dark side which has haunted so many humorists.

Cuppy, born in Auburn, Indiana, wrote numerous short witty essays, thousands of book reviews, and several darkly comic books that skewered the failings and fallacies of modern mankind: *How to Be a Hermit* (1929), *How to Tell Your Friends from the Apes* (1931), *How to Become Extinct* (1941), *How to Attract the Wombat* (1949), *The Decline and Fall of Practically Everybody* (1950) and *How to Get from January to December* (1951). While selling his work to high-profile venues, such as *The New Yorker* and *Saturday Evening Post*, Cuppy also edited several popular mystery anthologies.

The versatile Cuppy prided himself on his meticulous, fact-based research. He earned a bachelor's degree in philosophy from the University of Chicago and then spent seven years taking numerous graduate courses, eventually earning a master's degree in English. According to Wes Gehring, "He would often read two dozen scholarly books and assorted articles in order to write a single one-thousand word essay." Similarly, Gehring, approaches his book topics with dedicated scholarship. For his work on Cuppy, Gehring was immersed in months of archival research involving several special collection libraries, starting with the University of Chicago—the home of Cuppy's private papers.

Sadly, Cuppy's dark musing on humanity, though imbued with humor, reflected a depressive streak and hopeless worldview that foreshadowed his eventual suicide by sleeping pills at age 65. A lifelong recluse who sought a hermetic existence for years on Jones Beach, just off the coast of Long Island, and later, an obscure Greenwich Village apartment, Gehring says that Cuppy was plagued by a series of ailments, lingering health issues and a "tortured psyche."

While admiring Cuppy and identifying with his "loner writer's mentality" and cynical view of the absurdity of human nature, Gehring is quick to point out his own happy childhood in the 1950s and current contented family life as a new grandfather. However, he emphasizes that Cuppy's views are even more relevant in our information-overloaded, attention-challenged, social media-driven 21st century, where people still spend so much time on inane activities like trivia texting and Facebooking about mundane, meaningless topics.

"We were a much more literate society in the 1930s and 1940s," Gehring says, noting how he first discovered Will Cuppy's writings in a used bookstore as a 12-year-old Iowan. Gehring, who was one of "those kids who loved watching old black and white movies," was raised on a steady comedic diet, spurred on by his grandfathers and father, who especially enjoyed such performers as W. C. Fields, Laurel & Hardy and the Marx Brothers. Where does Cuppy belong in such a pantheon of great comic talents?

In the end, Wes Gehring states: "Cuppy's humor merges the biting cynicism of the Marx Brothers and W. C. Fields with the everyday Everyman frustrations of Laurel & Hardy. However, like much 'literature,' especially satire, many of the stories and the storytellers are about figures tap-dancing at the edge of the abyss. Cuppy held on for as long as he could."

Mark H. Massé (www.markmasse.com) *is a professor of literary journalism at Ball State University. A freelancer for 35 years, Massé has published two books of narrative nonfiction,* Trauma Journalism: On Deadline in Harm's Way *and* Inspired to Serve: Today's Faith Activists, *and the novel* Delamore's Dreams.

Preface and Acknowledgments

[Alexander the Great was often] extremely brutal to his captives, whom he sold into slavery, tortured to death, or forced to learn Greek.
— Will Cuppy footnote from *The Decline and Fall of Practically Everybody* (1950)[1]

As a child growing up in Marion, Iowa, I would sometimes bicycle to the neighboring larger city of Cedar Rapids in order to take in a first-run feature film in one of the old majestic downtown movie palaces then still in existence. However, no such adventure was complete without visiting a Catholic mission thrift shop near my favorite theatre, the Paramount. Though I would usually gift my mother with some small piece of crockery which caught my eye, the shop's real attraction for me was its used book section. There is nothing like the intoxicating smell of old book bindings and a pinch of dust — with all those bound-up voices waiting to be freed by simply opening their pages. On one such outing I came across three Will Cuppy books, *How to Become a Hermit* (1929), *How to Become Extinct* (1941), and *The Decline and Fall of Practically Everybody* (1950). I was immediately hooked. The time was the early 1960s, and I was no more than 12. I was captivated by both Cuppy's anthropomorphic satire, and his head-on derailing of historic figures. While I already had a budding fascination with all facets of history, Cuppy's iconoclastic quasi-scholarly dark comedy, complete with sarcastic footnotes, were an inspired revelation. I had soon read all things Cuppy, as well as the works of arguably his greatest later disciple, Richard Armour, including the latter's breezy skewering of literature and academia, *The Classics Reclassified* (1960). Yet, I would later recognize his "voice" in the writings of special cynics like Oscar Levant (especially *The Unimportance of Being Oscar*, 1968), Charles

Bukowski's *Ham on Rye* (1982), and my favorite Jim Knipfel text, *Quitting the Nairobi Trio* (2000).

While my future writing career would assume a more traditional approach to scholarship, with a definite focus on film comedy, Cuppy's work was never far from my mind, be it penning a biography of his favorite humorist, Robert Benchley (*"Mr. B" Or Comforting Thoughts About the Bison*, 1992), or trying my own hand at satire with *Film Classics Reclassified: A Shocking Spoof of Cinema* (2001).[2] Obviously, the gestation period for the book in hand was long. Yet, a key catalyst occurred while researching the biography of another Hoosier—film director Robert Wise.[3] While sifting through the archives at the University of Southern California (USC), I asked directions to the university's Warner Bros. holdings. Located just off campus, within easy walking distance, the reference librarian told me to exit the main gate of the walled downtown Los Angeles university and go to Hope Street. The large warehouse-like structure would be just to the right. However, what struck me by his directions were their inadvertently poetic darkness—"It's just beyond Hope." Appropriately, it was an apt axiom for the early horror/film noir genre beginnings of Wise's directing career, which paralleled the end of Cuppy's life. Yet, at the time it struck me as an equally fitting description of Cuppy's oeuvre, especially since I had brought along my well-worn copy of the humorist's *How to Tell Your Friends from the Apes* (1931) to reread on the flight to L.A.

Surprisingly, or maybe not so surprisingly, once I started writing the Cuppy biography, the words came more easily than any of the many other books I have authored. At the risk of sounding like a cliché (which life essentially is), I felt like I was channeling Cuppy's neglected story. Though I have profiled many prominent personages, a great number of my biographies have also been inspired by the attempt to shine a light upon a new slighted subject. Cuppy is such a figure. George Orwell was fond of saying that there was a degree of ego in all writing—the glory of seeing one's name on the binding of a book. While I would never debate that view, I would posit that, for many biographers such as myself, profiling is also about salvaging a largely forgotten figure. Erich Segal caught a sense of both perspectives (salvaging and the egotistical self) when he wrote, "What lies beneath that fear [of death] is the terror of insignificance. Of not being remembered, not counting."[4] So, one might say, this book is for Cuppy ... and myself.

Providentially, during the writing of this text I viewed Joseph Cedar's Academy Award nominee for Best Foreign Film, *Footnote* (2011, Israel). The story chronicles the rivalry between a father and a son who are both eccentrically dedicated professors. The elder is a neglected traditionalist, while his son is a pop-culture success. The father's one claim to fame, or at least a modest recognition, is being acknowledged in a footnote of another scholar's book, whose breakthrough revelations should have belonged to the older man. The film's title, *Footnote*, is a bittersweet, darkly funny satire of all the significance/insignificance to be found in one of academe's signature symbols.

How does this apply to Cuppy? The humorist had a love/hate relationship with the scholarly life, having spent years in graduate school at the University of Chicago. His brief, brilliantly comic essays are each anchored in copious research, which he then relishes in turning/twisting into treatises of topsyturvydom. Moreover, the jewels of Cuppy's satirical sabotaging of scholarship are to be found in his comic footnotes, such as the one which opens this preface—almost heckling the reader.

Besides the hauntingly chance comment, "It's just beyond Hope," which helped lead to this work, some preliminary Cuppy research seemed to suggest I was meant to tackle the biography. That is, my usually movie-related subjects necessitate research starting points at New York City's Performing Arts Library at Lincoln Center, and the Motion Picture Academy of Arts and Sciences in Beverly Hills, California. However, most of the archives for Hoosier-born Cuppy were in my own Middle-American backyard, including my University of Iowa (Iowa City, Iowa) alma mater, and the nearby Herbert Hoover Presidential Library (West Branch, Iowa). Sometimes life presents us with signs.

Interestingly, the closest such archive, the Lilly Library at Indiana University (Bloomington, Indiana), though having minimal Cuppy material (two letters), provided a rare slant upon comedy by the humorist, with an even more entertaining back story. As this biography will document, Cuppy was not into defining humor. Yet, when he once let down his guard for Max Eastman's study, *Enjoyment of Laughter* (1936), Cuppy's definition was bungled into something approaching nonsense.[5] However, it was the catalyst for an inspired letter to Eastman, in which we get a more viscerally clear reading on the subject. Cuppy said, in part;

> [My entry] doesn't make sense.... I [really] said something about if these half-witted serious writers [naming names, probably] ever had any feelings as strong as those which impel humorists to their [wise] cracks, the feelings would blow them to pieces.... I think humor springs from rage, hay fever, overdue rent and miscellaneous hell.[6]

Given that Cuppy was an often angry, hay fever suffering, financially strapped, devout believer in hell on earth, this is probably one of the most heartfelt (or is that *hate*felt?) takes on the subject ever recorded. Cuppy's passionate devotion to getting it right has only encouraged me all the more to honor the old axiom of the profiler — to get "the best truth possible."

Given that goal, as with all creative endeavors, no matter how great the individual dedication, numerous others help make the project possible. At the University of Chicago, which houses the Will Cuppy Papers, I would especially like to thank the Special Collections staff: Barbara Gilbert (Reading Room Coordinator), Julia Gardner (Head of Reader Services), Rena Schergon (Administrative and Reader Services Assistant), and Christine Colbert (Copying Services).

At the Herbert Hoover Presidential Library (West Branch, Iowa), Spencer Howard (Archives Technician) was tireless in his assistance and advice. At the nearby University of Iowa (Iowa City, Iowa), the main library's special collection guru Denise Anderson always went the extra mile. Cornell University's (Ithaca, New York) special collections staff member Jude T. Corina was more than helpful. At Indiana University's (Bloomington, Indiana) Lilly Library, reference staffer Rebecca Bauman greatly assisted me in my Cuppy research.

Closer to home, Ball State University's interlibrary loan staff— Sandy Duncan, Kerri McClellan, Lisa Johnson, Elain Nelson, and Karin Kwiatkowski — managed to track down my every research request. Darey Davidson, of the William H. Willenar Genealogy Center (Auburn, Indiana), assisted me in uncovering more about Cuppy's siblings. Research librarian Ray Ranier, from the Peabody Public Library (Columbia City, Indiana), was also helpful along these lines. Whitley librarian Joyce Hite (Genealogy Society of the South Whitley Cleveland Township Public Library, Whitley, Indiana) was always available for an assortment of Cuppy-related questions.

Will Cuppy scholars Tom Maeder and Robert Michael Walter were like foundation rocks in the construction of this text. Mike was especially there for me whenever I had a Cuppy puzzle to figure out. As with all of my books, Janet Warner supplied valuable editorial help, while Kris Scott was responsible for the computer preparation of the manuscript. BSU colleague Chris Flook was especially helpful with all of my technology questions. And my TCOM department chair, Tim Pollard, was most generous with his support and with facilitating travel funds for my research.

Finally, however, the intellectual energy level necessary to sustain a project of this scope begins with the love and support of my family and friends.

ONE

Hoosier Childhood, 1884–1902

"On Edward R. Murrow's normally serious CBS news program *See It Now*, host Murrow and a colleague read in turns from [Will Cuppy's 1950 bestseller] *The Decline and Fall of Practically Everybody* until the announcer cracked up." — From *Murrow: His Life and Times*, 1986[1]

Back in the golden age of humor books (from the late 1920s until the early 1950s), when pantheon wits like Robert Benchley, James Thurber, and S.J. Perelman were producing their signature works, there was another singular satirist who more than held his own with such fast company. His name was Will Cuppy (1884–1949), and his métier was dark comedy, which flirted with nihilism. His agenda is baldly stated in such classic Cuppy book titles as *How to Be a Hermit* (1929), *How to Tell Your Friends from the Apes* (1931), and *The Decline and Fall of Practically Everybody* (1950).

Though Cuppy was born and reared in Auburn, Indiana, his Hoosier legacy was tied to South Whitley, Indiana, where young Cuppy's widowed paternal grandmother Sarah Collins Cuppy (1813–1900) had a farm. That is, since he often satirized human behavior under the guise of natural history, he later confessed, "[It was on my grandmother's farm] where I acquired my first knowledge of the birds and flowers and all the other aspects of animate nature which I treated none too kindly in some of my writings."[2]

Yet Cuppy's shish kabobbing of humanity was often the subtext of these flora and fauna "studies," and is best summarized by the title of his aforementioned text, *How to Tell Your Friends from the Apes*. In the words of contemporary *New Yorker* critic Anthony Lane:

> Speaking as someone chained to the past — or to an imaginary version, if the one proves unavailable — I tend to inquire, when grading current humorists, not "How good are they?" but "How bright would their gleam have been measured against a past great?"[3]

Cuppy remains a neglected gold standard of laughter, whose black humor becomes more timely with each passing day. Moreover, with the possible exception of Benchley, no other American humorist was more gifted in the inspired christening of his books, with my personal favorite being *How to Attract the Wombat*.

His short comic essays, ranging from natural history to the history of man, would involve massive amounts of research. A visit to the "Will Cuppy Papers" at the University of Chicago reveals that the humorist would fill hundreds of note cards for a single essay of no more than 1,000 words. Thus, there is frequently a dry, darkly comic professorial air to his satire. For instance, in an essay from his *Apes* book, Cuppy writes, "Young normal Tigers do not eat people. If eaten by a Tiger you may rest assured that he was abnormal. Once in a while a normal Tiger will eat somebody, but he doesn't mean anything by it."[4]

Though his paternal grandmother's farm produced a love of nature which provided the perfect cover for his satire of the follies of mankind, he purposely kept this biting veneer razor thin. For instance, in an essay from *How to Become Extinct*, Cuppy does little to disguise his inspired contempt for Hoosier provincialism:

> Even as a child back in Indiana, whenever I took a Butterbelly off the hook I used to ask myself, "Does this fish think?" I would even ask others, "Do you suppose this Butterbelly can think?" And all I would get in reply was a look. At the age of eighteen, I left the state.[5]

Or, in another short piece from the same text and time, Cuppy's satirical digs are fairly obvious: "The fish people are pretty well agreed that animals cannot hear unless they have large, flopping outside ears like Elephants and the hired man on my grand-mother's farm. I wonder!"[6]

Ironically, the fact that even many Cuppy fans missed his veiled anthropomorphic use of animals merely underlined why he was a satirist: The human species definitely needed some remedial classes. Cuppy boldly addressed the subject in his biting preface to the posthumously published *Wombat* book. With comic angst, he revealed the question so often asked by his audience:

> "Why don't you write about people, Will?" They always [ask]. They have through the years.... To give you an idea, the first friend I met on the street after writing that book on Apes...shouted from afar, "Why

One. Hoosier Childhood, 1884–1902

don't you write about people, Will?" This surprised me the more since I had used that very lady as the model for my article on the chimp in that volume.[7]

Cuppy's smart-aleck heckling of history and/or authority is reminiscent of his contemporary Groucho Marx (1890–1977), particularly in the Marx Brothers' academic satire *Horse Feathers* (1932), in which the greaspaint-mustachioed brother is president of Huxley College. Of course, one might as well call Groucho Cuppy-like, because the print humorist had the same cutting wit from his earliest work. My favorite such Cuppy crack, which could have doubled as dialogue for Groucho, comes from the Hoosier humorist's preface to his *Apes* text:

> I grant you there are plenty of old-fashioned and pretty ineffective ways to tell one's friends from the Apes. What could be simpler, for instance, when you are at the zoo? The Apes are in cages. Yes, but when you are *not* at the zoo, what then?[8]

Prof. Quincy Adams Wagstaff (Groucho Marz, right) checking out one subject (anatomy) in *Horse Feathers* (1932), about which he might have some interest. A professor (Robert Greig, left) looks on warily.

Though it took a while, period critics eventually made the Cuppy-Groucho link, too. A decade after, in 1941, the aforementioned quote appeared, the *New York Times*'s review of the humorist's *How to Become Extinct* finally made the comparison. The catalyst was a Cuppy footnote chronicling how herpetologists had recently decided that the boa constrictor should have a new name. The humorist's response: "I have decided that it should not. Two can play at that game"— had the *Times* reviewer observing, "Somehow the judicious reader is apt to hear the tone of Groucho Marx in a statement like that."[9]

There is no easy formula for the making of a satirist. In Groucho's case, one might start along Freudian lines, with a domineering mother who clearly favored two of his other brothers, Chico and Harpo.[10] Unfortunately with Cuppy, his early years are much less documented than that of the Marx Brothers. But if there was one pre-existing Cuppy condition to assist in the nurturing of his darkly comic satire, being born into a somewhat dysfunctional family was undoubtedly a boon. The humorist's alcoholic father, with the all–American sounding name of Thomas Jefferson Cuppy (1844–1912), was the proverbial jack-of-all-trades and master of none. At various times he was a tool salesman, railroad man, grain trader, and lumber merchant. Cuppy scholar Thomas Maeder has ironically observed that even on his son's birth certificate his father was listed as a "traveling man," and that his "miscellaneous jobs took him farther and farther from home until one day he never came back."[11] During Cuppy's youth, the marriage of his parents, Thomas and Frances Stahl Cuppy (1855–1927), seems to have evolved into what was then called a "Victorian divorce." That is, there was no official dissolution of the union during Cuppy's childhood, but the two parties led largely separate lives.

However, the year after the humorist left for college (1903), Thomas and Frances did legally divorce. Cuppy's mother would subsequently marry two more times. Given Frances's strong anti-drinking views, borne of her first husband's alcoholism, the surname of her second spouse, married in 1912 — during the decade prior to Prohibition — had a most ironic ring to it: Benjamin F. Casebeer. He was a widowed farmer from Hicksville, Ohio, which is where they made their home. Sadly, he died only two years later, in 1914. Frances's final union was to the widowed minister John Wesly Lilly, the United Brethren (now the United Methodist) pastor at Hicksville, Ohio.

In Cuppy's voluminous letters to close friend, mentor, and fellow writer Isabel Paterson (1886–1961), he makes few but always comically disparaging remarks about his father. For example, in one undated letter [mid–1920s], he observes:

> Mother writes that things are a little worse, if anything, around [her Ohio] home and wants to know where I would like to be buried. She thinks maybe she'd like to be buried in Auburn, Ind., and maybe I'd like to lie there too with the proud poor Cuppys. No [I responded], the Cuppys are buried at South Whitley, Ind. We had to dig them all up when father sold the farm [family cemeteries were then sometimes maintained on private homesteads] by forging mother's name to the deed or something [and] then decamping Westward and dying of drink.... I really can't decide where to be buried. They don't tend the graves very well at Auburn but South Whitley is such a slow town, too. I yearn for cremation.[12]

(For the record, Cuppy would eventually get his wish about cremation, but the ashes did not find their way to South Whitley. Instead, he was indeed buried next to his mother in Auburn. And while there are no records of how Cuppy's grave site was initially tended, the plot went unmarked for decades.)

The humorist's surviving private papers provide minimal information about his stepfathers. But two passing references to Minister Lilly, in Cuppy's correspondence with Paterson, has the humorist making a comically nightmarish-like link between the pastor and his father. The first Cuppy excerpt is from an undated (1923) letter describing a visit to Hicksville to attend a memorial service following the untimely death, on August 2, 1923, of President Warren G. Harding, who had been born in Ohio. Cuppy's chronicle is relatively straightforward, although only his father has been dead over a decade:

> I suppose I told you all about my wonderful vacation in Ohio. Father delivered the address at the Harding Memorial Services at the Opera House. He staggered up the stair and told us (mother and me and a few of the neighbors) what a shame it was that President McKinley had died [assassinated 1901] and what a good man President McKinley was and so forth.... He had spoken at the McKinley exercise, too, and reverted to form.... Nobody seemed to mind.[13]

One's initial "reading" of this talk might simply be that Cuppy's *step*father was feeble of mind and body, and after a challenging navigation to the pulpit, had slipped into an old benediction for the startling death of yet another Ohio-born president. But in a later undated letter [circa 1924] to Paterson, Cuppy confesses: "It was only a beautiful dream. It was not a McKinley exercise. It was a Harding Memorial service, and father got up and delivered a memorial service on McKinley, the name of [the] current corpse having escaped him"[14] This added revelation does not necessarily negate the fact that a botched benediction was performed by a senile Pastor Lilly. But Cuppy's comments about it being a dream, describing a staggering (drunken?) father, and a McKinley memorial which occurred at a time when the elder Cuppy was still alive, all suggest another darkly comic memory of the humorist's father ... merged with an unflattering take upon stepfather number two.

Given the ongoing less-than-stellar comments about Cuppy's father, his ironic given name of Thomas Jefferson might be a starting point for discussing the humorist's propensity for a black humor-tinged satire of historic figures. As previously noted, Cuppy's biting wit was often channeled through an anthropomorphic cover. But during the last 16 years of Cuppy's life he labored over a history-slashing opus now often considered to be his masterpiece, the posthumously published *Decline and Fall of Practically Everybody*. Before a brief sampling, however, an added dimension of his satire necessitates more Cuppy family history.

Decline frequently couples Cuppy's sideswiping of historic figures with a comically casual take on the huge body counts attached to said personages, wars, coups, and assorted purges. Interestingly, the best times of Cuppy's youth were spent with a grandmother whose life revolved around the carnage of the Civil War. Indeed, the humorist was named for his father's brother, Civil War soldier William H. Cuppy, captain of Company E, in the 44th Regiment of the Indiana Infantry. William later died (July 15, 1862) of wounds he sustained during the Union siege of the Confederate-held Fort Donelson, Tennessee (February 1862). His commanding officer's (Colonel Hugh B. Reed) official report noted, "In the early part of the action Captain Cuppy ... was severely wounded while in advance of his men bravely cheering them on."[15]

While both sides suffered heavy casualties, the Union army ultimately prevailed. But a full reading of Reed's report reveals that the battle subjected Company E to the classic insanity intrinsic to any armed conflict, however just the cause, which has inspired such anti-war works as *Slaughter-House Five* and *Catch-22*. Invariably, these tales of carnage chronicle some Kafkaesque variation of what Reed reported:

> We took our position on the left wing of our brigade, in front of and in range of the enemy's guns. They were invisible to us, while we were exposed to their view. There was part of a regiment of Union troops (Colonel Logan) on the slope of the hill between us and the enemy. Colonel Logan came to our lines and requested we would not fire, as it would endanger his men. I gave the order to the men to withhold their fire. We remained exposed to the enemy's fire for fifteen or twenty minutes without being able to return it or to determine whether our friends were still in danger of our guns.[16]

Captain William's mother, Sarah (Cuppy's grandmother), would have been well aware of these absurdities of war, since she and her daughter

Martha (Mary) immediately traveled to the combat area to nurse her son and other wounded soldiers. Captain William survived for five months, ultimately being sent home to his mother's care in South Whitely, Indiana. After her son's death, Sarah turned their home into a hospital for wounded soldiers without families to nurse them. (Sarah's other son, Thomas — the humorist's father — worked for the Union in some unspecified non-battle zone supply capacity during the Civil War.)

Sarah soon became known as the "Florence Nightingale of Indiana."[17] Civil War veteran Allen Pence was so inspired by the patriotic service of both women that he had a granite memorial erected in their honor at the South Whitley cemetery, where so many Union soldiers lay buried. The inscription on the monument reads: "Sacred to the cherished memory of Sarah Collins Cuppy, wife of Abraham Cuppy, and her daughter Martha, for their sacrifice and unselfish devotion upon the alter [sic] of freedom for the cause of the Union, 1861 to 1865."[18] Though in her fifties after the war, Sarah maintained what was then known as the "Cuppy House" as an ongoing headquarters for a plethora of GAR (Grand Army of the Republic — Union Civil War veterans) meetings/activities. With the young humorist spending summers on his grandmother's farm, he would have been forever surrounded by tales of the Civil War's 600,000 casualties.

History has not recorded Cuppy's take on this backdrop, other than his fascination with nature on Grandma's farm, which may have been his means of escape. Yet, he eventually took no prisoners when it came to historic figures. Though generally granting American figures a pass, he wielded the most sardonically wicked pen against everyone else of note. For instance, of Nero he writes, "Since Nero's character leaves much to be desired, we are apt to forget his good side. We should try to remember that he did not murder his mother until he was twenty-one years old."[19] Moreover, the humorist frequently embraces the callousness of his targets, especially when it involves war. Thus, he reminds readers that under Frederick the Great, half a million "Prussians were killed [in battle] but there were a lot left."[20] Always the professorial type, his invariably fact-based humor was frequently peppered with the most casual asides about the common cruelties of war. For instance, Cuppy's treatise on Alexander the Great documents that the warrior's great opponent Darius:

> had chariots armed with scythes on each side for mowing down his enemies. These did not work out, since Alexander and his soldiers refused to go out and stand in front of the scythes. Darius had overlooked the fact that scythed chariots are effective only against persons who have lost the power of locomotion and that such persons are more likely to be home in bed than fighting battles in Asia.[21]

Neither having a derelict father whose patriotic-sounding name was a joke in itself, nor spending summers in a home which doubled as a Civil War shrine would necessarily give one a cynically blasé sense of history, but it would be a good foundation.

One is, however, on solid ground when documenting Cuppy, who was forever in need of pampering and support. His correspondence with illustrator William Steig bears this out. This neediness began in childhood, and had many causes. First, the humorist was a fair-haired child with allergies, including hay fever (then sometimes referred to as a "rose cold"), an excruciatingly distressful ailment in the pollen-happy rural Midwest, especially during a pre-modern medicine era. Undoubtedly, this contributed to both his grandmother and mother, two already strong-willed women, being protectively controlling about young Cuppy's health. In an undated letter to Paterson (circa August 1924), Cuppy reminisces about summers on the farm:

> Farmhands are really all right, though, I ... was one myself. [Well, as a child I was] a farm finger, mebbe, as I had no appreciable effect upon the crops and grandmother always would run and bring me home if she caught me plowing in the sunlight or otherwise doing anything that might have developed my physique or have given me a sane outlook upon hogs and such. So here I am fair, fat and damn near forty.[22]

Second, the adult Cuppy was a confirmed hypochondriac, again, the tendencies were there early. The humorist admits as much in a letter briefly sketching out his biography to professor/broadcaster/author John Towner Frederick:

> I was out of school a good deal, having what passed for recurrent attacks of appendicitis; I now think that this was merely my way of attracting attention and getting out of work. Nevertheless, to my lasting regret, I was considered bright enough to skip the eighth grade, so that I missed all tutoring in grammar, punctuation, and that sort of thing. As a result, I have always been wobbly in such matters.[23]

The latter portion of the preceeding quote segues to the third facet of Cuppy's personality. Being "bright enough to skip the eighth grade" seemed to foster his need for praise. Paradoxically, while others might have gained great confidence from success, Cuppy seemed ever more antiheroic. This Cuppy bugaboo is best described by journalist and literacy critic Burton Rascoe, a Cuppy friend from their University of Chicago days, and later the humorist's *New York Tribune* (and its successor, the *Herald Tribune*) editor. In Rascoe's 1937 memoir, while praising Cuppy's talent — "one of the wittiest of contemporary writers" — his friend is very candid about an inherent neediness he had always seen in Cuppy, and how Isabel Paterson became his early (1920s) mentor:

> He [Cuppy] always expected me to read his stuff immediately, to chuckle appreciatively, pat him on the back and tell him it was fine. Occasionally I was too rushed to do this. Then (as I learned later) he would go out into the other [*Tribune*] room where Isabel Paterson was and sink into a chair utterly dejected. He would say to her, "Burton doesn't like my reviews any more. I don't think he is going to print any more of them. Is my stuff that bad?" Mrs. Paterson would reassure him, compliment him on his last printed piece, spur him on. The job of encouraging Cuppy got to be too much for me.... [But] by working with Mrs. Paterson might and main to keep going, there was finally evolved the series [of essays] which largely go to make up *How to Be a Hermit*.[24]

As a youngster, Cuppy had received a dual dose of overprotectiveness and praise from his overly matriarchal world — widowed Grandmother Sarah, his mother Frances, who was what then was called a "grass widow" (husband largely gone), older sister Anna (1883–1940), and his aforemen-

Burton Rascoe and Isabel Paterson at an awards dinner (early 1930s).

tioned Aunt Martha (Mary)—Sarah's grown daughter, who remained at "Cuppy House" until Sarah's passing (1900). Since Sarah and Frances had also had a child precede them in death (Cuppy's namesake uncle, and the humorist's younger brother, Jack, [1887–1898]), the protective tendencies of both women were probably ratcheted up all the more.

The humorist's memories of his youth invariably began with Grandma Sarah: "My happiest childhood days were spent at the Cuppy farm ... where my widowed grandmother was the rallying point of G.A.R activities." And he obtained his aforementioned first knowledge of nature.[25] Undoubtedly, the fact that Sarah was a local legend added to her mystique. Her *Columbia City Post* obituary, to which young Cuppy might have contributed, given that small town newspapers traditionally depended upon family authorship, read, in part:

> Mrs. Cuppy was highly esteemed and greatly respected by all who knew her. In the community where she lived for so many years there is but one sentiment and that is, she was a grand and noble woman.[26]

Cuppy was also proud of his mother, whom he often credited with having

> most of the family sense. She was a singer of great talent, and I used to pump the organ while she sang in the choir in the Presbyterian church in Auburn—a circumstance that finally led to my membership in the Guild of Former Pipe Organ Pumpers.[27]

Frances, a former schoolteacher, was a strong-willed seamstress who maintained a small shop next door to the family's Auburn home. As the previous quote suggests, she was very active in her church, and the humorist's memories of his mother and two siblings were usually projected through a comic filter of their church chores. Thus, in a later undated letter (circa, 1929), he shared:

> Well, my [younger] brother Jack and I would pump the organ ... and my sister Anna would play the organ and my mother would sing in the choir and when Anna was gone I would play the organ and Jack would pump and mother would sing and when mother was gone I would sing ... and Anna would play and Jack would pump ... and I would also help carry the potato salad to the socials besides delivering [church] papers.... So one day [my teetotaler] mother made me get up in the choir and sing the alto of: "Water, water, pure and free, water is the drink for me." So I left home.[28]

While Cuppy reveals some affectionate chafing over his mother's controlling nature in this letter, the humorist is also capable of baring her persistently demanding nature, too. In one correspondence from 1924, he complains about her picking at a personal sore spot. At this point, the 40-

year-old Cuppy had yet to establish himself as a writer in New York, a city to which he had moved a decade earlier in order to write an important serious play. Though Cuppy would sporadically work on the project until the end of his life (1949), the play would never be completed. But the situation was already a millstone a quarter-century before his death, and his mother would periodically push his buttons over it. Thus, the humorist wrote:

> Mother wants to know and has for years why I have not finished [my] great drama, seeing that there are twenty-four hours in a day. Passing over the obvious that there aren't twenty-four hours in a day, what does one reply?[29]

As with most mother-child relationships, Cuppy's ties with Frances were complicated. She had been the parent who had been there for him. Sensing his talent, she also tended to encourage and/or push, which probably also explains that skipped grade. This is hardly an unusual phenomenon, and is now often referred to as being a "helicopter parent"—ever hovering about. Being essentially a single mother would only have exacerbated the situation. His correspondence sometimes amusingly kids his mother's focus on music and teetotaling, but it definitely influenced him. For instance, in a letter to John Frederick, he complains about a conflict in his schedule:

> The only catch in all this is that I'll miss the first half hour of the Metropolitan Broadcast.... But then, I know all the operas by heart anyway and maybe I better start trying to learn about books.[30]

But his mother's fostering of music appreciation can also surface as a random addendum in his comic essays. For example, in an inspired piece about the singing fish of California, he asks the reader, "You have often wondered, doubtless, how he does it [sing], and I can't say I blame you. I've wondered myself, and I came out of a musical family."[31] In another comic essay about German composer Karl Maria Friedrich Ernst von Weber, Cuppy deadpans, "He is perhaps best known to us lowbrows for his piano piece, *Invitation to the Dance*, every note of which is but too familiar to anybody whose sister ever took lessons.[32] Still, despite the affectionate kidding about his mother's influence upon him, music would always remain a pivotal part of his life. One gets an entertaining sense of its hold upon the humorist in two works: Isabel Paterson's novel *The Golden Vanity* (1934), and Cuppy's short essay, "Certainly, I Play the Piano" (1943, anthologized in May Lamberton Becker's *The Home Book of Laughter*, 1948). The former text concerns a piano-playing character based upon the satirist. Obviously, the latter piece has Cuppy himself amusingly chronicling his love of music.

Yet, the essay's revealing bombshell is that the boy was pleased Daddy was seldom home. It seems the elder Cuppy disliked music!

And though Cuppy was not above an occasional alcoholic beverage during his adult life, his writing (both private and for publication) also reflects his mother's disapproval of liquor consumption. In another letter from the 1920s, he observes:

> But taking up the matter of gin in a sensible way I should think most people would be very glad to go to a party where they get nothing to drink. We all have just sense enough, or almost, to think of your health once in a while, and personally, as you may know I do not care to drug myself in above manner.[33]

Cuppy reiterates this point in "The Peking Man," from his *Apes* text: "We do not know whether he was religious or promiscuous or both. He did not have love as we understand it because he had no gin."[34] (For the time, gin was a popular target, because it was usually the lowest-priced hard liquor available.)

Maybe, however, the most comically poignant Cuppy correspondence about his relationship to alcohol and Frances connects to the humorist's sense of frugality. This was a trait tied to necessity, since the 1920s found him inhabiting a rundown shack on Jones Island, just off the southern coast of New York's Long Island. During Prohibition, when bootleggers' ships bound for New York with illegal alcohol were threatened to be boarded by federal agents, their contraband cargoes were often tossed into the sea, sometimes to wash up on Jones Island. Now, what is a light drinker to do when liquid fun occasionally appeared with the driftwood? Cuppy confessed in correspondence that

> one of the main reasons for patrolling beach is to find booze.... You see just how low we all are out here. Pray God I do not get this [note] mixed up with the letter I am going to ... [write] to mother later in the evening. She would rather see me in my grave than so much sniff a glass of harder cider.[35]

A more Freudian moment concerning Cuppy's relationship with his mother occurs in a provocative quote he cites in another letter from the period:

> The pleasure that many persons find in the retirement to small islands ... is one of the forms of the "idea of returning to the mother's womb and of resuming there the life enjoyed by the child in the prenatal stages."[36]

But before one keys too much on a mother fixation for Cuppy, a simpler explanation might be offered by Charles Bukowski (1920–1994), another comically iconoclastic writer. In his autobiographical novel, *Ham on Rye*, his protagonist could be describing the forever reclusive Cuppy, who also avoided conventional work/obligations and never married:

> I wanted someplace to hide out, someplace where one didn't have to do anything. The thought of being something didn't only appall me, it sickened me. The thought of being a lawyer or a councilman or an engineer, anything like that, seemed impossible to me. To get married, to have children, to get trapped in the family structure. To go someplace to work every day and to return. It was impossible.[37]

Or, put more succinctly, with another Bukowski quote which also perfectly describes Cuppy, "There would never be a way for me to live comfortably with people."[38] That being said, both men were quite capable of interacting with humanity when necessary. But it was an experience they preferred to avoid.

Interestingly, while Bukowski came out of an abusive childhood, Cuppy had been coddled, even spoiled. But, in each case, strong parental control had been in place. Thus, Bukowski's sense of freedom/escape was later fueled by alcohol abuse. Cuppy simply craved quiet isolation ... with only a periodic surrogate parent type (such as Isabel Paterson) to pat his hand. Cuppy's neediness, however, negated a total break from his mother's purse strings. For instance, Frances's final will (1927) states, "Any unpaid notes which may be in my possession at the time of my death, which are against my son William J. Cuppy, shall become and constitute a part of his share of my estate."[39] In other words, Frances was still loaning her son money in the final years of her life.

Consequently, Cuppy's mother was a multi-faceted ongoing presence well into his forties, and the humorist invariably noted her with pride in any biographical material he provided for publicity use. Besides the strong-willed Frances, and the Hoosier famous Grandmother Sarah, Cuppy did have some creative fun with his ancestry. As a biographer I have found that many subjects embrace almost tall-tale dimensions in retelling their stories. Indeed, in one extreme, the Paul Bunyon nature of the whoppers even impacted my book's title — *Red Skelton: The Mask Behind the Mask*.[40] But Cuppy's exaggerations were refreshingly playful, and when he allowed them to segue to the ludicrous, as was his habit, the humorist made clear that it was *all* a joke. For example, he was fond of pretending to be descended from the ancient French dynasty of the Capets, a term which he felt, fittingly for a humorist, had been corrupted into the funny-sounding name Cuppy. But he would occasionally use this phony French family tree as yet another reason he had never married: "The Capets, noble folks, can't afford to marry anybody but royalty. And royalty is so broke nowadays that I can't even afford that."[41] One is reminded of a similar satirical "family" tendency in a humorist Cuppy greatly admired, Mark Twain (1835–1910). In Twain's *Innocents Abroad* (1869), a humor/travel book about the author's first visit to Europe and the Holy Land, he allegedly wept at the grave of his early ancestor ... Adam. (Surprisingly, given all the watershed texts Twain produced, including *Tom Sawyer* and *Huckleberry Finn, Innocents Abroad* remained the humorist's best-selling book during his lifetime and Cuppy's youth.) Since both men's writing had fun at the expense of French history, Cuppy would probably also have enjoyed a favorite Twain tongue-in-cheek axiom best paraphrased as, "It's un–American, it's unBritish ... it's French."

Like filmmaker Leo McCarey (1898–1969), whose many cinematic accomplishments included teaming and molding Laurel and Hardy, Cuppy also enjoyed periodically sharing antiheroic moments from his youth. While McCarey's favorite boyhood anecdote involved a tumble down an elevator shaft, Cuppy was fond of recalling how, as a child, he had once pulled a goldfish bowl over on his head.[42] This Cuppy antiheroic miscue was only rivaled by his tale of somehow surviving a accidental trip through the spinning and whirring inner workings of a thrashing machine on his grandmother's farm. Certainly, Alice's fall down a rabbit hole had little on the early misadventures of young Cuppy.

Will Cuppy as a young man (circa 1902).

Regardless, by 1902 Cuppy's Indiana cocoon had started to unravel and it was time to find another safe haven. After providing some musical support at his own Auburn High School graduation, the future humorist would establish his next cocoon at the University of Chicago.

TWO

University of Chicago Years, 1902–1914

> "[Sexy coed Edith Ward] owned a smile ... that would soften the heart of a trigonometry professor."—From Will Cuppy's *Maroon Tales: University of Chicago Stories* (1909)[1]

The year 1902 was a good time for Cuppy to leave Auburn, Indiana. His parents' marriage had been over forever, and they would make it official in 1903. His beloved Grandmother Sarah had died in 1900. His little brother Jack had already passed in 1898, after an attack of appendicitis. The humorist's sister Anna, whom he later idealized, would marry in 1902, and soon leave Auburn for Columbia, Indiana. Moreover, Cuppy, the voracious reader, had exhausted the contents of Auburn's public library, which was only a block from his family's home. Of course, he did not have a clue as to what career to follow. But colleges have always doubled as an excuse for a prolonged adolescence.

Throughout Cuppy's adult life he toyed with the antiheroic idea, both in print and private, that there was a "Hate Cuppy Movement." The humorist was a personification of the old gag definition of a paranoid agnostic: he did not believe in God, but he was convinced there was some Mighty Force out there trying to screw him. Pivotal evidence for the humorist included the publication of *How to Be a Hermit* coinciding with the 1929 Stock Market crash that precipitated the Great Depression, and *How to Become Extinct* appeared almost simultaneous to the Japanese attack on Pearl Harbor in 1941. But by the end of his life, it took little to elicit the phrase, as this passing reference in a letter to professor/broadcaster/author John Towner Frederick demonstrates: "I am honestly thrilled to think you are taking me up in this way [as a guest on your radio program *Of Men and Books*]. Maybe it [will] make some of the Cuppy Haters take notice of me."[2] Ironically, even this honor could be construed as a "Cuppy

Hater" slur, since the appearance was not to discuss his writing but rather mystery books he had reviewed in his *New York Herald Tribune* column. Regardless, while this alleged "movement" will be addressed further in forthcoming chapters, there is appropriateness to noting it here, as Cuppy's college years are examined.

Thankfully, there is more documentation of Cuppy's time at the University of Chicago, including the autobiographical fiction of the aforementioned *Maroon Tales*, than his time at Auburn High. Indeed, between school consolidation in his home county (DeKalb), a flood, and a fire, there are not even any surviving high school yearbooks prior to 1904.[3] If Cuppy were alive today he would undoubtedly have added such natural disasters to his list of concerted efforts by the "Hate Cuppy Movement" to minimize and/or erase his presence here on planet Earth.

A good composite picture of Cuppy the college student comes from Burton Rascoe, a university friend and later the humorist's editor at the *New York Tribune* (and its successor, the *Herald Tribune*). Rascoe's autobiography, *Before I Forget*, wryly describes Cuppy, given his 12-year college tenure, as the "oldest infant prodigy in the history of active American student life."[4] Though Rascoe first knew him only during the humorist's seven years of graduate school, he suggests Cuppy had established himself early as a campus writing star. Unfortunately, according to Rascoe's profile, this status had made the humorist affected: "Cuppy lived at the Phi Gamma Delta Fraternity House. He spent most of his time in the English library, reading dramas from *Gammer Gurton's Needle* to Shaw and Pinero. He was a plumpish, fair-haired, droll young man with a constant air of fatigue and boredom, lightened only by the occasional chuckles which followed his own observations

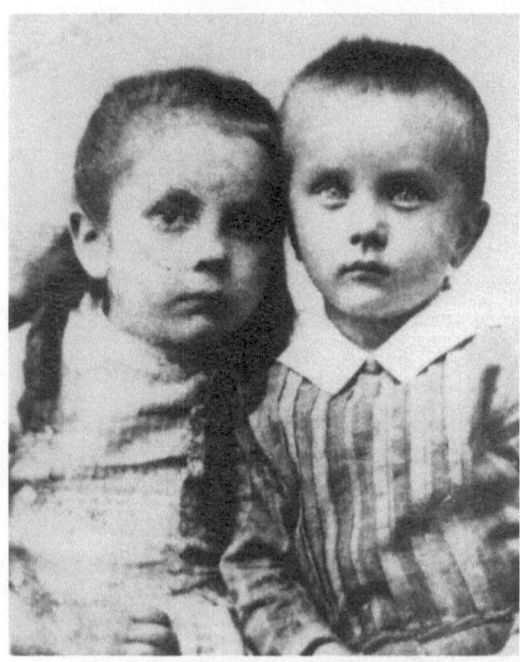

Will Cuppy used this childhood picture of himself and his sister Anna as a Christmas card in the early 1940s.

on comic manifestations of human nature, including his own."[5] In other words, it was the final incubation period of the later hypochondriac-prone satirist known as Will Cuppy.

Cuppy's prodigy status at the university had resulted in an honor he initially described as "fantastic," only to turn into the most humbling of experiences for a wannabe author:

> A publisher [Chicago's Forbes & Company] asked me to write a book of University of Chicago college stories, and I did. [The university had handpicked him to help create the "traditions" of what was then still a young university.] After purchasing and reading all the books of college stories available, I almost immediately produced a sizeable volume entitled *Maroon Tales* [for a university called The "Chicago Maroons"], as much like the others as possible but worse.... Mercifully, Most of the first edition was drowned in a flood which visited the cellar of the university press shortly thereafter.[6]

Cuppy later enjoyed telling how this experience had stunted his writing for 20 years, with his next book, *How to Be a Hermit*, not coming out until late 1929: "I used the ... [time] between my first and my second book in trying to achieve the first faint glimmerings of how to write English."[7]

As with all things Cuppy, there is a great deal of antiheroic posturing here, maybe even the beginnings of his "Hate Cuppy Movement." *Maroon Tales* is not a bad book but merely what one might expect of a young, first-time author writing to order on a subject not of his choosing. Though not a commercial success, this now public-domain property is an invaluable time capsule of Cuppy's university days. Because, while the book's framework is an allegedly fabricated series of stories following the lives of several young University of Chicago students, Cuppy has peppered the text with materials which now read as subtextually autobiographical.

To better demonstrate these connections, however, one needs to state some Cuppy basics. First, the humorist excelled at writing about goofy-looking, often extinct creatures. For instance, one of Cuppy's later inspired essays addressed how

> the Dodo never had a chance. He seems to have been invented for the sole purpose of becoming extinct.... I'm not blaming the Dodo but he was a mess. He had an ugly face with a large hooked beak, a tail in the wrong place, wings too small ... and a very prominent stomach. You can't look like that and survive.[8]

Fittingly, in Cuppy's *Maroon Tales*, one of his student characters loved to visit the university's Walker Museum because

> he liked to look at the ... remains of queer animals: funny little skulls and bones and disjointed skeletons of strange monsters that must have

been remarkable when they were alive ... [he] wondered if the long one with the flat, triangular head used to crawl, or hop, or what.⁹

Another later comic Cuppy essay discusses the difficulty of deciphering ancient Egypt's language: "Their hieroglyphics, or picture writing, consisted of owls, canaries, garter snakes, and the insides of alarm clocks."¹⁰ Over 40 years before, one of his *Maroon Tales* chronicles another student who was fascinated with the university's Haskell Museum, where

> he greatly fancied the perspectiveless reliefs of kings of Egypt going forth behind six-legged, three-headed hobby-horses [more unusual animals] to hunt tame-looking wild beasts ... and the personal effects of the princess with the impossible name.¹¹

Third, Cuppy spent years in a graduate school working towards a Ph.D. in English literature, after obtaining a B.A. in philosophy (1907). But, by 1914, he was burned out on college; he later comically confessed:

> [I] had almost completed a doctor's thesis on the subject [of Elizabethan prose]. One day I decided that all that would never do, so I cut my thesis in half, took the degree of Master of Arts in English and hopped a train for New York [to write my play].¹²

But what might have initially motivated him to tackle a Ph.D? In the *Maroon Tales*, written *early* in his graduate career, Cuppy describes the advanced degree aspirations of another student character:

> Red skipped most of the other degrees. Bachelors

Burton Rascoe was known as being somewhat affected, as suggested by this publicity photograph (mid–1930s).

of Divinity and Masters of Art are usually people you never heard of, anyhow. Doctors of Philosophy are more interesting; you have to do such an impossible amount of work to be one.[13]

Fourth, Cuppy greatly admired several of his university professors. Appropriately enough, in a letter the humorist wrote decades later to a then-contemporary professor of note, the aforementioned John Towner Frederick, Cuppy revealed three of his favorite college teachers, as well as an ironic bias against mystery stories — given that he spent much of his adult life reviewing works in this genre: "In my day profs of English wrote books but not mysteries. I took all the courses offered by Robert Herrick, Richard Morss Lovett, James Weber Linn."[14]

While these professors are not mentioned by name in *Maroon Tales*, any research applied to the trio leads to a subtextual sense of them in Cuppy's now-neglected first book. For example, while both Lovett (1870–1956) and Linn (1876–1939) wrote and taught at the University of Chicago for over 40 years each, these two liberal academics doubled as activists trying to make the greater Chicago area a better place in which to live. This is best symbolized by their joint connections to the Jane Addams Hull House, a pioneering community center that attempted to improve social conditions for underserved people and communities in and around Chicago. It was founded in 1889 by future Nobel Peace Prize winner (1931) Addams (1860–1935), whose goal was to "aid in the solutions of life in a great city, to help our neighbors to build responsible, self-sufficient lives for themselves and their families."[15]

Linn's mother, the former Mary Catharine Addams, was the sister of Jane Addams. When Linn lost his mother as a teenager, Jane Addams made it possible for him to finish his undergraduate studies at the University of Chicago. Among his later publications was a celebrated biography of his aunt. Linn's passionate humanism surfaced not only as a caring publishing professor but also in his work as a local politician and a columnist for various Chicago newspapers, including the *Herald*, the *Herald Examiner*, and the *Daily*. Linn later modestly linked his many talents in the following manner:

> It seems to me that it is a natural for a novelist and a newspaper writer, who is first of all an observer of the human scene, and for a teacher, who is necessarily a student of society, to go into politics, as it is for a duck to hunt water to swim in. Politics is neither law nor business. It is applied social philosophy.[16]

Academic/author Lovett was a stormier activist than Linn. When Lovett arrived in Chicago as a young Harvard graduate, he immediately involved himself in a myriad of liberal causes. This necessitated a great deal of bravery, because "he was often on the picket lines where strike violence [against the picketers] was worst, and was a friend and confidante of most of the leaders of the radical movement."[17] Most prominent among the young left-wing writers he helped nurture was John Dos Passos (1896–1970). Lovett's many causes included Hull House, fueled, in part, by his wife being a close friend and associate of Jane Addams. Indeed, during the couple's declining years they resided at Hull House. Cuppy's *Maroon Tales* includes passages which seem reminiscent of Linn and Lovett:

> [Student] Petey's independent quest led him among the professors. The stories he heard about them were most exciting. Some, he learned ... were helping the city of Chicago take care of its problems, and some were spending years on the queerest problems imaginable. Most of them seemed to be doing things that made their teaching in class look small and un-important in comparision. And these things ... were what made the University really great.[18]

Among the student characters Cuppy uses as mouthpieces in *Maroon Tales*, the above quoted Petey sounds especially like the future humorist, because Cuppy's indecision about what to do with his life drove him to take a vast random assortment of classes. Whatever romanticism his earlier comments associated with getting a Ph.D., he later confessed to a quiet desperation upon the eve of graduate school: "Deciding, after graduation that I know nothing whatever about anything, I hung about the campus for the next seven years, taking courses in practically everything, with or without credit, as the spirit moved me."[19]

Regardless, Cuppy's admiration for humanists Linn and Lovett is not without some irony, given the broadness of the humorist's later satire — a sautéing of society, regardless of class or station. The paradox is compounded further by the fact that Cuppy's later friend and mentor, pioneering libertarian Isabel Paterson (1886–1961), was as far to the political right as Linn and Lovett were to the left. For example, the latter duo would later become ardent New Dealers under President Franklin D. Roosevelt, whereas Paterson was one of FDR's most vociferous critics.

Naturally, there are a variety of explanations for this apparent incongruity, starting with an individual simply having a broad range of friends and contacts. Second, satirists, of course, by way of their acid wit in pointing out the follies of man, are also attempting to improve the human condition. It is just that Cuppy's take on the genre often nihilistically skates beyond satire to the thinner ice of dark comedy, where the only message is: there is no message.[20] Third, one could also argue that since there was a 20-year period between the optimistically youthful publication of the *Maroon Tales*, and Cuppy's first critical and commercial success as an author, *How to Be a Hermit* (a period in which he had suffered a great deal of personal frustration), his cynicism had simply had more time to stew. Moreover, Linn and Lovett's "can do" attitude might simply have reminded young Cuppy of his sainted grandmother (Sara, see Chapter 1), who, prior to her outreach work as a Civil War nurse and GAR advocate, had made her home part of the illegal "Underground Railroad." (This represented a network of safe houses used by black slaves to escape to free states and Canada — with the most traffic occurring during the decade prior to the Civil War, 1850–1860.)

The best explanation, however, for any disparity between Cuppy's later dark satire and his young enthusiasm for Linn and Lovett is probably anchored in something which never changed about the humorist — he forever needed caretakers. Unlike Blanche du Bois's signature line in Tennessee Williams's *A Streetcar Named Desire* (first produced in 1947), "I have always depended upon the kindness of strangers," Cuppy always depended upon *everyone*. He most certainly would have gravitated towards compassionate professors. And if truth be told, the staunch *Individualism* expounded by the aforementioned Paterson (to be addressed later in the text), was completely absent from her caretaker-like nurturing of Cuppy's potential as a humorist. Moreover, Paterson's biographer would suggest Cuppy was essentially apolitical, as he would periodically exasperate Paterson with "his absurdly uninformed questions about politics."[21]

The most interesting Cuppy-professor connection at the University of Chicago, however, involves Robert Herrick (1868–1938), whom the humorist billed ahead of Linn and Lovett in his aforementioned letter to John Towner Frederick. Like Lovett, Herrick was a Harvard-educated native New Englander before coming to the University of Chicago. But whereas Linn and Lovett were entrenched at the school before Cuppy's arrival, Herrick's tenure there began in 1905, two years before Cuppy received his B.A. As with all of Cuppy's favorite professors, Herrick was a humanist later described as having "a truly democratic attraction for his fellow-man, he brought into his liberal politics [he, too, became a New Dealer] the kindliness and a wisdom which were deeply appreciated."[22]

Other than Herrick's delayed arrival in Chicago, this third Cuppy English professor sounds a lot like Linn and Lovett. But what made Herrick number one on Cuppy's list — the first academic to be remembered by the humorist? One might simply assume the elevated status was a product of Herrick being the most prolific and acclaimed writer of Cuppy's pantheon of three. But a better answer can be found in a brief capsule definition of Herrick's oeuvre — a poignant overview which could double as a description of the future reclusive Cuppy, a humorist who founded his work on first becoming a hermit, away from the tumult of New York City: "[Herrick's] novels deal with the turbulence of industrialized society and the turmoil it can create in sensitive, isolated people." [23]

Comic capsule variations of this Herrick summation occur throughout Cuppy's later correspondence and published essays, with my favorite example appearing in, fittingly enough, *How to Be a Hermit*:

> There are worse things than rabbits. Rabbits are among the few remaining vertebrates which neither bark, sing, whistle, play the piano, lecture nor invent new machines to make more of the same or other loud noises.[24]

Cuppy was more subtextually comic when addressing urban distractions and other satirical targets early in his humor, as was his habit, via the animal kingdom. But later on, Cuppy's wit was more direct about this subject and other human follies. For instance, in an essay from another aptly named text, *How to Tell Your Friends from the Apes*, he faults psychologists who suggest "something amiss with a bookish old recluse who does not enjoy the combined yawpings and yowlings and yammering of the entire brute [urban] creation while he is trying to get some ... writing done."[25]

Herrick was part of a new school of American realists, though not to the naturalist extremes of muckrakers like Upton Sinclair (1878–1968). Interestingly, each man's greatest novel, Herrick's *Web of Life* (1900) and Sinclair's *The Jungle* (1906) is set in Chicago and made its mark in literary circles during Cuppy's college years. Coincidentally, Cuppy's later work is sometimes referenced as "whimsically realistic." Along related lines, one critic described Herrick's fiction as achieving "its power from a melancholic fatalism."[26] And despite Cuppy's wit, his mantle of satire often also derives its power from a "melancholic fatalism," as in this *How to Attract the Wombat* axiom: "Intelligence is the capacity to know what we are doing and instinct is just instinct. The results are about the same. [Then in Cuppy's footnote to this he adds:] But we do it on purpose."[27]

With Herrick still in mind, there is another character in *Maroon Tales* who might be described as a comic muckraker à la American humor's "wise fool," who "innocently" makes satirical points in his student articles for the local newspaper. (Cuppy put himself through college by writing for several Chicago area newspapers—another link to the extensive journalistic activities of his aforementioned Professor Linn.) Cuppy described his student reporter, Silver, as someone "possessed with an evil affinity for the unpropitious phrase," such as:

> When he informed the readers of [the university newspaper] *The Maroon* that one of the deans was about to "take a vacation in order to

find some new ideas, as [he has not had one] for three years...." [the dean] scratched his head reflectively while the campus giggled with delight.[28]

Cuppy's Silver character also flirts with comic trouble when covering the "Old Man" and the college football program. This is as close as the *Maroon Tales* come to essentially citing an actual college personality, since this was the nickname of famed football coach Amos Alonzo Stagg (1862–1965), who led the University of Chicago to two national championships (1905,1913) during his 40-year tenure (1892–1932) at the school, when Chicago was one of the charter members of the Big Ten. Stagg was already a sports legend before he arrived in Chicago. As an undergraduate at Yale in 1888 he pitched the baseball team to a 2–1 victory over the major league Boston Braves, followed by being selected to the first College Football All-American Team in 1889. His obituary would later note:

> His teams won six Big Ten Conference titles and were unbeaten in five seasons. He became the first football coach to have a field named for him, the first athletic director to achieve faculty status and to thousands of students and fans, was as much a part of the university as its imposing Gothic buildings. [29]

Among his many additional accomplishments, Stagg pioneered the use of the forward pass and the T-formation.

Cuppy's references to the "Old Man" and/or university football in the *Maroon Tales* are affectionately respectful. But there is sometimes a sense of wink-wink double standard regarding college football players. For instance, one of Cuppy's student/journalist characters made the "mistake" of doing an article in which

> he featured the captain of the football team in describing a "midnight lark" on the [city's famous] Midway, and ... [the reporter compounded the mistake by also being] interviewed by that worthy [errant athlete], who was supposed to be in bed at ten every night.[30]

Cuppy had modestly hit upon a subject which would soon be a source of college humor for decades. A more polished later example of this double standard would be James Thurber's chronicle of a struggling student athlete at Ohio State in "University Days," from *My Life and Hard Times* (1913). Thurber drew from his own Big Ten college experience, which began in 1913, when Cuppy was still in school. Thurber's tale involves a tackle on

> one of the best teams in the country.... In order to be eligible to play, it was necessary for him to keep up in his studies, a very difficult matter, for while he was not dumber than an ox he was not any smarter....
> None [of his professors] gave him more hints, in answering questions ... than the economics professor, a thin, timid man named Bassum.... All

> of us [students], of course, shared Mr. Bassum's desire that ... [the player] should stay abreast of the class..., for the Illinois game, one of the hardest and most important of the season, was only a week off.[31]

This shared feeling (by both teachers and students) being totally behind a university as football factory is also anticipated in Cuppy's *Maroon Tales*. The book entertainingly chronicles some school pride/vigilante justice against a rival team's football spies:

> These villains ... had been caught red-handed while taking voluminous notes on the Old Man's [Stagg's] formations, and after confessing their crime, had been ducked in the Botany pond until they yelled for mercy.[32]

Maroon Tales's stories about the "Old Man" and college football were not written, however, just because the coach was a campus legend. Cuppy's aforementioned college friend, Burton Rascoe, later suggested that one of the few journalistic tasks the future humorist enjoyed was periodic short "interviews on athletic matters with 'the old man' (Coach Stagg) or Assistant Coach Pat Page."[33] In an earlier 1930s Cuppy profile, the humorist even admitted his sessions with the coach were on par with his fun fraternity life:

> [My college] degree shows that I did not study Greek — another of my tragedies. I was interviewing Professor [and coach] Amos Alonzo Stagg about the prospects of the football team and having high jinks with the members of the Phi Gamma Delta fraternity when I should have been studying Greece — but I'd do it over again.[34]

Regardless, sometime early in the 1910s the graduate college experience started to sour for Cuppy. His inability to finish the Ph.D. dissertation begins a pattern of life incompletions, including the play he would soon spend the rest of his days writing ... but never finish. Even his greatest critical and commercial success as a humorist, *The Decline and Fall of Practically Everybody* (1950), was unfinished at the time of his death. Cuppy had worked intermittently upon the essay collection for 16 years. Only the extraordinary efforts of his friend and sometimes editor Fred Feldkamp had made the book possible, just as Isabel Paterson would be so instrumental in getting his early humor texts in print.

To reframe this Ph.D. incompletion, however, one might simply suggest that Cuppy had outgrown the experience. Hidden in one of Cuppy's later letters to Paterson, he randomly notes the birth of his cynicism:

> I break down in the attempt [at hope] owing to the damnable fact that I had an education. That is, from the age of [twenty-] four to about twenty-six or eight [1912] I did nothing but prepare lessons for the

The legendary athlete and coach Amos Stagg (circa 1900), whose many honors include the fact that the team winning the Big Ten Football Championship Game receives the "Stagg Championship Trophy."

professors, so that the natural resiliency of my mind was probably destroyed.[35]

This entertainingly hyperbolic description of the first pinprick to pop a long-term goal bubble is only flawed by the fact that his 1920s letters are regularly peppered with various explanations as to why he became the most cynical of satirists. Still, the comment suggests he had outgrown his professors, and it was now time to move on. The letter is reminiscent of the pivotal Cuppy quote from the previous chapter, in which he recalled, as a boy positing the question as to whether fish could think. Cuppy then claims that when he had realized that such deep thinking was beyond anyone else in Indiana, he immediately left the state. Such was now the case with college.

Yet, his protracted stay at the University of Chicago had hardly been a waste. Besides the ongoing joy of spending every available moment in the university library, he later built from this experience a comedy style, which would paradoxically couple scholarship with a propensity for puncturing the pedantic. First, there was the academic-based side to his satire. The aforementioned Fred Feldkamp revealed:

> [Before Cuppy wrote] a line on any topic ... he would read every volume and article on the subject that he could find.... In some cases, he would read more than twenty-five thick volumes before writing a one-thousand-word piece.[36]

Moreover, prior to writing, the Cuppy system had first necessitated the humorist transfer an exhaustive amount of information from his research to hundreds of 3-by-5 index cards.[37] This attention to detail sounds very much like someone who spent seven years in graduate school.

After such an academic foundation, Cuppy equally relishes mocking the make-up of a scholarly treatise. First, and most obviously, he has a wonderful propensity for reinventing the footnote — a reference or comment seldom conjuring up descriptions which trade in fun or funny. John Barrymore (1882–1942), a Cuppy contemporary and arguably the 20th century's greatest stage Hamlet, provides the best lack-of-enthusiasm definition for the category when he observed, "[A footnote is] like running downstairs to answer the doorbell during the first night of marriage."[38] Of course, given Cuppy's own master's thesis, "The Elizabethan Conception of Prose Style," it is possible to demonstrate one of the future humorist's own traditionally straight dry footnotes. What follows is only a portion of a scholarly footnote comprising *two-thirds of a typed page*. Yet, even here, as Cuppy questions several authority figures, one witnesses the iconoclastic heart of his later satire:

Professor Courthope affirms, apropos of Sidney's mention of Xenephon, and Shelley's instancing of Plato and Bacon as poets, "The fallacy of the examples given by each of these critics is, that they do not take into account the different aims of the writers they cite."[39]

In contrast, Cuppy's later funny footnotes almost steal the satirical thunder from the witty main texts of his humor books. For instance, in Cuppy's study of gorillas, from his *Apes* collection, a footnote deadpans, "The Gorilla is said to have hidden depths but if they are so hidden, what good are they? He has small ears, generally a bad sign."[40] In Cuppy's essay of Lady Godiva in *The Decline and Fall of Everybody*, his first note states, "Godiva was the sister of Thoroid the sheriff. This would mean more if we knew who Thoroid the sheriff was."[41] And in a squirrel essay from his *Wombat* book, Cuppy plays at being an intellectual tease in one note: "What the Squirrel says about the Owl is extremely amusing. We won't go into it here."[42] Cuppy's footnotes were a hit not only with the public but with his fellow humorists, who sometimes hired him to add funny notes to their own comic work.[43]

The scholarly side of Amos Stagg (circa 1906), which would have drawn Cuppy to him even more.

Second, when Cuppy's merry mix of fun and facts are not derailing academe by way of the footnotes, the text itself doubles as an astute skewering of all things intellectual, from animals to iconic humans of history. Or, Cuppy is just as happy to take down John Q. Public, too:

> The Modern Man or Nervous Wreck is the highest of all mammals because anyone can see that he is. There are about 2,000,000,000 Modern Men or too many.[44]

Maybe Cuppy excels best, however, with his satirical take downs of specific iconic scholars whom he considered to be overrated. (Once again, this brings to mind Cuppy the graduate student feeling superior to his professors.) Regardless, a typical example of his humorously hamstringing a so-called expert occurs in his study of Darwin's *The Descent of Man*, from the Cuppy collection most reminiscent of Darwin, *How to Become Extinct*:

> "Male snakes, though appearing so sluggish, are amorous." Isn't that just like Darwin? It was one of his main ideas, you know, that the males of almost all animals have stronger passions then the females. Since then we've learned a thing or two.[45]

Cuppy's favorite intellectual whipping boy is no less than the poster child of Western civilization — Aristotle. His comic riffs on this intellectual behemoth are scattered throughout Cuppy's books. Sometimes they occur in brief asides, such as the following footnotes from two essays included in his *Apes* book. First, in a short piece on the chimpanzee, Cuppy writes, "Aristotle did not mention Chimps but they got along somehow."[46] Then, in writing about the monkey-like lemur, which Cuppy describes as a creature which "sleeps all day long and nobody tells him that he is a tramp," he adds, "Aristotle would not have known a lemur if it came up and bit him."[47]

Cuppy's *pièce de résistance* on Aristotle occurred, however, in an *Extinct* essay in which even the title zings the ancient Greek Professor: "Aristotle, Indeed!" The catalyst for the essay was a response to a reader offended by Cuppy's cracks about the oft-revered watershed scholar in another article included in this collection, "Own your Own Snake." In the latter essay Cuppy writes:

> I ask little credit for my victories over the Father of Learning, as they call him. They're too easy. Every time I look up something in his works, darned if the old boy isn't screwy. I suppose the rest of his stuff is fine. I just happened to look at the worst places.[48]

In "Aristotle, Indeed!" Cuppy slyly pretends to balance previous attacks on the Greek with biting false praise:

> Aristotle ... was frequently right, for it is almost impossible, under the laws of chance, to be wrong all the time.... [For instance, he] denied that Hyenas change their sex every year. He was only guessing but it sounds like a good guess. I don't know what to say of his theory that flat-footed people are treacherous. Some of them are, very likely ... Aristotle's discovery that snakes and fish have no feet is a keen bit of observation for an ancient Greek but why should it make him the Father of Learning?[49]

If "hell hath no fury like a women scorned," Cuppy's under-appreciated graduate student would run a close second. Though his satirical gestation period took 20-plus years after the publication of *Maroon Tales*, Cuppy's work still resonates with readers. But there is a wonderful paradox in the wit and twisted wisdom of his writing. His short essays undoubtedly attract many enemies of deep dish studies. Yet, Cuppy's offbeat scholarship is still so impressively based upon all his research (those oodles of note cards), that the heart of higher education still shines through: Do your homework and never be afraid to question the status quo. Thus, his humor is just as likely to attract academic fans, including this author. Indeed, while many of my books feature those dreaded-by-some traditional footnotes, Cuppy's work (and the Cuppy disciple Richard Armour) inspired me to do my own periodic satirizing of scholarship, such as *Film Classics Reclassified: A Shocking Spoof of Cinema*.[50] Moreover, as future chapters will document, Cuppy would soon have many fans among deep-dish scholars, too.

As noted earlier, Cuppy spent much of his post-college life reviewing mystery books, a genre for which, in private, he expressed little affection (also, interestingly, the then-prevailing view in academe). Yet, as author Roger Rosenblatt has so wisely suggested:

> All writers are mystery writers. We may not employ detectives in our work but as seekers of guilty parties we can identify with ... [private eyes]. Like them, we muck about in a world studded with clues, neck-deep in motives ... we are foolhardy, preposterous, noisy, irritating. No one wants us around. We work alone, yet like Sam Spade, we operate within a tradition of our own, of which we are respectfully aware. Write and you are in the company of all who have written before you.[51]

The reclusive Cuppy mocked mankind in a multitude of ways, from subtextual satire via animals, to lancing science and history by way of targeting celebrated historical figures. But ironically, his comic art was based upon — depended upon — spending most of his time "in the company of all" those writers he enjoyed dismantling. The mysteries never end.

THREE

A Wannabe Playwright and His Humor Mentor: Isabel Peterson

"To Isabel Paterson, to whom I always dedicate my books."—Will Cuppy's dedication from *How to Tell Your Friends from the Apes*[1]

Art critic Jed Perl once wrote, "Biographers are forever readjusting our sense of the fantastically mutable relationship between an individual and society."[2] In other words, nothing is created in a vacuum. But the *degree* to which people are sculpted by the world around them always remains open to interpretation. That is why some of history's unique and/or most provocative figures continue to generate so many books. Angles of vision are constantly changing. Along similar lines, biographers are also frequently called upon to gauge the "mutable relationship" between their subjects and special individuals in that profiled person's life. This chapter, and much of what follows, will be filtered through arguably the most influential person in Cuppy's life: Isabel Paterson. But just as the study of the relationship between society and the individual is a slippery slope, so is the examination of one person's impact upon another. Still, it behooves a biographer to study these relationships as best s/he can. To paraphrase profiler Paul Murray Kendall, "A biographer can never be sure of the absolute truth, but what he engages to tell is the *best truth* he can find, to the best of his abilities."[3]

Cuppy's move to New York (1914) from his extra-inning cloistered college cocoon of a life at the University of Chicago did not immediately result in his creating another safe hideaway. Plus, his fortuitous connection with friend and mentor of mentors Paterson would not occur for several years. Sadly, his stated reason for the migration east, to write his "Great

Three. A Wannabe Playwright and His Humor Mentor

American Drama," was just not getting done. Between the distractions of Greenwich Village nightlife and trying to get by writing advertising copy for various newspapers, midlife creative panic was setting in. Of course, on the plus side, Cuppy had found his new favorite place in the world — the Bronx Zoo — an invaluable inspiration for later satirical pieces masquerading as comic essays on animals. Also, another new, much beloved locale which would be instrumental in his future writing was the New York Public Library's main branch at Fifth Avenue and 42nd Street.

Sometimes a setting can be an added catalyst for creativity, either through the accumulated history of one place or an artistic "well" of a broader domain. In contrast, a more ephemeral yet specific inspirational location is encapsulated in Christopher Buckley's description of the Metropolitan Museum's (New York) Temple of Dendur, the stunning Egyptian blocklong "room" with a glass wall view of Central Park — "the coolest space on the planet."[4] While I happen to share this sentiment, a close second for this researcher/writer is Cuppy's own follow-up favorite, the main branch of the New York Public Library — "the one with the stone lions," as my daughter Emily labeled it as a child. The importance of this library to Cuppy brings to mind legendary basketball player and passionate athletic artist Bill Russell's thoughts upon departing his creative space: "Whenever I leave the [Boston] Celtics locker room, even heaven wouldn't be good enough because anyplace else is a step down.[5]

Though such wonderful Cuppy distractions as the Bronx Zoo and the New York Public Library would eventually benefit his comic art, they still did little for his aspirations to be a playwright. American's entry into World War I (1917) created a more formidable distraction for Cuppy, though the over-30 future humorist never made it overseas. Second Lieutenant Cuppy was stationed in Washington, D.C., serving as a Motor Transport Corps publicity writer.

According to Cuppy aficionado Thomas Maeder, after the war the writer "took the strange and radical step of becoming a hermit" — for creative privacy.[6] For most of the 1920s he inhabited a rundown shack on Jones Island, just off the southern coast of New York's Long Island. From this hovel by the sea, which he affectionately names "Tottering-on-the-Brink," Cuppy becomes a sort of comic Thoreau, fashioning his affectionately anti–*Walden* guide to contemplation, *How to Be a Hermit*. Paralleling the beginning of his Jones Island sojourn (1921), Cuppy indirectly lobbied his University of Chicago friend Burton Rascoe for a job. Rascoe was then the literary editor of the *New York Tribune*. But, as was Cuppy's habit, he needed to be praised into production. Rascoe later recalled:

> [I received] a very droll letter, largely concerned with Aldous Huxley's *Crome Yellow* [1921]. I printed it and wrote urging him to do some book reviews for me. It took a great deal of urging to keep him going once he got started. He has to be pampered and encouraged and told he is good every minute or he will think you consider his stuff too rotten to print.[7]

(Appropriately for Cuppy the future satirist, early Huxley fiction might best be described as expressing disgust at the hopeless, self-inflicted problems of humanity.)

As Cuppy's constant need for coddling became draining for Rascoe (see chapter one), Cuppy was increasingly dependent upon the encouragement of fellow *Tribune* writer Isabel Paterson. From this haphazard beginning was born a pivotal mentoring friendship. Though the Canadian-American Paterson wore many titles in her long and illustrious writing career including journalist, novelist, literary critic, and political philosopher (one of the founding figures of American libertarianism), for Cuppy she was best described as a "cheerleader" and "catalyst for comedy." Though two years younger than Cuppy, she was already an established columnist/critic at the *Tribune*. Cuppy would log several years as a freelance *Tribune* reviewer before also receiving a column.

Beyond Paterson's generous tendency to help talented people better realize their potential, and Cuppy's overwhelming need to be propped up with praise, several basic traits linked the two writers. First, and most importantly, they enjoyed each other's dry, dark sense of humor. Paterson called Cuppy a "bright spot in a dismal world," and often quoted him in her column.[8] Indeed, Paterson's early showcasing of Cuppy's funny comments from his correspondence in her "Turns with a Bookworm" column had many readers initially assuming that she had simply made him up! When Cuppy first heard about this notion of his being merely a "figment of Isabel Paterson's imagination" he responded, "I know of nobody at all of whose imagination I should feel prouder and more signally honored to be a figment."[9]

More to their mutual enjoyment of each other's comedy company, however, is Cuppy's confession to Paterson in an undated (circa 1927) letter: "Why is it that only you and I are able to make me laugh? Why? Why?"[10] Thankfully, Cuppy preserved the flavor of their banter in two essay-length dialogues from his *How to Be a Hermit* text. Besides usually giving Paterson/Pat the best lines, the first Cuppy excerpt/example chronicles her more driven nature:

> PAT: I've too much much work on hand to-day [to be interviewed]. I have to write [my column] "Turns with a Bookworm" and two

> articles and a chapter of the novel and go to a party and deliver a lecture and—
>
> CUP: Do you call that work?
>
> PAT: Well, it cuts into the afternoon.[11]

The second snippet from these exchanges satirizes the fact that Cuppy's eventual column, "Light Reading" (later renamed "Mystery and Adventure") keyed upon a genre for which Cuppy had little interest:

> CUP: Detective stories serve a worthy purpose. They rest the mind.
>
> PAT: Sure they do, if you have that sort of mind.
>
> CUP: You think detective authors should eat more spinach?
>
> PAT: No, more strychnine.[12]

Regardless of the quotes, if Paterson had focused upon satire, we might now be mentioning her in the same breath with period wit Dorothy Parker. For instance, here is columnist Paterson's 1934 take on a literary icon:

> Gertrude Stein, author of "The Autobiography of Alice B. Toklas," is coming over soon [from France] for a lecture tour. One of her lecture topics will be "The History of English Literature as I Understand It." That should be a very brief lecture.[13]

Fittingly, given their comedic talents, both Cuppy and Paterson agreed upon superior nature of the art form, or as Paterson succinctly phrased it, "Wit and humor are the highest forms of intelligence ... the balance wheel or perspective element in the human mind."[14] Of course, as was his nature, Cuppy pumped up the genre's importance by playing upon the pain and difficulty of its creation. For example, in another letter to Paterson, which also documents Cuppy's sense of ego, when he is not running his "woe is me" ploy for attention, the humorist writes:

> You may think, as I've heard about myself, that my exceedingly laughable witticisms just purl out of me by the mile, but the fact is I beat my brain against the wall and endure untold agonies to get each one out of my petrified dome.[15]

Despite their ongoing celebration of comedy, Cuppy, like many humorists of this era (from Benchley to fellow Hoosier Red Skelton), had strong feelings against publicly critiquing comedy. But instead of the standard superstitious explanation, that the magic of laughter disappears when the joke is dissected, Cuppy felt great anger towards the professorial types who merely attempt to explain humor. To illustrate, in an undated letter (circa 1924) to Paterson, Cuppy was happy to rain down caustic comments of agreement with an unnamed critic who panned one such book-length study by Gilbert Seldes. To place Cuppy's attack in a historical context, the presumed Seldes text is *The 7 Lively Arts* (1924), which is now considered a groundbreaking collection of entertainment-related essays on a myriad of pop culture subjects/figures, from Charlie Chaplin to Krazy Kat (a newspaper comic strip favorite of Cuppy's).[16] Most of Seldes's topics, with the exception of Chaplin, had never before received such serious critical attention. But Cuppy felt reviewers like Seldes often simply missed the point of the humor:

> I love to see these godamned nits stepped upon.... It is again ... [the] fault of not being able to see a joke. That is why he writes about humor ... the people who analyze jokes are always that way.[17]

This anti-professorial rant (please see chapter two) anticipates his later satirical essays which take on any and all experts in Western civilization, starting with Aristotle. And Cuppy's views against publicly dissecting humor never changed. Note the following opening to his *New York Herald Tribune* "Mystery and Adventure" column from 1946, "It is now the fashion, in reviewing books of comic intent, to explain exactly how the thing is done — a vain and villainous pursuit, in our opinion."[18]

Along less off-with-their-heads satirical lines, Cuppy also had propriety reservations about humorists reviewing humorists. He would confide to Paterson, "As you know I think it is a little immodest for an alleged joker to write about other alleged jokers."[19] That being said, Cuppy did allow for certain exceptions, especially when it included humorist Robert Benchley (1889–1946), a special favorite of both Paterson and Cuppy.

The now-neglected wit Isabel Paterson (mid–1930s).

Indeed, in Cuppy's extensive correspondence with Paterson, Benchley was the humorist he spent more time praising and/or defending. In one such letter to Paterson (circa 1925), Cuppy even took his friend to task for dragging her feet on publishing his critical Valentine to Benchley:

> Do you mean to tell me that you have not yet printed the [praising] masterpiece I wrote about Robert Benchley? Save it, by all means, until everybody else has reviewed it [Benchley's latest book, presumably *Pluck and Luck*, 1925].[20]

What provoked such passion in Cuppy is undoubtedly tied to the style of humor influence Benchley had on the *Tribune* writer. Though these links are examined further in the forthcoming chapters, suffice it to say that Benchley's earlier in-print MO, like Cuppy's, assumed a derailed professorial tone, though without the Hoosier's ranchor. One pertinent Benchley quote which merits noting at this time, finds the comic writer in perfect agreement with Cuppy on not analyzing humor:

> In order to laugh at something, it is necessary, (1) to know *what* you are laughing at, (2) to know *why* you are laughing, (3) to ask some people why *they* think you are laughing, (4) to jot down a few notes, (5) to laugh. Even then, the thing may not be cleared up for days.[21]

Besides Cuppy and Paterson's joint talent for amusing each other and their general celebratory nature towards all things funny, there was also a very practical side to their humor connection. Cuppy sometimes used his conversations with Paterson as either a comedy catalyst and/or a final polish to his satirical essays. That is, when they got together for their late-night riffing sessions, Cuppy would sometimes bring along a stack of his aforementioned note cards — covered with the humorist's detailed research on a specific animal or historic figure through which he would channel his nihilistic wit. The satirical barbs Paterson and Cuppy would trade on assorted subjects (not unlike their previously cited exchanges) would help Cuppy shape his material.

These wee-hours-of-the-night bull sessions normally took place in Paterson's small *Tribune* office, though sometimes they met at her lower Manhattan apartment (508 West 34th Street), the beginning of the once tough Irish neighborhood known as "Hell's Kitchen" (between 34th and 59th Street, and from 8th Avenue to the Hudson River). Fittingly, for a location which would help give birth to Cuppy's biting comedy, the origins of the name "Hell's Kitchen" is drenched in dark humor.[22] One explanation goes back to the 19th century writings of Davy Crockett. He explained how his frontier experiences with the Irish were always excellent, but in the area of New York, "They are too mean to swab hell's kitchen." Or, another

Cuppy's comedy hero, Robert Benchley (mid–1920s).

popular take on the phrase is attributed to a veteran cop from the area, "Dutch Fred." When he was teamed with a rookie partner on a particularly ugly case, the youngster was said to have described the neighborhood as hell-like. Dutch Fred deadpanned, "Hell's a mild climate. This is hell's kitchen."

Three. A Wannabe Playwright and His Humor Mentor

Whatever the name origin of Paterson's area, when Cuppy was forced out of his year-around residence on Jones Island (to be addressed in the following chapter), he rented an apartment in Greenwich Village (130 West 11th Street) within easy walking distance of his friend's place. Besides this common New York geography, and putting wit on a pedestal, many other traits linked the two. Like many writers, they were late-night people who treated cigarettes as one of the major food groups. (Ironically, the chain-smoking Cuppy, who was convinced the world was forever conspiring against him, puffed away on Lucky Strikes.) Also, neither of these confirmed cynics had a high opinion of humanity. In a Paterson letter (1933) to another friend, she confirms this tie with the humorist:

> Cuppy came in for an hour last night but it was so hot we sat morosely in the dark and I said I didn't care what happened to a nation of halfwits, not if they all starve in breadlines, and he said earnestly: "Now you are talking in a constructive way." So it was too hot to add to that and he went home.[23]

Along similar lines, Cuppy observes in a footnote from *The Decline and Fall of Practically Everybody*, "It's easy to see the faults in people, I know, and it's harder to see the good. Especially when the good isn't there."[24]

That being said, Paterson was quite passionate about her position regarding people who could not take care of themselves, and one sees the natural bridge to the rugged individualism at the heart of her later libertarianism. Not surprisingly, she was a major critic of President Franklin Roosevelt's "New Deal" social programs of assistance. In contrast, while Cuppy's correspondence and published satire is dripping with scorn for the masses, the humorist's tough shell had a soft underside — maybe because he was so dependent upon others himself. Thus, he confessed to Paterson in a mid–1920s letter:

> I spend my life trying to pretend that I have no [good] intentions towards people. Of course they know I have but they are right that I keep up the bluff, and I exact the same from them, on the pain of banishment. That is why I think God intended us to lie and nothing else. It is probably why the folks distrust anything that savors of what we think is the truth.[25]

As the latter portion of this quote suggests, Cuppy's iffy feelings about humanity are based as much, or more, in a tortured psyche belief— most often bared in his correspondence — that the world was out to get him. This is best crystallized in Cuppy's writings, both published and unpublished, by his periodic blaming, when something goes wrong, of the aforementioned "Hate Cuppy Movement." Cuppy's self-pity addiction moved

Paterson's biographer, Stephen Cox, to wryly suggest that if there was such a movement, Cuppy was its leader.[26]

The manner in which Cuppy's sharp tongue masked a haunted soul (revealed in his unpublished letters) anticipates the later humor books of pianist/composer/actor/writer Oscar Levant (1902–1972), whose signature line, "There's a thin line between genius and insanity. [pause] I have crossed that line." In Levant's *Memoirs of an Amnesiac* (1965) and *The Unimportance of Being Oscar* (1968), he comically bares his Cuppy-like neurotic, hypochondriacal, humanity-baited, self-declared genius core.[27] Had Cuppy also been able to reveal his much earlier similarly brilliant bittersweet private ramblings with such cathartic bestselling success, he might not have taken his own life. But the humorist eventually reached that place where there are no road maps home. Regardless, in an earlier Levant memoir, *A Smattering of Ignorance* (1942), he had revealed to a friend a normally well-hidden vulnerability which might have also doubled as Cuppy's convolutedly complex axiom on humanity, "Well, you know I hate 'em 'till they say hello to me."[28]

Another parallel between Cuppy and Paterson was a loner mentality. While Cuppy demonstrated it in a more high-profile nature by literally becoming a 1920s hermit and writing about the experience, that was essentially the mindset of Paterson. Her biographer even described the Cuppy-Paterson late-night dialogues as "hermit to hermit."[29] But the paradox of their personalities was that both writers were winsome in social settings, if necessity demanded it. In fact, Cuppy would later briefly host a NBC radio program, *Just Relax* (1933), fueled by the subject of his pet peeves. But the nature of Paterson's newspaper column, which was heavily laced with literary gossip, made her more a slave to the cultural soirée scene. Still, she admired Cuppy's Jones Island statement, and it probably also helps explain her putting up with his never-ending neediness.

Herein was another paradox. Cuppy was a *hermit* who needed constant help, varying from Paterson's psychological support to more basic assistance (the odd meal, or rowing him to the mainland) provided by the Coast Guard personnel (stationed three hundred yards down the beach from his hovel). Paterson was the founding mother of the fiercely *individualistic* libertarianism movement, yet she constantly went out of her way to assist struggling talent as different as Cuppy and Ayn Rand. Doubling the irony, some of Paterson's most satirically biting lines attack the angst-ridden literary neediness of the times. For instance, her take on the post–World War I "Lost Generation" movement: "We wish they'd stay lost. Nobody would go to look for them."[30] Yet Cuppy was both the king and court of self-pity. For instance, in a mid–1920s letter to Paterson, he writes,

> I'm only a poor silly little playwright, but I do think as long as I heap flatteries upon you all the time you might give me a human word now and then about my great works. I don't insist upon [it] ... but I mean don't pooh-pooh me any more at your peril. Are you trying to KILL MY SOUL?[31]

For humorists like Cuppy, if his letters are not a window into the soul, they at least provide a peek into the fruit cellar neediness of his day-to-day existence. Cuppy's extensive correspondence with Paterson is full of such demands; similar Cuppy requests to other friends are chronicled later in the text. Thus, for the fan of Cuppy's dark comedy bravado, the letters provide a startling glimpse at the vulnerability behind the curtain of a self-proclaimed "hermit."

The paradox of the *personal responsibility* lady (Paterson) constantly helping *needy* man/child Cuppy is further ratcheted-up by another shared trait: both felt victimized by deadbeat dads. Paterson's early frontier-like life in Canada and the Western United States was dependent upon a working mother and the efforts of multiple siblings. Her father did not leave the family, à la Cuppy's dad, but he might just as well have. He left the care of his family to others; from this was born Isabel's philosophy of personal responsibility. In contrast, the dereliction of duty by Cuppy's dad seemed to make him more needful of those around him, starting with his mother, and eventually morphing to friends like Paterson. Besides playing mother hen to Cuppy, there were additional Paterson personality traits which were reminiscent of the humorist's mom, including a talent for seamstress work, cooking, and a love of books.

Though Cuppy and Paterson had all these things in common, it was a stressful relationship. Like Burton Rascoe before her, Cuppy's constant neediness (and his apolitical nature) eventually caused Paterson to break with Cuppy in the late 1940s (to be addressed later in the text). But an early prickly point between the always-practical Paterson and the wannabe playwright Cuppy involved her suggestion that he stop trying to write his self-proclaimed "masterpiece." But it was something with which he was obsessed. Though it is frequently referenced in Cuppy's correspondence as a respite from the burden of his murder-mystery review column, he would never finish the play. Moreover, the hundreds of pages he composed over the decades never got beyond a first act! In fact, his working title for the seemingly jinxed project, "Not That It Matters," suggests Cuppy possibly felt the play would neither be produced, nor even finished.[32]

As even Cuppy's early *Maroon Tales: University of Chicago Stories* demonstrates, the writer's strength was in characterization rather than narrative. His eventual "voice" as a humorist, which Paterson helped him find, was essentially that of a Groucho Marx–like personality comedian of the printed page. His forte was a series of controlled anger riffs (short essays), what humorist Frank Sullivan affectionately called Cuppy's "chip on the shoulder" approach, driven by both his relentless attack mode and by a bevy of funny facts which satirized humanity back to its primitive past.[33] Paterson's instincts were correct in encouraging Cuppy the comic commentator over Cuppy the struggling playwright.

Be that as it may, Paterson granted Cuppy a playwright's success in fiction which he would never achieve in real life. In her novel *The Golden Vanity* (1934), she casts him as the accountant Jake Van Buren, a wannabe writer who somehow concocts a commercial hit play. She laced this poignant gesture with other ties to Cuppy, including his sometimes nickname among friends, Jake. One would assume that making his character an accountant was their in-joke, since his letters to her are frequently full of monetary numbers. These figures range from review fees he either has not received, or requests for more books to critique — to bolster his always bare bones existence. In a late–1920s letter to Paterson about his character, the humorist writes: "You may go to the limit insulting me in your novel. All I ask is don't make me fat. If you do I will haunt you." [34]

Like many people, Cuppy had constant concerns about his weight. One might even couple it with his ongoing worries over his health. Ironically, for such a published cynic, all these things tied into Cuppy's wish to look like the stereotypical, romanticized sickly (on the verge of TB) intellectual. While he ultimately makes a joke about it in his profile from *Authors Today and Yesterday* (1933), variations of the publication's description occur frequently enough in his correspondence to suggest it was more serious than he let on:

> Mr. Cuppy is 5 feet, 10 inches tall, and constantly in fear of becoming a trifle too plump. He begins a rigid diet on the first day of every month but by evening he is up to his old tricks. He has blue eyes and a complexion of somewhat rosy hue. He has always wanted to be pale, thin, and Hamletish.[35]

Just such an example of Cuppy's Hamletish tortured writer philosophy occurs in another mid–1920s letter to Paterson: "You can't amount to much until you have been drug through hell and gone, backwards and forwards and round about, preferably while in a state of youth."[36] Fittingly, in a follow-up letter, he almost builds a case for his various alleged ailments and their link to artistry. Also, keep in mind, when Cuppy was not throwing himself a pity party, he was comfortable calling himself a genius and other superlatives: "Haven't you noticed that geniuses are never what you would call well ... they always have a fever when they should be cool and [having] palpitations and so on...."³⁷

Flash-forward 14 years (1939) and nothing has changed regarding Cuppy's pained perspective on creativity. Paterson plays straight man to the humorist as she quotes from his latest letter in her *Tribune* column. But first she sets the proper tone for her angst-ridden friend: "An author's life is mostly grief ... here's a note from Will Cuppy":

> I have been about stumped [writing wise] for a week.... It's hard, what with newspaper and radio and all [the bad news] out here in the desert [isolated on Jones Island] and also a combination of hay fever and common cold and the usual mental break-down.... Honestly, no mental bust-up you ever had (if you ever had any) can be as bad as this one of mine.³⁸

In marked contrast to Cuppy's antiheroic "Hamletish" perspective of himself and the arts, he fittingly paints a much stronger profile of Paterson when he subtextually writes about her in a comic essay on the ancient Egyptian Queen Hatshepsut, from the humorist's *The Decline and Fall of Practically Everybody*.³⁹ Hat/Pat was forced to be strong because she had a "lazy and shiftless" father.⁴⁰ Hat/Pat was too practical and independent to ever be happily married. (Paterson's only marriage was a brief one.) And Cuppy's admiration for the focused, I-won't-take-no-for-an-answer Hat/Pat knew no bounds: "[This leader] has been called the first great woman of history. She simply appointed herself King of Egypt and that was all there was to it."⁴¹

The strong ties between Cuppy and Paterson are reminiscent of an old Marty Feldman comedy routine, recorded years before he became famous as the pop-eyed assistant "Igor" to Gene Wilder's title character in *Young Frankenstein* (1974). The recurring punch line of this Feldman bit was, "Funny he never married." But as Feldman's less-then-bright stage persona innocently shares more and more information about his story's fictitious figure with periodic repetitions of the "Funny he never married" line, the explanation slowly becomes comically obvious — he's gay. With regard to Cuppy, however, Cox's biography of Paterson is the only source which makes that claim about the humorist. While this may have been true, it is based upon a rather thin premise: Cuppy claiming at a small party that homosexuality was as "natural" as "anything people did."⁴² After all, Cuppy was a curmudgeon-based comic writer who enjoyed being provocative. And sadly, among conservatives, this is still a controversial statement. And keep in mind, the newspaper for which Cuppy and Paterson wrote, the *Herald Tribune*, was then the most conservative of New York City's dozen-plus publications. Regardless, there are also many potentially conflicting statements in Cuppy's extensive correspondence with Paterson. For example, in a letter from the mid–1920s, apparently following an argument, Cuppy wrote, "We need not continue the discussion of marriage plans you mentioned.... I am not so simple and bourgeois as to insist upon the usual order of events."[43]

In a late 1920s letter to Paterson, Cuppy seems angry at her for a lack of respect for his work, and his missive is tinged with a vague sense of romantic jealously. Cuppy also mixes in a threat of suicide, as was his habit, when he was upset:

> The hell of it is, I have no gas to turn on ... I guess I'll keep on going. This latter remark means that some day I will meet the DREAM GIRL, for whom I have been saving my love.[44]

In a later letter seemingly resigned to a platonic fate with Paterson, Cuppy would add, "I may have and probably did say that you were the only woman I have ever adored." [45]

There is also the fact that several James Thurber biographers (including arguably his definitive profiler, Harrison Kinney) have noted that during the 1930s, Cuppy "courted Ann Honeycutt," a radio producer/writer.[46] Evidently, Thurber, who conducted an on-again-off-again affair with Honeycutt for years, was of the same opinion about Cuppy's interest in her. In a late-1930s letter to a friend, Thurber sadly includes Cuppy as one of his main romantic rivals for Honeycutt:

> I offered her all that a man can offer a woman.... [But] It was the same as a letter from Will Cuppy or a dinner date with [St. Clair] McKelway. It began to get me: it curdled my humor, it stopped my imagination, it drove me crazy.[47]

Though Thurber's work is most synonymous with *The New Yorker*, Cuppy was a regular contributor to the magazine, too; McKelway was also a writer and editor for the journal. Needless to say, as another Thurber biographer suggests, the "vivacious blonde Southerner" Honeycutt was a bit of a *New Yorker* groupie.[48] But Thurber was always married to someone else during his Honeycutt years, whereas Cuppy never married anyone — and only McKelway eventually wed Ms. Honeycutt.

Of course, none of these details provides a definite answer as to whether Cuppy was gay. In a conservatively closeted time, Cuppy might even have been using Honeycutt as a "beard" (cover) for being homosexual. When I put the sexuality question to Cuppy scholar Thomas Maeder, his answer continued the ambiguity, "I think he was mostly asexual." [49] One cannot help thinking of the title to James Thurber's first humor book, a volume admired by Cuppy — *Is Sex Necessary?* (co-authored by E.B. White,

1929). Regardless, the humorist's sexual persuasion is immaterial. The only point of this exercise is to eliminate a simplistic explanation as to why Cuppy and Paterson never married: the "Oh, he was gay" answer. Indeed, the duo probably never made it official for the same reason Paterson eventually severed their friendship — Cuppy's overwhelming need for attention. Besides, in the long run, both Paterson and Cuppy were essentially loners, and they felt a certain comfort in that mindset. The mere fact that Cuppy played at being a hermit on Jones Island (living the loner dream) probably helped Paterson put up with him for as long as she did. Cuppy indirectly addresses this solo perspective in a philosophical note to Paterson, concerning an argument she had with their *Tribune* editor, Burton Rascoe. Cuppy's letter also reveals a certain crass resilience he normally kept buried under his usual cries for assistance:

> I can't believe that you and Burton are to part mad. It seems strange that friendship, like love, is only a bubble that bursts but I think it does. Re Burton, what you ought to do is simply tell the poor dear how grand he is. If you stopped doing that to me I would toss you aside like a broken blossom.[50]

Once again, Cuppy's letters are reminiscent of the later work of another hermit-like, cantankerously comic writer, Charles Bukowski: "I didn't want a woman anyhow. Not to live with. How could men live with women? What did it mean? What I wanted was a cave in Colorado with three-years worth of foodstuffs.[51]

However, a more period-based artistic slant to Cuppy, concerning the subject of relationships, might simply be found in the period's newspaper comic strips. Cuppy, the sometimes self-described "genius," was especially fond of pop culture's first intellectual strip, the reclusive George Herriman's (1880–1940) *Krazy Kat*. Fittingly, Herriman's inspired Coconina County was filled with comic creatures just perfect for the future anthropomorphizing Cuppy. That is, Harriman's fantasy world had a cast of humanized animals which focused upon a dysfunctional love triangle of the title character for Ignatz Mouse and Offissa Pupp (the cop pooch) for Kat. But Ignatz loved no one, and the signature scene in strip after strip is for him to perform his one joy in life — to "krease that Kat's bean with a brick." But "Krazy" Kat always took this as a show of affection — a literal *love tap*. And Offissa Pupp, ever attentive to the disinterested-in-him Kat, would then briefly jail Ignatz. This circular theatre of the absurd look at love sounds a lot like Cuppy's aforementioned analogy that all relationships are nothing more than a "bubble that bursts."

At the risk of making Cuppy rise from his grave, it seems appropriate to quote the aforementioned Gilbert Seldes (a critic with whom the humorist had issues), on the *Krazy Kat* strip and Cuppy: "Like Charlot [Chaplin's Tramp], he [Kat] was always living in a world of his own, and subjecting the commonplaces of actual life to the test of his higher logic."[52] Like Kat, Cuppy was always in "a world of his own," and "his higher logic" seemed to dictate no relationships. And though his letters to Paterson, at times, suggested the romantic inclinations of Kat, Cuppy's image and his satire were more in line with a paraphrasing of Ignatz Mouse: "Krease [everyone's] bean with a brick."

FOUR

Writing
How to Be a Hermit

"A hermit is simply a person to whom civilization has failed to adjust itself." — Will Cuppy (1929)[1]

When Will Cuppy moved to his shack on Jones Island, the aforementioned Tottering-on-the-Brink hovel just off the southern coast of New York's Long Island, his plan was not to write a comic version of Henry David Thoreau's celebrated philosophical account of his two-year sojourn (1845–1847) spent living in a woods near Concord, Massachusetts. No, Cuppy's goal was something even more lofty and poetic. Well, not exactly poetic, because he hated verse. Still, Cuppy wanted time — quiet time — to work on his "masterpiece," the humorist's ironic term for the serious play on which he would fruitlessly labor for decades.

The time was the early 1920s and Cuppy was trying to get away from the New York rat race, live frugally by the sea, and eke out a living as a book reviewer for the *New York Tribune* (which later became the *Herald Tribune*). Unfortunately, the going rate for each critique was a mere two dollars. While that sum went further a century ago, no one was going to get rich on it during the Jazz Age. Of course, living in an abandoned hut in a then-remote area, with periodic free assistance from the nearby Coast Guard and the odd friend, Cuppy's expenses were modest.

Although his newspaper eventually rewarded him with a review column, the focus was upon critiquing mysteries, a genre he found less than artistic. Thus, his freedom came with a price — unsatisfying, time-consuming reviews. Still, Cuppy persevered, because besides needing the money, he found he had a knack for tongue-in-cheek criticism, with elements of his future talent for comedy surfacing. Also, he was occasionally allowed to review non-mystery material, and more importantly, he found an all-important *Tribune*-based mentor in columnist Isabel Paterson (see previous chapter). Her non-stop praise for everything Cuppy (except his playwright aspirations) helped make his first popular success a reality— *How to Become a Hermit*.

However, before examining both the *Hermit* text and the times that produced it, the chapter opening reference to Thoreau's *Walden* deserves some embellishing. Upon my first chance reading of *Hermit* as a boy, back when the world was young, I was reminded of a book report I had just done on *Walden*. That is, while the Cuppy experience was one of those wonderfully fortuitous accidents, a fun "read" of a random text found in a little Catholic mission used bookstore (in my hometown of Cedar Rapids, Iowa), *Walden* had been an assigned project I forced myself to soldier through (this an unfortunate example of how some classic books are taught rather than enjoyed). Regardless, if there is any benefit to growing old, and I have my doubts, one sometimes has a fleeting sense of clarity. Whereas before I had seen the two works as miles apart — a guilty pleasure versus homework — I now see several parallels between the books and their author/philosophers.

First, neither Cuppy nor Thoreau (1817–1862) planned to write about their hermit experience per se. While Cuppy had a play in mind, both men could still be bracketed under Thoreau's simple explanation for getting away: "My purpose in going to Walden Pond was ... to transact some private business [discover how to live] with the fewest obstacles."[2] Second, while Thoreau is remembered as reclusive, and Cuppy was a self-proclaimed "hermit," both men were always tethered to civilization and general assistance. Thoreau's cabin at Walden Pond was built upon the estate of his poet friend and benefactor Ralph Waldo Emerson (1803–1882). There was always a hot meal and good conversation available at the drop of that proverbial hat. Moreover, Thoreau would stroll into the nearby town of Concord on an almost daily basis. And as will be fleshed out shortly, Cuppy's hideaway was in the shadow of New York, a destination to which he returned frequently (with the help of the Coast Guard), just as he also had a great deal of assistance in his getaway by the sea.

Third, both Cuppy and Thoreau were fascinated by nature and made it central to their writing. Granted, Cuppy satirized the public through his anthropomorphic use of animals, but that intent is not alien to Thoreau. For instance, in his *Walden* "village" chapter he observes:

> In one direction from my house there was a colony of muskrats in the river meadows ... in the other horizon was a village of busy men, as curious to me as if they had been prairie dogs, each sitting at the mouth of its burrow, or running over to a neighbor's to gossip. I went there frequently to observe their habits.[3]

Ah, comparing mankind to gophers — Thoreau was clearly a writer after Cuppy's heart. Such satiric impulses often spring from curmudgeonly characters, as past pages of this text have documented about Cuppy. The same has been said of Thoreau. Like the humorist, Thoreau could inspire close friendships, but there was a prickly opinionated tic to his nature, too. After Thoreau's death, Emerson's memorial address found much to praise about the writer, but he also footnoted his former gardener's dark side, including a comment from another of Thoreau's friends: "I love Henry but I cannot like him, and as for taking his arm, I should as soon think of taking the arm of an elm-tree."[4]

Fourth, as this text has established, when Cuppy was not in need of praise, he was never shy about proclaiming his sense of "genius." From such a perch it is always easier to sauté society with satire. The following Thoreau quote from *Walden* would not be out of place in one of those provocative Cuppy letters cited in the previous chapter:

> I was more independent than any farmer in Concord, for I was not anchored to a house or farm but could follow the bent of my genius, which is a very crooked one, every moment.[5]

A "bent" or "crooked" genius would also double as an inspired description of Cuppy.

Fifth, *Walden* and *Hermit* also represent non-traditional autobiographical works, which were not the initial plan of either author. Thoreau found that some fans of his occasional lectures on a myriad of other subjects expressed a greater interest in his Walden experiment. Cuppy's college of one (Paterson) kept after the budding humorist to string together his random essays about his Jones Beach mis-adventures. Sometimes the most honest memoirs are the unplanned ones. Or, as Garrison Keillor, the writer/critic and host of public radio's *A Prairie Home Companion* once described another casually eclectic memoir, in which "rich contradictions abound — with little attempt to explain them away, a mark of the honest autobiographer."[6]

What do the parallels between these two "bent" geniuses tell us? Most basically, their alleged retreats from society were really an indictment against a phony and misdirected society — an attempt to find a better and more honest way of living. Or, to borrow a famous phrase from another Thoreau work, *Walden* and *Hermit* were acts of "civil disobedience." Granted, Thoreau's primary focus was philosophical inspiration, while Cuppy's aim was satire. But the subtextual message was the same — society sorely needs to improve.

Hermit also reads, at times, as an affectionate spoof of *Walden*, given

Cuppy's gift for mixing philosophy with humor. For example, late in Cuppy's text he coins the hauntingly honest axiom about the loneliness of being: "It is an ancient and inviolable rule for hermits not to tell exactly where they live. The truth is they hardly know themselves."[7] Also, in later works (see the following chapter), Cuppy even comically chides Thoreau for suggesting that birds are pleasant creatures. Moreover, while *Walden* hints at mythology, with Thoreau's comments about "heroic books" seemingly being a veiled reference to his own text, Cuppy's *Hermit* begins with the most amusingly philosophical of talking cats (a Mr. Finnegan), the author of the epigraph of this chapter: "A hermit is simply a person to whom civilization has failed to adjust itself." Finnegan's early presence suggests to the reader that *anything goes* in the text, which follows ... and possibly offers another clue that Cuppy's favorite comic strip character was "Krazy Kat."

Speaking of parody, however, one should now more closely examine the 1920s for some history basics pertinent to Cuppy's spoofing book. The decade had begun with Warren G. Harding's election to the White House—a successful campaign which might best be summarized by his signature promise: a "return to normalcy." Nothing symbolized this "normalcy" phenomenon more then a publication bonanza for magazines like *Better Homes and Gardens* (founded in Des Moines, Iowa, 1922), which focused upon "how-to" tips regarding decorating, cooking, and overall healthy family living. The publication was an instant mecca for spoofing which has yet to cease. (Even decades later, as a child of the 1950s, I remember *I Love Lucy*'s title character joking about *Better Homes and Garbage*, or *Mad Magazine* entitling an issue *Bitter Homes and Gardens*.) But such satirical riffs were there from the beginning. Indeed, America's premier humor magazine then and now, *The New Yorker* (founded 1925), was dedicated to a reader covenant which sounds very much like a jab at *Better Homes and Garden* (and its Iowa-based Meredith Corporation, which subsequently published a similar series of follow-up magazines, such as the *Family Circle*): "*The New Yorker* will be the magazine which is not edited for the old lady in Dubuque [Iowa]."[8]

Keep in mind, moreover, everything about Cuppy's *How to Be a Hermit* text, with the important but generally neglected subtitle, *or A Bachelor Keeps House*, satirically derails the aforementioned *Better Homes and Garden*'s filtering of feel-good family via proper decorum, culinary tips, and wholesome "how-to" tips. Cuppy's comic *breakdown* of these correct rules of social engagement might begin with his number-one *Hermit*-based etiquette hint: "ETIQUETTE, or dog, in the original Coptic, means behaving yourself a little better than is absolutely essential."[9] Of course, what would be more natural than burlesquing all things proper, when a special night out for Cuppy might entail spoofing a gourmet meal with a banquet of canned beans ... shared with Coast Guard buddies like Portygee Pete and Hot Biscuit Slim.

Cuppy's disgruntled comic battle cry in *Hermit* reflects a major change sweeping through American humor during the early 20th century. This transition to a more vulnerable comic antihero had gained great momentum by the late 1920s. The dominant American humor type prior to this time had been a capable crackerbarrel Yankee figure, whose roots might be traced back to the traditions of *The Book of Proverbs*, *Aesop's Fables*, the essays of Bacon, and Benjamin Franklin's *Poor Richard's Alamnac*.[10]

The Yankee was capable; he could take care of himself. Legendary humor historian Walter Blair called these capabilities "horse sense," even entitling a book *Horse Sense in American Humor*:

> [The Yankee] learned everything from experience. When he gets into a new situation, he whittles his problem down to its essentials, sees how it compares with situations in his past and how it differs from them, and then he thinks out what he should do —figures out the right answer.[11]

For the Yankee it was a rational universe and life could be planned in a rational manner. Comedy resulted from *other* characters who had trouble planning their existence. But the Yankee established a positive, rational plan an/or advised others of the correct procedure open to them.

This generally rural and/or small-town character, sort of an American Solomon, has never totally left the scene. For instance, witness the ongoing popularity of *The Andy Griffith Show* in television syndication. The homespun wisdom of Griffith's Sheriff Andy Taylor is the epitome of the American crackerbarrel figure. Even in Cuppy's initial heyday (early 1930s), the most popular comic figure, in both motion pictures and print, was another crackerbarrel icon — Will Rogers.

Still, the breakthrough of the comic antihero took place in the 1920s. The antihero, who tries to create order in a world where order is impossible, is actually not new to American comedy. He even surfaces on occasion in the 19th-century world of the New England Yankee, as well as the wild and woolly frontier humor of the Southwest. In fact, few comedy types are ever entirely new. But what is different about the American antihero of the early 20th century is his advancement to center stage. Previously he had been a character often on the fringe of American humor, an irrational figure in a world still considered rational. Now, he was busting out all over popular culture from the comic essays of Cuppy's favorite print humorist (Robert Benchley), to the newspaper comic strip Cuppy most admired — George Herriman's *Krazy Kat*.

One could differentiate between the crackerbarrel Yankee and the comic antihero in five key ways.[12] The crackerbarrel is capable; the antihero tends to be frustrated. The Yankee defines and draws his life lessons from a work ethic—the school of hard knocks. The antihero is more likely to address leisure-time activities. The former is a small-town/rural advocate; the latter is an urban victim. The crackerbarrel character generally has a political and/or social agenda. But the antihero avoids overt issues by focusing upon the day-to-day frustrations of modern life and/or he is simply overwhelmed by them. Lastly, the crackerbarrel Yankee is foremost an adult/parent figure, and the needy antihero is simply childlike. If Will Rogers was a defining cinema crackerbarrel example for Cuppy's time, Laurel & Hardy were the poster children for the comic antihero.[13] With regard to print humorists, pivotal pioneers of antiheroic comedy would key upon Robert Benchley, James Thurber, Clarence Day, S.J. Perelman, and Frank Sullivan.

Cuppy's *Hermit* text could double as the antiheroic template. Of its five-point criteria, the volume is strewn with riffs of the first component—*frustration*. The signature example would be an early in-print variation of the humorist's comic paranoia about the world's aforementioned "hate Cuppy movement." Thus, he is always "wondering what everybody has against me ... I forgot to say that worrying, in moderation, is part of the Cuppy plan. Worry a little every day, folks, I mean it."[14] In contrast, Cuppy's comedy hero, Benchley, was more likely to couch his displays of antiheroic frustration in terms of self-depreciation. For instance, Benchley confesses in *Love Conquers All* (1922): "I would be classified ... 'Low Average Ability,' ... and preparing for a career of holding a spike while another man hits it."[15]

Perhaps Cuppy's *Hermit* frustrations find their most entertaining fruition over the love-hate relationship he has with his Jones Island shack, which is referenced under assorted titles, including the "crooked little house," "house horrible," and the "mansion of Krazy Kat."[16] Because complaining is so central to the Cuppy persona, both on and off the printed page, what could be a more convenient subject for comedy than one's daily self-destructing hermit abode? This ongoing battle/source of material is best captured in the following *Hermit* passage:

> Some day I plan to repair the roof, the walls, the four sides and the underpinning, not from love ... but in instinct to survive. My ["holey"] shack is a house ... but you could just as well call it the great outdoors.[17]

Benchely did a variation of the same scenario with his own metaphorical New York island getaway—the humorist's small Royalton Hotel suite.[18]

Four. *Writing* How to Be a Hermit

When he first retreated to the Royalton, a place the humorist called home nearly as long as Cuppy had his Tottering-on-the-Brink hovel, Benchley mistakenly encouraged friends to contribute bric-a-brac. His green-shaded brass library lamps soon cast incongruently scholarly light on an ever-growing menagerie which included stuffed animals, old busts of Sir Walter

Laurel & Hardy at the time (circa 1927) of their teaming and molding by Leo McCarey.

Scott, an abandoned cello, four-foot-tall electrified statues, an Erie steamboat model, and assorted knickknacks, ranging from miniature glass penguins to figures carved from roots. As with Cuppy, a frustratingly bemused Benchley comically complained in his writing:

> [When I] invited contributions ... I didn't mean that I was starting a whaling museum or that I planned to build more rooms. I ... [wanted] a mid–Victorian study of the "what- not" variety. Well, I got my "what-nots."[19]

The second antiheroic element generously peppered throughout Cuppy's *Hermit* text is his ongoing tutorial on leisure time, or, more aptly phrased, the humorist's study of *anti-work* techniques. Keep in mind, such thoughts are blasphemy in the world of crackerbarrel populism. Indeed, in Will Rogers's book, *Letters of a Self-Made Diplomat to His President* (1926), he includes the telling fact that on his Oklahoma ranch, there was "a sign on the barbed wire gate at the section line: 'Nothing Allowed in That Will Interfere With the Work or Scare the Animals.'"[20] Cuppy's book never misses a chance to take a jab at this honored work ethic.

Moreover, unlike his fellow antiheroic writers, Cuppy's comedy in this area could legitimately be called a direct attack on the crackerbarrel figure—yet another variation of the humorist's one-man war against expert figures. The beauty of Cuppy's satire here is its mutli-faceted levels. First, just as a crackerbarrel populist might methodically itemize a rational game-plan to manage one's workload, Cuppy systematically plans ways to defuse reasons to work. For instance, under the "Cuppy Plan of Motionless Housekeeping," he suggests that these tasks are unnecessary ... and if you still have any lingering bursts of energy or guilt, simply compose an "official list of things not to do."[21] Cuppy, the satirical wordsmith, also periodically justifies his plan by turning a phrase associated with work into topsyturvy-dom—"You may not be able to eat off the floor of my kitchen, but who wants to?"[22] Second, by drop-kicking common sense into nonsense, Cuppy reinforces the irrational world view at the core of antiheroic comedy. That is, Cuppy's comedy, like most iconoclastic humorists, argues that life is a treadmill to nowhere. For example, he argues against making one's bed because "next morning where are you? Right back where you started."[23] Third, Cuppy's happy snowballing of leisure time (including skipping the laundry, so there is no ironing to do) not only obliterates the arbitrary work standards of the crackerbarrel Yankee, it also spoofs the values inherent to publications like *Better Homes and Gardens*.

While Cuppy's most original contribution to the leisure component of pioneering antiheroic writers remains his direct derailing of the crackerbarrel work ethic, his *Hermit* text also showcases more eccentrically basic examples of the individual at play. Thus, just as Benchley had a gift for such short offbeat leisure essays as "Penguin Psychology," or "How to Break 90 in Croquet," Cuppy was also up to the more zany antiheroic task.[24] Fittingly, for an author who would go on to write such nature-based satires as *How to Tell Your Friends from the Apes* and *How to Attract the Wombat, Hermit* is at its eccentric best on subjects like clams! For instance: "No single component of our modern, highly advanced civilization (laughter) is so little understood ... as the common, or soft clam ... unless it's the hard clam, or Freud."[25]

The third antiheroic component in *Hermit* abundance is Cuppy's spoof of urban life. But he tackles the target in a misdirected manner. Unlike his comedy contemporaries who are writing as urban victims, curmudgeon Cuppy, living on the fringe of New York, sees "the risks [from overt danger, to the absurdities inherent to modern life] ... quite as omnipresent and grave [to hermits] as in Manhattan itself, or Indiana."[26] Indeed, his talking orator of a cat, Finnegan, even diagnoses one of Cuppy's lingering urban "Riveting Age" ailments as "auditory hyperesthesia [he hates noise!], which might easily develop into schizophrenia."[27] Cuppy's complaints about maddeningly disruptive noise resonates even more today, when cell-phone etiquette translates into social rudeness to everyone in the receiver's immediate environment, through either disrupting real in-progress conversations, or forcing strangers to be party to such mundane questions as, "Whatcha doing?" Benchley suffered through similar noise pollution problems and addressed the scenario in assorted essays, such as "Traveling in Peace," in which his tips for the urban traveler include "pretending to be a deaf-mute."[28]

The fourth antiheroic element also common to Cuppy's pioneering *Hermit* "study" involves a decidedly apolitical nature. The humorist is much more concerned with such so-called pressing issues as the demand that anything called salad should have lettuce as its main ingredient; the difficulty for hermits to acquire adequate quantities of free paint in the same shade for their shacks (even if it only measures 20 feet by 20 feet); how dependent hermits are on pancakes for all their crucial enzymes; the lack of references to ham and eggs in ancient Greek literature, the neglected art of molding spinach into attractively shaped birds and animals, though he is a sardine addict — they might be the greatest of all modern cures — and how hot black coffee trumps all other things. The preponderance of food items in this abbreviated list of decidedly nonpolitical topics might explain why the Library of Congress originally catalogued Cuppy's *Hermit* text as a cookbook!

A Benchley essay from his delightfully titled collection, *From Bed to*

Worse, or Comforting Thoughts About the Bison (1934), provides a tongue-in-cheek reason for the lack of politics in antiheroic literature. Throughout the ages these befuddled underdogs were forever looking the wrong way during historic events.[29] Of course, for Benchley and Cuppy and other antiheroic humorists, it was a very conscious decision to avoid the issue-orientated wit of the crackerbarrel Yankee. A later example of just how casually adept Cuppy was at deflecting unpleasant topical issues occurs in a radio interview the humorist gave to the Municipal Broadcasting System (New York City, January 18, 1942). The session was part of the promotion for Cuppy's recently published *How to Become Extinct*, which, unfortunately, paralleled the United States' sudden entry into World War II. In discussing the book's then-somewhat controversial title, Cuppy observed:

> Whether there is any pressing need at the moment to learn how to become extinct, my answer would be No.... A much more timely title would be HOW NOT TO BECOME EXTINCT.... I know some people [the various Allied leaders] who are working on [the] problem right now ... but that's another story.[30]

Given what has already been chronicled in this chapter, with regard to *Hermit*'s other basic antiheroic components, addressing the final characteristic (a childlike nature) seems almost superfluous. Here's a 45-year-old man/child (at the time *Hermit* appeared) who is obsessed with Krazy Kat, who does not make his bed, who embraces pancakes as a panacea, who designs elaborate schemes to avoid household chores, and who extols the significance of the common soft clam (or was that the hard clam, also known as Freud). Regardless, this boy/adult's ultimate career goal is to make his life "one long holiday."[31]

Thanks to Cuppy's extensive 1920s correspondence with his mentor/friend Isabel Paterson, the darker side of the humorist's 1929 antiheroic *Hermit* components can be further plumbed. Of course, as a fierce skeptic of all dogmas, except Cuppyism (the most persecuted ism in history ... according to Cuppy), the humorist was adept at baring much correspondence angst on his Jones Island tribute to Thoreau—what the *New York Times* reviewer of *Hermit* called "the 'Walden' of a rose-fever [hay fever] addict."[32]

To revisit Cuppy's five-part antiheroic framework, via the window of reality provided by the Paterson correspondence, necessitates starting again with the subject of *frustration*. The most dramatic demonstration by correspondent Cuppy revolved around his constant threats to kill himself, or someone else (especially if his latest positive review of a Benchley book was not published). This became such an ongoingly dark comedy joke that *Tribune* friends often sent him macabre reading material for possible review. One such submission is discussed in a Paterson letter:

> Thanks for the essay on arsenic ... the book saddened me much more by saying over and over again that cyanide ... does not kill you right away ... you have plenty of time to swallow it ... and give orders for your funeral.[33]

Sometimes his suicide comments were less dark comedy and more absurd, such as his frustration about yet another review not appearing in a timely fashion: "I may decide to stay out here and commit suicide by feeling madder and madder."[34]

As the latter quote suggests, many of Cuppy's letters of frustration, or correspondence comments in general, are on a par with his published work. Unlike rare letter writer Charlie Chaplin, who felt his creative riffing should be saved for a screenplay, Cuppy was not averse to sharing his wit in correspondence. In fact, decades before Gilda Radner's (1946–1989) *Saturday Night Live* character Roseanne Roseannadanna made a national catch phrase of "It's always something!" Cuppy was frequently using a variation of the same line in his letters *and* essays. Radner/Roseanne always credited said bit to her father, who was a young man during Cuppy's heyday, so maybe the elder Radner was simply recycling the humorist's pet peeves mantra. Regardless, what follows is an early Cuppy variation upon the expression in an undated [circa 1926] letter to Paterson, concerning a nearby brush fire:

> If the wind shifts and the flames tear towards me, I will dump all works of genius into the tin boxes I have for the purpose, bury them in the sand and collect insurance. But I'll be asleep at the time [and die]. O well, there's always something.[35]

As with many authors, writing letters often doubled as a warmup exercise for their art. Thus, several variations of the "something" statement would later appear in Cuppy's published work, such as this excerpt on Cleopatra from *The Decline and Fall of Practically Everybody*: "Caesar might have married her but he had a wife at home. There's always something."[36]

The second antiheroic component in the Cuppy correspondence to Paterson keys upon *leisure* time and again occurs with a strong dose of frustration. Ironically, Cuppy writes about a seemingly health-proof subject—lying on Jones Beach and looking for astrological figures in the nighttime sky: "I've been trying to read star maps tonight and have all but dislocated seventeen vertebrae and the godamned things are cock-eyed liars."[37]

Just as leisurely salubrious outings like star gazing could result in pain for Cuppy the chronic hypochondriac, danger even lurked in the most iconic symbols of rest—yawning! Cuppy warns Paterson in another late 1920s letter, "Please be careful about yawning. I have meant to tell you that yawning sometimes dislocates the jaw and one has to be rushed to the hospital in anything but a dignified expression on [your] face."[38]

For Cuppy, even the joy of cooking was fraught with peril. In more amusingly complaining correspondence to Paterson he confesses, "Every time I eat my neck swells up, so I can't eat anymore.... I won't last long at that rate."[39]

Moving in a more poignant leisure-time direction comes a Cuppy correspondence confession about the pleasant escape to be found in working on his never close-to-completion play. Couched as it is in romantic terms, it may even serve as more evidence of Cuppy's asexual nature: "I would rather stay out here [on Jones Island] and do this than be in New York holding someone's hand."[40] This passion for the escape of writing the play helps explain why it was the one thing his mentor/friend Paterson could never get Cuppy to drop from his schedule, despite her strong belief that the material was simply mediocre. Sadly, though Cuppy's self-proclaimed "Great America Drama" is now apparently lost, Paterson was not alone in her assessment. When I put the question to Cuppy scholar Tim Maeder, who was privy to the work years ago, he responded:

> [Cuppy] never got very far [on his play] but rather kept reworking the same incredibly tedious [first act] bits. This was certainly a case where ... [Paterson] was absolutely right in advising him to drop his dramatic aspirations and focus on what he did best [comedy].[41]

The third antiheroic element to investigate in the Cuppy correspondence, which parallels the writing of *Hermit*, is the maddening nature of *urban* life. There is a decided suggestion in early 20th century pop culture that the ever-escalating pace of the industrial urban age could lead to an individual jumping the tracks mentally, à la Charlie Chaplin's Tramp in *Modern Times* (1936). Such instability represents an excellent catalyst for exploring the possible correspondence-based inspiration for Cuppy's aforementioned talking cat (Mr. Finnegan) in his *Hermit* text. In a mid–1920s letter to Paterson, the recent death of some stray cats on the island was the catalyst for a morose Cuppy to share:

> Of all the ghosts I know of, commend me to a dead cat. I had one follow me one night in Chicago ... it was the soul of a friend who had just committed suicide ... and he followed me home and disappeared into the air, howling every step. I suppose he was sorry he done it.... I might do the same thing tonight.[42]

Charlie Chaplin literally being swallowed by the machine work of *Modern Times* (1936).

Beyond the "boogie boogie" nature of ghosts, Cuppy's period correspondence is equally full of standard urban complaints about losing his hold on reality. He does not like his mystery book-reviewing job, and complains to Paterson, "I am growing half-witted by the minute reading those books. I can't stand it and won't."[43] And along even more conventional city-based frustration lines, the same letter documents how his alleged but ever-so-flawed escape (Jones Island) from New York has been betrayed:

> My house is a hell, with crickets in the walls, and outside is a double hell, with a steam dredge drudging up the bay to make a road over here to [to the island] so that human worms can drive their Fords over here and make it a triple hell.[44]

The comic anger inherent to so many of these letters is much more apparent in the Cuppy books which follow the *Hermit* volume.

The fourth antiheroic element, a *nonpolitical nature*, surfaces in a surprisingly provocative manner in the Cuppy letters to Paterson. Earlier in this chapter I demonstrated how Cuppy's position on practically everything was the antithesis of the populist political crackerbarrel Yankee, especially as personified by Will Rogers. Indeed, I went so far as to quote from Rogers's 1926s text, *Letters of a Self–Made Diplomat to His President.* What if an off-the-record Cuppy letter sideswiped not only Rogers's writing in general but even that book in particular? Cuppy seldom dated his rambling letters to Paterson, and then only noted authors by name and not the title of their books. However, by referencing other historical information in Cuppy's correspondence, one can be assured that in a 1926 letter to Paterson he sent the most damning verdict on *Letters of a Self–Made Diplomat,* given this was the only text published that year by the crackerbarrel humorist:

> To add the last camel [the straw that broke the camel's back, the *Tribune*'s] Miss Moore sent me Will Rogers' new book to review, which is the most ghastly godawful collection of knockneed and pitiful skulduggary [*sic*] I have witnessed so help me.[45]

Cuppy's letters are full of such diatribes against crackerbarrel Rogersisms; the above quote was simply the most colorful. But other period American heroes of potentially populist possibilities, though decidedly not humorists, are under satirical attack in Cuppy's correspondence. Populism is all about celebrating Americans via American heroes — learning from ordinary people doing extraordinary things. Cuppy's later books mute his cynicism about American populist figures by either subtextualizing his crack through anthropomorphic use of animals, or by focusing his satire on famous folks from foreign lands and distant times. And his *Hermit* humor is much more likely to dwell on something as far from politics as sleeping with his

A typical Will Rogers crackerbarrel pose (circa 1930).

vegetables during the winter, in order that the food does not freeze. But as concerned Rogers, Cuppy's private ramblings pulled no punches against what he saw as a potential demigod, whose attitude was just too positive to be believed. Along similar lines the following year (1927), when seemingly everyone was singing the praises of Charles Lindbergh (1902–1974), when "Lucky Lindy" became the first pilot to fly solo across the Atlantic Ocean, Cuppy was equally upset about the hero-worshipping mob mentality of Americans. If possible, Lindbergh symbolized an even greater danger to Cuppy, because while Rogers represented a program of "knock-kneed junk," Lindbergh was simply a 1920s take on today's "flavor of the month," with no program at all ... and yet the masses treated him like the Second Coming:

> paper states man jumped off bridge leaving note that since there is so much Lindbergh in the newspaper life isn't worth living any more. They took him to Bellevue for observation.... That man is probably one of us.[46]

Within 12 years Lindbergh's reputation was tarnished by his anti–Semitic statements and other Nazi-sympathizer actions. But even if Lindbergh had simply disappeared after his *Spirit of St. Louis* touched down in Paris, Cuppy's main point would still be golden — modern pop culture, with the most gullible mass audience, is ordaining heroes right and left, and seldom are these figures up to the task.

Cuppy's antiheroic contemporary James Thurber indirectly referenced Lindburgh in the short story "The Greatest Man in the World" (1931).[47] Thurber's story asked what if a person of comparable accomplishment turned out to be pond scum as a human being despite the hero-demanding needs of the public? Thurber's fictional "greatest man" is another flying hero, Jack Smurch, from populist Iowa. But as the name "Smurch" suggests, despite his accomplishment, Jack is just this side of a Neanderthal. Members of the press whitewash him as long as possible, but this character, whose own mother wishes he had drowned during his historic flight, cannot be muzzled forever. Consequently, during Smurch's meeting with statesmen, dignitaries, and newspaper editors, this human embarrassment is sent on his final flight, (so to speak) by "accidently" falling out of a ninth-story window. A cover-up is concocted by the press, and so Smurch remains the hero in death that he never really was in life.

In Jean Renoir's classic film *Rules of the Game* (1939), yet another Lindbergh-like aviator does not know how to act as a hero, despite experiencing mob adulation. Renoir's figure comes across as a pouting, whiny child whose toys are not to his liking. Before he does irreparable damage to the image of heroes everywhere, however, the plot kills him. Though not a deliberate murder, as in Smurch's case, the flyer's death serves the same purpose. To utilize Renoir's inspired title, neither character has lived up to society's "rules of the game." But once they are safely dead, the media can maintain their manufactured heroic image. As the sometimes-populist director John Ford later had a film figure observe, "When the legend becomes a fact, print the legend." This could be called Ford's justification for a cover-up. It implies, as with the stories by Thurber and Renoir, that people need heroes to look up to, whether the real individuals merit the honor or not. But since these artists reveal the alleged heroes' feet of clay to their audiences (only the public within the stories remain fooled), the real villain/fool remains a naïve populous, forever ready to drink whatever Kool-Aid is offered. Cuppy's correspondence on the subject suggested simply cutting through the hypocrisy and killing himself, which was his favorite solution.

Still, Cuppy was in perfect agreement about the less-than-lofty potential of the masses. He probably never publicly pursued the point to the extent of a similar contemporary like author/editor/humorist H.L. Mencken (1880–1956), because of the potential firestorm of political venom it might produce. Note how the respected even-tempered period reference, *Living Authors: A Book of Biographies* (1931), opens its entry on Mencken, and how much his "crimes" parallel the correspondent complaints of Cuppy:

> Mencken has been denounced more copiously and violently than any American of the present age. His attacks upon Babbitts [he actually preferred the term "Booboisie" for the bourgeois], professors, and politicians met with excessively hearty [negative] response.[48]

The fifth and final antiheroic component to be examined in Cuppy's Paterson letters is that of a *childlike nature*. One might start by merely referencing the previous chapter's documentation of the non-stop nurturing he demanded of Paterson, his intellectual nursemaid. But with regard to Cuppy's more basic survival needs on the island, his relationship with the Coast Guard station, located a mere 300 yards from his beach house, is always front and center in his correspondence. Cuppy would ladle on the heavy praise for all their kindnesses, especially during the island's ugly winter weather. For example, in one undated Paterson letter (circa 1924) he shared, "A brave coast guard has just carried your message to ... me ninety-five thousand miles through snow and ice and hellishness [which is] unspeakable."[49] In another letter referencing the delivery of countless books to be reviewed for the *Tribune*, Cuppy simply calls them "those angelic coast guards."[50]

Cuppy's letters chronicle, however, a litany of additional Guard services to him, including rowing and/or motoring the writer to the mainland;

fixing everything and anything mechanical (especially his typewriter); providing the occasional hot meal; posting his reviews and letters; providing him with paint and odd building materials to maintain his "Tottering on the Brink" hovel; and gifting him with affectionately comic jabs, which Cuppy then recycles. For instance, the humorist asks Paterson in one letter:

> Please tell me by return mail if this is a popular joke one of the Coast Guard told me, "If knowledge was power, Bill, you'd be helpless." Sounds like a factory made jest but I hain't heard it before [and] might use in article.[51]

"Helpless" Bill was not really that helpless, but he certainly played that card. Paradoxically, an aggressive ploy of this boy/man was his petty, childish feelings toward actual children, paralleling the curmudgeonly W.C. Fields (1880–1946). Perhaps the most paraphrased Fields line upon the subject is "Anyman who hates dogs and kids can't be all bad."[52] For Cuppy, the worshipper of quiet, his greatest complaint about what he usually called "brats," was their propensity for creating disruptive noise. In one letter he complains about their use of fireworks; in another he anticipates the quiet of his beach being lost: "The brats have a vacation from school next [Easter] week so they will be all over the place [;] is that what the good Lord died for [?][53] In a third letter he comically suggests not even wanting to be seen holding a book about children:

> Why do I not review "A Century of Children's Books"? Why Indeed ... I never took the gol darned thing out of the [*Tribune*] office ... [having] decided that I couldn't have it with me on the train [back to the island].... You know my feelings about children, those hateful little brats ... I shall never cease regretting that I didn't get "Doggy Woof and Pussy Meow" to review last year.[54]

Could it be that the self-centered, often self-loathing Cuppy saw a lot of the spoiled "brat" in himself, too?

The all-important New York reviews for Cuppy's *Hermit* were uniformly good, no small task for a humorist whose day job was with a competing Gotham publication (the *Tribune*). But one of the most entertaining takes upon the book was an interview/review in the *Brooklyn Eagle*, whose critic felt compelled to share with readers:

> Most hermits are supposed to wear dirty beards and possess bitten and broken fingernails.... [Not the] rather goodlooking [Cuppy, who] wears, when in the city on business, neat shirts, sedate cravats and pressed suits. On Jones Island he relaxes ... but still manages to cling to the more conventional garb of masculinity.[55]

Egbert Sousé (W.C. Fields) throttles yet another bratty kid (Bobby Larson) in *The Bank Dick* (1940). The boy's mother (Jan Duggan) is not pleased.

The *Eagle* critic was most interested in Cuppy's comparisons of himself to Robinson Crusoe, which the humorist was only too happy to expand upon at tongue-in-cheek length. After setting the record straight upon Crusoe's given advantage of having 12 raft loads of supplies from his wrecked ship (versus Cuppy dragging everything out from the city over a period of years), the humorist played at being honest and modestly confessed:

> Naturally, I'm a little jealous of Robinson Crusoe because he has had all the attention. But I do think he was a clever chap because he could

make bread, which I can't. He also sopped his bread in milk, showing that hermit etiquette is much alike at all times and places. I had it on him in one thing. Where he had only Friday I had nine Coast Guards. I never found out what the Coast Guards think about me and my hermitage. They probably think I'm a poor, harmless lunatic who needs help. Those Coast Guards are certainly swell fellows.[56]

Just as Cuppy manages to plug his sainted surrogate parental Coast Guard in this *Hermit* review, the humorist also gets in a dig at a "brat" in a freelance article he pens on the new book. Written for the *Author League Bulletin*, with the wonderfully self-promoting title, "The Hermit Looks at Bookshops," Cuppy credits a rare sale of *Hermit* to an "old-fashioned grandmother" who:

> was leading by the hand ... fair-haired, blue-eyed lad of some four summers, apparently with a beastly temper; every few steps he would break away, run ahead, and kick his grandmother in the shins. She, angelic soul, had obviously come to buy the little monster a book.[57]

But in a surprise twist to this pugnaciously poignant look at the plight of authors waiting ... and waiting ... on book signing sales, the "little monster" actually does a good thing. Well, sort of. The brat shoplifts Cuppy's book, and Grandma is forced to buy it.

Of course, *the* Cuppy critical coup de grâce for *Hermit* was his home newspaper, the *Herald Tribune*, allowing him to review his own book! Comically entitled, "Little Brothers of the Clam," Cuppy initially assumes a seemingly unbiased perspective by noting that he is largely drawing from the publisher's catalog "where some unprejudiced reader has set forth the [book's] details ... [only to later add] it is a well known fact that most authors write their own catalogue stuff ... Mr. Cuppy is no exception."[58] Like everything Cuppy wrote, including his book-critique column, "Mystery and Adventure," he essentially turns his *Hermit* review into a comic essay. And, yes, while there are tongue-in-cheek plugs, such as his comment that "the author achieves real eloquence at times, notably in his defense of the sardine," Cuppy was much more likely to go for straight-out comedy:

> Students of morbid psychology may be interested in ... the Liveright [his publisher] archives ... a confidential letter from the author (also suppressed): "I am unable to analyze my creative method. It just comes to me. As for the inner meaning ... a few readers will easily identify ... [it] with the great outside world but these readers will be crazy. Age: I'm getting along but look younger. Favorite flower: None. Favorite bird: None. Clubs: The Guild of Former Pipe Organ Pumpers. Purpose in life: To borrow $1,000."[59]

Though Cuppy's *Hermit* text received critical praise from other writers, besides his own self-promotion, no one approached the sheer volume of loyal hosannas from his mentoring friend Paterson. This assorted quantity, via her own *Herald Tribune* column, "Turns with a Bookworm," is best broken down into several categories. First, before the book even appeared, Paterson produced what might be called, à la the movies, "coming soon trailers." For instance, on September 22, 1929, she closed her Sunday column with the tease, "Watch for the big Cuppy Number [the showcasing of Cuppy's *Hermit* in the *Herald Tribune*'s "Books" section] next week."[60] Second, there was Paterson's non-stop praise following the text's publication, such as:

> We've been carrying ... "How to Be a Hermit" under our left fin all week, and reading it at odd intervals, especially when we should be doing something else.... It has deranged all our literary schedules, deprived us of sleep, made us forget to order coal, so that when the cold snap hit us last week we nearly perished — "fashionable but frozen."... Common sense compels us to admit that it is the funniest book we have read for years.[61]

Third, Paterson excelled at obtaining entertaining *Hermit* raves from numerous authors, ranging from Burton Rascoe claiming, "It is nothing short of inspired ... it practically cured Burton of pneumonia," to Edward McKenna stating, "Cuppy is one of God's own cuckoos. His talent is very serious.... Did we say so, or not?"[62] Fourth, Paterson was relentless in her support. What follows is the opening to her column of November 10, 1929:

> As a whole week has elapsed without our recommending "How to Be a Hermit," we feel that the time has come to take this up again in a serious way. Especially in view of the current performance of the stock market.... Going or coming, "How to Be a Hermit" is now an absolute necessity.[63]

Fifth and finally, given that *Hermit* was dedicated to Paterson, she was fiercely funny in stating that her championing of the book was completely aboveboard, with no ties to their friendship. Given what we now know about the challenging/demanding nature of any ties with Cuppy, Paterson was barely stretching the truth:

> It may be intimated that we praise ... out of personal friendship.... The fact is, if it wasn't for the way he writes, we couldn't stand Will at all.... As for the dedication, we are very choosy about dedications ... a book has got to be good or we don't care to have it dedicated to us. If this seems harsh, ask yourself, what other chance have we of having our name go down in history?[64]

The fittingly glum Oscar Levant (center) in *An American in Paris* (1951, with Gene Kelly on the right, and Georges Guetary), playing a Cuppy-like character.

Besides Paterson's literary army of one, watershed humorists (such as Frank Sullivan, recently selected as one of the *50 all-time Funniest American Writers*), endorsed Cuppy's book in their newspaper columns.[65] For Sullivan, Cuppy's island "struggle for existence" tale was at its best when the humorist shared his "actually bizarre hints on cooking ... that food has to be cooked occasionally."[66] But the *New York Times*'s reviewer makes one of the more insightfully amusing links between how Cuppy's food interests tie into the world of the nonpolitical comic antihero: "The great questions of the day reach Jones Island, and Mr. Cuppy is properly perturbed ... [with] the relation of spinach to the good life."[67]

Pianist/composer/actor/writer Oscar Levant, whose later tortured psyche memoirs are so reminiscent of Cuppy's angst-ridden letters to Paterson, always believed that a particular decade in an individual's life defines or shapes him. For Cuppy, that decade was the 1920s. Though the humorist would soon lose his permanent resident status on the island when it became a public beach area, he would forever after characterize himself as the "Hermit of Jones Island." Moreover, Cuppy exited the 1920s as a major satirist, whose period correspondence foreshadows the increasingly darker work to come. In Sam Kashner and Nancy Schoenberger's definitive biography of the aforementioned Levant, these profilers celebrate how their subject emerged as a 1940s movie actor presence because Levant embodied a type coming into vogue at this time. The irony of this cinema character profile is that it better describes Cuppy's "Hermit of Jones Island" persona more than a decade earlier:

> [He is] a kind of resident cynic who's brilliant but intrinsically lazy, a nocturnal creature with a good heart who is nonetheless capable of turning on you but who is always harshest on himself.[68]

Cuppy, this comic connoisseur of catastrophe, both real and imagined, was just that far ahead of the times.

FIVE

Early Greenwich Village Years, Groucho Marx, and *How to Tell Your Friends from the Apes*

"The family life of the Baboon is known as hell on earth."—*How to Tell Your Friends from the Apes* (1931)[1]

After the failure of *The Maroon Tales* (1909/1910), it took Cuppy 20 years and an aggressively stubborn mentor champion (Isabel Paterson) before the humorist produced a second book, *How to Become a Hermit* (1929). But despite the lengthy gestation period, and *Hermit*'s popular publication paralleling the birth of the Great Depression — a key component in the humorist's burgeoning belief that the fates were always against him (the "hate Cuppy" nonsense with which he loved to pepper his letters and literature) — his next hit humor book appeared a mere two years later, *How to Tell Your Friends from the Apes*.

Apes is arguably Cuppy's greatest text, and brings out more of the satirical anger present in the previously cited Paterson letters. Moreover, while the *Hermit* book put Cuppy on the humor map, *Apes* would be the prototype for the Cuppy books to follow. But before addressing three distinct differences toward which the humorist morphed in those two short years (again with the help of Paterson), one should begin with the things the *Hermit* and *Apes* texts continued to have in common.

First, though Jones Beach becoming a public park forced Cuppy to abandon permanent residency on the island, *Apes* still documents an individual directly pinpricking, though ever so affectionately, high-profile naturalists like Henry David Thoreau. For example, Cuppy states that, while

A caricature of Cuppy used to promote *How to Be a Hermit* (1929).

Thoreau and John James Audubon (1785–1851) were perfectly within their rights in producing the watershed works *Walden* (1854) and *Birds of America* (1827–1838), the humorist felt "they encouraged certain unfortunate [bird loving] tendencies [to be praised]."[2]

Second, in the opening pages of *Apes*, Cuppy continues to spoof Thoreau's broader philosophical core. For instance, critic Stanley Cavell suggests that the key task of *Walden* is to help one "discover how to earn and spend our most wakeful hours — whatever we are doing."[3] Fittingly, in Cuppy's preface to *Apes* he suggests, with a literary wink, that his text's primary goal is addressing the "need [for] more and yet more of these how-to-tell books, for isn't it high time that we learned to tell a few things apart in this topsy-turvy old world."[4]

Third, and most obvious, both *Hermit* and *Apes* are subtextual satires of mankind which camouflage their barbs, first through a journal-like memoir, *Hermit*, and then through a pseudo-naturalist text, *Apes*. But as will be showcased shortly, starting with the *Apes* book, Cuppy's work evolved into tight little essays that managed to include inspired footnotes which did not slow the marvel of each article's craftsmanship. Cuppy's pet peeves were a bittersweet anticipation of the CBS *60 Minutes* commentator Andy Rooney's weekly whine, which started with his signature opening, "Did you ever notice...?" This print version of a sour expression after tasting something funny was vintage Cuppy. But if one does not relate to the Rooney comparison, there is always a period link to Presidential Calvin Coolidge (1872–1933), whose White House tenure (1923–1929) paralleled Cuppy's years on Jones Island. The description of Coolidge coined by Jazz Age wit Dorothy Parker might double as a visual icon of Cuppy's comic complaining mindset about life: "It looks like he was weaned on a dill pickle."

However, before more fully fleshing out these new wrinkles in Cuppy's career, one should briefly expand upon his migration from Jones Island (though he was still allowed to maintain his shack on a part-time basis) to Greenwich Village. For most of the 1920s, the humorist's address was:

> Will Cuppy
> c/o U.S. Coastguard Station 87
> Zach's Inlet Seaford, Long Island, New York

In the previous chapter much was made of his ever-so-helpful primary neighbors, the Coast Guard. But in 1926 Cuppy and the Guard were joined on the island by a small city surveying party led by Sidney Shapiro, who occupied another Jones Beach hut. Shapiro answered to New York's parks czar Robert Moses (1888–1981), who exercised considerable constructive or destructive power, depending upon your vantage point, on the physical face of New York for decades. Indeed, Moses was so controversial that he opened his later memoir on the defensive:

> Despite my reputation for ruthless destruction of familiar landmarks, let me assure you: I would not hasten by one hour the day when the whole town will look as if it had been designed by Frank Lloyd Wright.[5]

Such a reputation also gives a darkly comic double meaning to the title of Moses's autobiography *Public Works: A Dangerous Trade* (1970).

Regardless, Moses's orchestration of the Shapiro surveying party was to devise a plan to turn the island into Jones Beach State Park by the end of the 1920s. So, the unraveling of Cuppy's "paradise lost" occurred early in his tenure on the island. But even before this "progress" saw fruition, with waves of tourists flooding Cuppy's hideaway, the building of the mainland-linking roadway would be the catalyst for the humorist's darkly comic correspondence complaints to Paterson. In an undated letter [circa 1929, the year the park officially opened], Cuppy whined, "Just a word to let you know that the steam drudge has now decided to blow a siren whistle every fifteen minutes a day and night. It is the end."[6]

Still, Cuppy fought to stay in his hovel by the sea, and he won his modest victory based upon three factors. First, it never hurts to be modestly famous when you are requesting favors from powerful people. The eccentric humorist and columnist was well known in New York long before the August 1929 opening of the Jones Beach State Park. Cuppy's popular *Hermit* text underscored this reputation when it was published to critical and commercial acclaim shortly after the park's opening. Second, and even more importantly, powerbroker Moses seems to have had a sense of humor: he reportedly enjoyed Cuppy's book, and based upon his later memoir, he played at being comic himself. Third, in reading his autobiography, Moses clearly enjoyed the enormous czar-like power and patronage he had over the greater New York area: it seemed to amuse him to grant Cuppy's quasi-hat-in-hand request to let the humorist maintain at least part-time access to the Tottering-on-the-Brink shack. What follows is Moses's memoir account of his seemingly act-of-charity edict:

> Every now and then Will journeyed reluctantly to the big town, sold his stuff to the slicks and pulps, slept after hours on the operating table of a kindly doctor in Greenwich Village, and then hurried home to his beans and sardine cans. He lived on handouts from the nearby Coast Guard gobs and from our engineers and for variety snatched some of the clams the gulls dropped on the spreading concrete.... In the race between progress on Jones Beach and Cuppy, we had to make an agonizing appraisal. We saved Will ... but hermits must move a little further from town.[7]

Now, if that does not sound like a prince granting a pauper special dispensation, I do not know my Mark Twain and his 1882 book, *The Prince and the Pauper*. But Cuppy being Cuppy, one assumes the humorist made his appeal with the most groveling of game plans given his ability to assume, at times, a falsely flattering/fawning attitude, which would not be alien to Dickens's obsequious Uriah Heep, from *David Copperfield* (1849–1850). But as luck would have it, Moses' memoir memories of Cuppy were drawn from an earlier column the parks czar had written for *Newsday*. This article both expands upon Cuppy's situation prior to the fateful year of 1929, and actually includes the satirist's initial begging letter to Moses's subordinate Sidney Shapiro. First, here is Moses setting the *Newsday* scene for what he describes as Cuppy's "irresistible appeal": "In 1928 Will, whose shack was in the way of the big dredges and bulldozers, wrote a pathetic Christmas letter to Sid Shapiro ... begging for a few months' respite."[8] Cuppy's letter reads, in part:

> I have got to have a few days there somehow or go mad. As you have a kind face and I am not afraid of you, I will count on your firmest

support ... Jese [*sic*, Jeez], to put it strongly, I hate to leave.... I will be flat broke this spring ... if anything should occur to you ... will you be angelic enough to let me know, thereby saving what remains of my reasons?[9]

Presumably, the letter won Cuppy an island extension, and then the publication of the humorist's popular book helped cement a long-term arrangement, whereas the writer could maintain his beach shack on a part-time basis until his death. Moses's *Newsday* article also documents the czar's enjoyment of Cuppy's comedy by including several of his favorite quotes from the humorist's books. As a footnote to Moses's vivid memories of Cuppy the moocher, the humorist's *Hermit* text includes a panhandling section. Before Moses's park people made Jones Beach a tourist mecca for New Yorkers in the early 1930s, the island still had summer vacationers. At the end of the holiday season, Cuppy assumed/hoped visitors would not want to lug extra groceries home. Thus, the humorist attached a contribution sign to a "large cardboard grocery box ... placed in a conspicuous position on the [island exiting] dock in such a manner as practically to block the only passage to the boat."[10]

Of course, part of Cuppy's comedy payoff here was then chronicling the goofy collection of largely useless items he received, including soap flakes, shoestrings, and a "damaged portrait of a Cunard [ocean] liner."[11] This blatant begging also reinforced his spoofing of Thoreau's *Walden*. That is, Cuppy's dockside cardboard box was an obvious plea for practical foodstuffs. Thus, unlike Thoreau's idealized self-sufficiency (raising his own foods), and independence from the machine age, Cuppy (the connoisseur of canned goods ... especially sardines) and his begging box represented an antiheroic compromise/surrender to the industrial age, an "I can't do it alone" admission. But there was comic honesty in Cuppy's confession, too, because, as chronicled in the previous chapter, Thoreau was not quite up to the "home alone" task either.

There is also a raw humor inherent to Cuppy implying a sense of personal inferiority (e.g., the begging box), which takes the reader back to a primal explanation for laughter. Literary giant John Updike once wrote, "Perhaps one reason we laugh so much in childhood is that so much is unexpected and novel."[12] I would posit that much the same explanation is at work regarding the world-weary nature of Cuppy's bald faced mooching move — he surprises the reader with his comic admission of an almost universal human fear: the overwhelming nature of life. Cuppy squeezes a laugh from Thoreau's signature insight, "Most men live lives of quiet desperation."[13]

A final funny addendum to czar Moses's coming to the aid of Cuppy went beyond just saving the humorist's access to the shack by the sea. Again, like any good prince, Moses also granted Cuppy an honorary military title/cover: "[My] engineers put up a sign at Cuppy's shack with the name 'Captain August Johnson.' This alias kept beachcombers and exploring celebrity seekers away and ensured privacy."[14] While such kindnesses forever elevate Moses in the eyes of the Cuppy faithful, fans of old-time baseball will forever hold the park czar in contempt for contributing to the Dodgers leaving Brooklyn for Los Angeles. (Moses made it economically difficult for Dodgers' owner Walter O' Malley to build a new stadium in Flatbush.[15]) What would have been quasi-fan Cuppy's reaction to the game's most infamous exit act? Well, as a self-proclaimed "hermit," beach bum, he probably would have felt bad about losing the affectionately nicknamed "Bums" (Dodgers). But his periodic baseball references would seem to make him a Yankee fan, since that is the only team he notes and/or kids in his writing, and New York had three major league clubs throughout his lifetime: the Yankees, the Dodgers, and the Giants. For instance, in *How to Attract the Wombat*, Cuppy noted that when he asked an individual "whom I had always supposed to be fairly civilized if he had ever heard of the Wombat, he replied, 'Sure, he played third base on the Yankees in '35.'"[16]

If the 1920s island years were the decade which molded or shaped Cuppy, I would argue that the 1930s were what might be called his "zeitgeist" period. Contemporary screenwriter/director Alexander Payne more fully defines this phenomenon:

> They say ... [an artist] can do honest, sincere work for decades but you're given in general a 10-year period when what you do touchest the zeitgeist— when you're relevant."[17]

While I would argue that Cuppy has never been more relevant than he is today, the decade from 1931–1941, which is bookended by the publication of the humorist's *Apes* (1931) and *How to Become Extinct* (1941), represent Cuppy at his zenith. And it all began with three distinct changes the humorist brought to his work between *Hermit* and *Apes*.

The first and most obvious difference is a streamlined style. The *Hermit* essays are eclectically gathered under the broad umbrella of a Jones Island lifestyle. But the topics range from recipes/budgets to random vaudeville-like dialogues between Cuppy and Isabel Paterson. Moreover, the *Hermit* essays can entertainingly ramble along for several thousand words. Though often brilliantly amusing, this verbiage is more reminiscent of Cuppy's college excursion into writing in *The Maroon Tales*. In contrast, *Apes* is a methodically organized, spoofingly scientific "study" of various creatures in the natural world, from Neanderthal man to the platypus and the aardvark. Plus, each tightly crafted essay is the model of economy — running roughly 1,000 words (or two printed pages). The satirically professorial tone is further reinforced by gifting each piece with two or more bitingly tongue-in-cheek footnotes. In this joint comic streamroller effect, Cuppy uses his scientist persona to satirize humanity. To illustrate, he describes lemurs as having "huge bug-eyes, elongated ankles and knobby toes. He is sometimes confused with Delirium Tremens."[18] This particular crack is reminiscent of W.C. Fields. When asked if he had ever had DTs, Fields replied, "I don't know. It's hard to tell where Hollywood ends and the DTs begin."[19]

Second, *Apes*, and the Cuppy parody manuals for naturalists assume a consistently darker satirical tone than that of the *Hermit* text. Naturally, an element of this bipolar muse exists in everything he wrote, starting with the *Hermit* book. Yet with *Apes* and the subsequent texts, his contemptuous nihilistic anger is more front and center. For example, in *Apes* he writes that the irritating noise caused by the howling monkey "can be cured by a simple operation on ... [his] neck with an axe."[20] Bear in mind how this differs with his contemporary Walt Disney's (1901–1966) gushingly "cute" anthropomorphism in animated features like *Snow White and the Seven Dwarfs* (1937) and *Bambi* (1942). Cuppy was arguing, to reference scholar Sanda Lieb, "We (humans) are so similar to [lower animal] brutes that we need guides to make any distinctions."[21]

If one were to cobble together an epitaph to cover the more darkly comic transition represented by the *Apes* text, it would simply be: "Life is utter futility." Thus, just as a later Cuppy book would chronicle *How to Become Extinct* (based upon some late, not so great, *former* species), *Apes* provides suggestions as to how we might begin the process with the pesky, still-living creatures, such as the aforementioned howling monkey. Also, Cuppy and canaries just did not mix — the noise factor again. So the frustrated humorist diabolically dreams that "[this bird is used] to detect the presence of deadly gas in mines but there are not enough mines to go around."[22]

Consistent with this satirical survival of the fittest philosophy, Cuppy can comically support a bird which fights back. For instance, "Owls teach us to keep our hands out of hollow trees."[23] But Cuppy's *Apes* text is an equal opportunity guide to the potential extinction of all, even if it involves lesser animals bringing down man. Listen to his casually deadpan commentary about individuals with unusual pets: "Persons who raise Tiger cubs in their homes are sometimes known as missing persons."[24]

So why the more focused anger in *Apes* and the Cuppy books to follow?

While there can be no definitive answer, one could start with a change of address. After 1929, the humorist's primary residence would be the city — 130 West 11th Street, Greenwich Village. Ironically, though he would tuck himself away here as an urban hermit for the remaining 20 years of his life, this man who hated noise (especially from children), had an apartment next to a school playground. Moreover, his building seems largely populated with young couples and wailing babies. Cuppy's childlike manner of coping with this stress was to periodically pull out a New Year's Eve style noisemaker (the type which uncoils when blown) and literally blow/whistle in the direction of the offending sound. These daily catharses would get him through the worst noise problems. But Cuppy's dilemma was complicated by the fact that, as he reserved the quietest time for his writing (the wee hours of the night), the humorist's sleep-during-the-day schedule paralleled the period of maximum noise from the playground set.

Still, one could make the case that not even an army of noisy tykes could be as eardrum rattling as what Cuppy had endured during the final two years of his Jones Island sojourn. Besides the building of Moses's epic causeway to the beach, enormous dredges moved into the area in order to elevate the level of the island. Since the island all but disappeared during winter storms, the height of some sections were raised as much as 12 feet. And, during 1928, hundreds of New York park commission people roamed the island, planting a special variety of beach grass to hold the new sand/soil in place. No, when the dredges and the legion of workers are measured against a mere playground and the intermittent squawking babies, Cuppy, paradoxically, had it quieter *out of* the country.

Yet, could one argue that being forced from his onetime sanctuary and/or having it ruined (by tourists) contributed to his more bitingly sour satire? Possibly. But Czar Moses seems to have been unusually generous in accommodating Cuppy. Plus, in an undated [circa 1929] letter to Paterson, the humorist also appears to dare one to use the "moocher" term again: "Did I tell you that I have a new [Greenwich] apartment in town? 130 East 11th Street, given to me by old friend — only two rooms. When I stay there I can give parties upstairs"[25] (a fourth-floor walk-up). Between the references to "given" and "parties" Cuppy seems to have been coping quite nicely with the forced move.

No, I believe the best explanation for the darker tone of Cuppy's comedy starting with the *Apes* text is simply tied to the unexpected success of the *Hermit* book. The latter work was a safe last chance for the book reviewer to establish a literary beachhead. Once he became a "somebody" in humor circles, he could let more of the real Cuppy come through — the fully formed funny/sad, suicide-threatening, middle-aged grouch of the pre–*Hermit* Paterson letters. In baseball terms, I would liken Cuppy's easing into mainstream humor (before going more satirically rogue), to when the Brooklyn Dodgers integrated baseball (1947) with Jackie Robinson (1919–1972), the first African American to play in the modern major leagues. Robinson, a passionate player and activist, was strictly forbidden to show his confrontational tendencies until *after* he proved his legitimate talent and the public became accustomed to seeing a person of color playing in the major leagues.

One could also couple this newfound freedom of expression with his tighter writing style. Cuppy sometimes blamed his later brevity on a fear tied to his college-age wordiness. But the humorist merely stumbled onto what most disciplined writers discover over time — "less is more," or, as the sign over the door of my university mentor worded it, "When in doubt, leave it out." Of course, Cuppy's morphing into streamlined style was undoubtedly assisted by paralleling the career of the king of concise prose, Ernest Hemingway (1898–1961), whose arguably greatest novel, *A Farewell to Arms* (1929), appeared the same year as *Hermit*.

The third new nuance symbolized by the publication of *Apes* is an extension of Cuppy's darker wit — a persona whose tone sometimes suggests a print version of Groucho Marx. While the link between these two professional grouches also dated its beginning from the publication of *Apes*, every post–*Hermit* Cuppy quote cited in this biography further chronicles the satirical parallels with Groucho. Moreover, many of the Cuppy correspondence excerpts noted herein to Paterson further reinforce the two men's dark humor ties and sometimes document how Cuppy's original wit predated the legendary cinema lines manufactured for Marx. One of my favorite such examples keys upon the verbal gem from *Monkey Business* (1931, co-scripted by the great S.J. Perelman), in which an insulted woman complains to Groucho, "I don't like this innuendo," he responds, "That's what I always say. Love flies out the door when money comes innuendo."

Approximately six years earlier, in an unpublished letter (circa 1925) to Paterson, Cuppy coins a similar turn of phrase. On the subject of a rocky romance, he comically advises (Cuppy was more serious when his favorite indoor sport — complaining — involved himself), "Your boy friend probably has some libidinous fixation on you which complicates it [your relationship with him], too. When the libido flies in the window, logic flies out the door."[26] While the Cuppy-Groucho link is a comedy composition only completed by including the influence of Benchley upon the Hoosier humorist, making the Marx Brother tie is also important for another reason. To readers unfamiliar with Cuppy, the parallels with the more universally known Groucho provide an immediate take upon the "voice" of this neglected print humorist.

Of course, there is an irony involved with the Cuppy-Groucho comparison. Cuppy's work became progressively darker after *Apes*, culminating with the posthumously published *Decline and Fall of Practically Everybody*.

The ultimate Marx Brothers take on chaos — the team (left to right), Harpo, Chico, Groucho and Zeppo, casually play cards during an apocalyptic scene deleted from *Duck Soup* (1933).

In contrast, the personae of Groucho and Harpo Marx were homogenized with the team's move to MGM, which culminated with *A Night at the Opera* (1935).[27] The Marx Brothers' greatest picture, *Duck Soup* (1933, for Paramount), had initially proved too satirically dark for period audiences. MGM's more mainstream *Opera*, under the personal guidance of "Boy Genius" producer Irving Thalberg, gave the team a major critical and commercial comeback smash. This often very funny film created a second chapter to the Marxes' movie career, which had stalled. But there was an artistic cost to be paid — the compromising of the iconoclastic nature of Groucho's and Harpo's characters. No longer figures of pure anarchy (their norm at Paramount), in MGM's *Opera*, as well as their subsequent work for this studio, even the team's basic narratives often lack the undiluted comedy chaos of their Paramount pictures. Moreover, there are disturbing attempts to give the two Marxes pathos in *Opera*: Harpo is beaten by Walter King's villain, and Groucho is booted down three flights of stairs by a minor character. This is a comedy comedown for the duo, especially Groucho, the president of a college in *Horse Feathers* (1932, Paramount), and the leader of a country (Freedonia) in *Duck Soup*. In addition, the singing romantic subplot of MGM's *Opera* (involving Kitty Carlisle and Allan Jones) often threatens to supplant Groucho, Harpo, and Chico. Paradoxically, Groucho and company even assist the high-art narrative of *Opera*, while one would normally expect them to attack this cultural walk in the park, à la their anti-opera, fruit-throwing conclusion to *Duck Soup*.

No, as the 1930s progressed, it was easier to find Cuppy's increasingly dark Depression-era comedy in the period's broad political arena, the setting which best served Groucho in *Duck Soup*. For example, President Franklin Roosevelt's first vice-president, John Garner (serving from 1933–1941) was so disappointed with the insignificance of his office that he likened the post "to a bucket of warm spit [or worse]."[28] And pioneering Soviet communist Leon Trotsky (1879–1940) would say of literary critic Dwight Macdonald, "Every man has a right to be stupid but comrade Macdonald abuses the privilege."[29]

Fittingly, if even Groucho was getting his satirical wings clipped by the mid–1930s, Cuppy's ongoing bite might help explain why he was not quite the popular success of the gentler Robert Benchley and James Thurber.

Interestingly, Cuppy had launched a trial balloon subtextual warning on the possible darker comedy writing to come in his 1929 comments about the publication of *Extinct*. When his newspaper, the *New York Herald Tribune*, allowed him the happy assignment of reviewing his own book (which he naturally praised), Cuppy did manage a somber qualifier to surface near the critique's close:

> The truth is that the author achieves real eloquence ... in his defense of the sardine; indeed, with the energy he has devoted to the sardine and condensed milk sandwiches he might have written some- thing more serious, say a book proving that we all ought to go out and take poison. This apparently, was not to be.[30]

"Not to be [yet]," might have been an improved phrasing for the Cuppy books to come. Of course, while the humorist's letters to Paterson showcase his macabre mindset, Cuppy's friends were happy to occasionally reveal it, too. In doing so, they often confessed to also having similar views. For instance, in a late 1929 column for the *Herald Tribune*, Paterson discusses a visit to a sick friend (editor Burton Rascoe), with Cuppy in tow. In the course of the evening, which included the musical humorist playing piano duets with Rascoe's wife, Paterson shares how the radio was turned on:

> to hear Alexander Woollcott's first "Town Crier" talk on the drama.... And very entertaining, too, we all agreed.... Will conceded handsomely: "At least, it's not about the boll-weevil."... Then he said he'd assassinate us if we printed that, because he was merely thinking of the usual [boring radio program] and he admires Woollcott's work immensely.... But we might as well be dead as have to work, and we're tired of being told: "Now don't you print that."[31]

Along related lines, while Cuppy was always quick to disparage the subject of his *Herald Tribune* review column, "Mystery and Adventure," the entertainment value of his critiques was also tied to his dark comedy pitch. For example, he recommended *The Death Fear* novel for those "who want a few violent shocks and surprises in the way of assault, battery, kidnapping, false trails, paranoia, young love and Hubbard the butler ... [a character known to remark] that things are not what they seem."[32] And, like Hubbard the butler, Cuppy's reviews also feature winning macabre phrases, such as his closing description of a suspicious character in *The Perfect Murder Case*:

> This one deals with the exploits of a nut who writes letters to the [Scotland] Yard and the papers warning them that he's going to murder someone in postal District N. 22 on the night of October 11. And sure enough ... [he does] with a nephew acting twice as suspicious as life.[33]

If it was not already apparent that the column was purely an inspired platform for Cuppy's propensity for black humor, he often found inventive ways to accent that fact, such as playing upon the name of the star victim in his review of *Lady Can Do*: "Cuppy murder stirs the nation. N. Jonas Cuppy (of the Long Island Cuppys) immensely rich Orientalist, seducer and rum hound, found dead of ax troubles."[34]

Naturally, Cuppy's critiques also allowed the humorist/critic space to underline anew his low regard for fellow Homo sapiens. For instance, here are Cuppy's opening comments on *The Poison Plague* mystery: "Terror stalked through the great city, striking with apparent impartiality both high and low grade morons."[35] Though most of what he was asked to review was less than classic, Cuppy seldom gave overt pans. Instead, a flippant demeanor often suggested that a merely mediocre mystery was at hand. But this mode of critical attack seemed less harsh, even pleasantly palatable, by the nature of the subject matter — black humor seems almost intrinsic to dissecting stories of murder and mayhem. Only rarely did Cuppy let his sense of slumming as a mystery critic slip beyond his damning use of dark comedy. One such instance occurred in his review of Thomas Kingdom's *Murder in the Moon*, a critique which also includes more Cuppy sarcasm about the questionable intelligence of the general public:

> Kingdom is a real author, [though still] a mystery author, to be sure but not one of the dime novelists ($2 net) [$2 was the standard price of these books] so much esteemed by the great minds of these degenerate days.... All fans who have lost their self-respect reading tripe ought to try this engaging yarn about the corpse in light underwear and heliotrope [purple flowered] socks.[36]

One might be tempted to call Cuppy a hypocrite, given the length of time he reviewed a genre he generally disliked. But, here, dark comedy can also double as a defense for Cuppy. Think of his column not as a series of reviews but rather a showcase for more Cuppy comedy. With the humorist regularly critiquing as many as seven books a column, each capsule review seldom exceeded 200 words. But with Cuppy's rapier wit, the *Herald Tribune* seemed to be giving him a blank check to do what he did best. Indeed, if these reviews were ever anthologized, they would best be categorized under a humor heading instead of criticism. Moreover, as these early (1929) column excerpts have demonstrated, Cuppy's evolving style was as apparent here as in his overtly humorous pieces. Only the subterfuge of technically being a reviewer obscured that fact.

A final subliminal sign of *Apes* being a more macabre example of Cuppy comedy can be linked to the book's introduction. Written by celebrated British comic novelist, lyricist, and playwright P.G. Wodehouse (1881–1975), this is the first and only time during Cuppy's lifetime that any author, let alone such a prominent one, provided the humorist's work with an introduction. Why, if not to help facilitate the transition to a tougher Cuppy from the friendlier confines of the *Extinct* text? Wodehouse seems to underline that point: when, after much praise and quoting of

Cuppy quips, he segues to a modest qualifier — even when he disagrees with the humorist, Wodehouse admires Cuppy's "frankness and fearlessness ... [on subjects] which more timid [writers] have been content merely to think."[37]

One might also push the envelope a step further by asking, "Why Wodehouse?" The obvious reason is that he genuinely liked Cuppy's work. In fact, Wodehouse also wrote the most glowingly positive *New York Herald Tribune* review for *Apes*, stating the text "shows that it *was* possible to write a funnier book than 'How to Be a Hermit' (which I, for one, had always doubted)."[38] Yet, of equal importance, there is a provocative disparity between the tone of the two humorists. Wodehouse's modus operandi is light theatrical farce, whether written for the stage, or the printed page — a million miles from Cuppy's deathly dark musings. In contrast, a typical line from the prolific Wodehouse could be his Jeeves series' Bertie Wooster's light literary wordplay, "What sort of cove was Macbeth, and how could he have coped with Aunt Agatha?"[39] What better way is there to legitimize and/or make more socially acceptable increasingly edgy art (in this case, the writings of Cuppy), than to have said text open with a metaphorically affectionate letter of introduction to readers from a very popular (read *safe*) personality/author?

Regardless, *Apes* and its comically darker mindset appeared in bookstores at a particularly bleak time in America history (1931). Even seemingly "Depression-proof" industries like the escapist movies were starting to struggle. Paradoxically, Cuppy's life was experiencing a modest upturn (for a hermit anyway), and he no longer found it necessary to sleep with his vegetables to keep them from freezing in winter!

SIX

Easing into the 1930s, and Two More Important Friendships

"Self-pity — it's the only pity that counts." — Oscar Levant[1]

The above comment from the Cuppy-like Levant was a basic truism for both men. Indeed, years before Levant coined his ironically cryptic axiom, Cuppy had composed a similar rambling perspective on the subject in a letter: "I find it [self-pity] one of the noblest of emotions and practically the only thing of any interest.... It promotes humility, sympathy, maliciousness, hatred and all the bigger and better reactions."[2] But after the successes of *How to Be a Hermit* and *How to Tell Your Friends from the Apes*, as well as his ongoing popular book review column in the *New York Herald Tribune*, "Mystery and Adventure," and his freelance pieces appearing in such prominent publications as *The New Yorker*, there was less ready justification for the self-pity. Yet the beauty of Cuppy's self-pity was that he never felt the need to leave home without it, despite the 1930s upturn in his career. Of course, given the fact that hermits seldom leave home anyway, maybe he simply chose not to acknowledge his success. Just as Oscar Levant's later writing echoed Cuppy's nihilistic self-absorption, Cuppy was also following in the sardonic satirical tradition of another Hoosier, Ambrose Bierce (1842–1914?), whose pocket definition of misfortune — "the kind of fortune which never misses" — seems written with Cuppy in mind.[3] Better yet, Bierce's dialogue between a mother and child, entitled "The Humorist," anticipates all the Cuppy bugaboos, including self-pity, rejection of a traditional job, and the ever-present depression and/or thoughts of suicide, packaged in a dark comedy wrapper:

"Does he [the humorist] suffer,
  Mother?"
"God help him, yes!— A thousand
  and fifty kinds of distress."
"What makes him sweat so?"
"The fear of having to go to work."
"Why doesn't he end, then, his life
  with a rope?"
"Abolition of Hell has deprived
  him of hope."[4]

Indeed, when one factors in Cuppy's reclusive tendencies with his Bierce-like "open a vein" philosophy of life, one could diagnosis him as suffering from a twisted variation of the plight which later befell the French editor Jean-Dominique Bauby (1952–1997), chronicled in his hauntingly poetic memoir, *The Diving Bell and the Butterfly* (1997).[5] In late 1995, Bauby suffered a stroke so severe that he was left permanently paralyzed and speechless — a prisoner of what medical science calls the "locked-in syndrome." With his mental faculties remaining intact, Bauby's only means of communicating was by blinking his left eye. Amazingly, he managed to dictate his book by blinking when the correct letter was spoken by an assistant slowly going through an abbreviated alphabet (most frequently used letters) *over and over* again. Bauby's feat of "writing" this uplifting ("butterfly"-like) modern classic — based upon imagination, memory, and persistence — despite the almost "diving bell" death sentence of a stroke, initially seems miles away from Cuppy's self-pitying cynicism. But the "locked-in syndrome" doubles as a powerful metaphor for any affliction, whatever its origins, which threatens one's ability to communicate and brings about the death of one's spirit.

Loner curmudgeons like Cuppy have a corner on their own special brand of "locked-in syndrome." For someone who preferred to be left alone in various diving bell hermitages of his own creation, Cuppy still had a special need to get the words out — tightly polished little essays, just as Bauby's slim memoir is composed of brief, brilliantly poignant life-lesson chapters. Both men seemed to explore their own personal horrors through a sense of befuddled shock. Given their long histories of self-absorption, dire thoughts dovetailed into thoughts of suicide. Though Bauby moved beyond this escape while Cuppy eventually embraced it, Bauby's ultimately whimsical and ironic *Diving Bell* affirmation of a life still offers insights into Cuppy's world. For example, neither Cuppy nor his mentor Isabel Paterson were fans of the famous Algonquin Round Table group of New York literary wits, who called themselves the "Vicious Circle."[6] Their heyday was the 1920s and '30s — a comic force of nature holding noon court at the Algonquin Hotel, with an ever-fluctuating cast. Nominally led by Alexander Woollcott, the group included George S. Kaufman, Franklin P. Adams, Ring Lardner, Heywood Broun, Donald Stewart, Harold Ross, Marc Connelly, Charles MacArthur, Edna Ferber, Dorothy Parker, Robert Benchley and an occasional Marx Brother (Harpo or Groucho). While Cuppy and Paterson were fans of several of these humorists individually, especially Benchley (a pivotal star of the circle), the Algonquin Round Table's "chumminess and forced sophistication meant nothing" to inherent loners like Cuppy and Paterson.[7] Still, the Cuppy-Paterson correspondence suggests he might have sat in on a session or two of the Algonquin group.[8] Along related lines, Bauby's comments about the "Parisian snobbery," of which he was once a member, making ugly comments about his condition resembles the Cuppy/Paterson thoughts on the Algonquin's "Vicious Circle":

> The city [Paris could double for New York], that monster that knows nothing but says everything, had written me off.... Instead I would have to rely on myself if I wanted to prove that my IQ was still higher than a turnip's.[9]

Indeed, the turnip reference sounds exactly like something the spinach-obsessed Cuppy might say.

Even more movingly Cuppy-like is a story Bauby recalls about a series of bets on long-shot horse, Mithra-Grandchamp (the animal's only claim to fame in fact, was based upon the likelihood of failure). Sadly, Bauby and a friend had been so distracted by the racing establishment's exquisite food and wine that they missed placing their bets. Naturally, the horse won in a major upset and paid a great return. Bauby's poetic summing-up echoes the private side of Cuppy's correspondence. But, like all inspired writing, there is an everyman quality to it:

> The memory of the event ... [is] regret for a vanished past, and above all, remorse for lost opportunities. Mithra-Grandchamp is the woman we were unable to love, the chances we failed to seize, the moments of happiness we allowed to drift away. Today it seems to me that my whole life was nothing but a string of those small near misses: a race whose result we know beforehand but in which we fail to bet on the winner.[10]

Though Cuppy left no suicide note in 1949, the aforementioned Bauby lament would not have been out of place at the humorist's death scene.

One can also read Cuppy's "locked-in syndrome" as the mountain of work (hundreds of research note cards) he assigned himself for each of his brief satirical essays. Though Cuppy's obsession with detail reflects an academic background, some friends (including editor Burton Rascoe) felt part of that extreme scholarship for a mere 1500-word piece (what *The New Yorker* called a "casual"), masked Cuppy's growing anxiety about simply performing the task of writing ... or what many authors reference as the challenge of "getting black on white." For years the humorist followed a philosophy of life which anticipated Woody Allen's do "whatever works" axiom — as long as it gives you pleasure and does not harm anyone and helps pass the time. Sadly, at some point, Cuppy's "whatever" ceased to work. While no single Rosetta Stone explanation has yet to surface for his suicide, in later years Cuppy sometimes noted the increased difficulty of creating quality verbiage. But it remains to be seen if that would have been enough for Cuppy to decide that life were no longer worth living, or to use a period colloquialism, "to keep a dog in the hunt."[11]

Even in the best of times, meaning early in Cuppy's humor writing days, the process seemed to take forever. In one of Isabel Paterson's columns, "Turns With a Bookworm," she addressed the subject at length. Tired of responding to the question, "What has become of Will Cuppy [and his 'Mystery and Adventure' column]," she revealed he that

> has been hiding out at Jones Beach, under a clam-shell, while finishing his "*How to Tell Your Friends from the Apes.*".... When last heard from, he had one hour and fifteen minutes in which to write the last four chapters and the preface.... At his usual rate of progress, which is three days per page, with an additional week for repolishing.... Were we making an official forecast, we should say that he has turned the corner, going in the wrong direction as usual.... Will's last words, heard faintly over the telephone, were: "Do you know anything about the hyena?" ... we said yes, we have known it for years; we know its whole family.... The operator then cut us off.[12]

Cuppy was not alone in his writing struggles. Robert Benchley, for instance, officially retired from the craft in 1943, self-deprecatingly claiming: "I don't think I write funny any more. I've run out of ideas, and from now on I'm [only] an actor. It's a lot easier and the pay is good."[13] The then-54-year-old Benchley rationalized that humorists were not funny after the age of 50. (Cuppy was 59 at the time.) Also, the pressure of competing with either humorist's lofty comedy reputation would have contributed to both men's fear of a writer's block. The closing of Benchley's writing career was big news. Interestingly, Cuppy's home newspaper (the *Herald Tribune*) even ran an editorial about it. Naturally opposed to the decision in Benchley's case, the *Tribune* supported the idea, at least in

Six. Easing into the 1930s 93

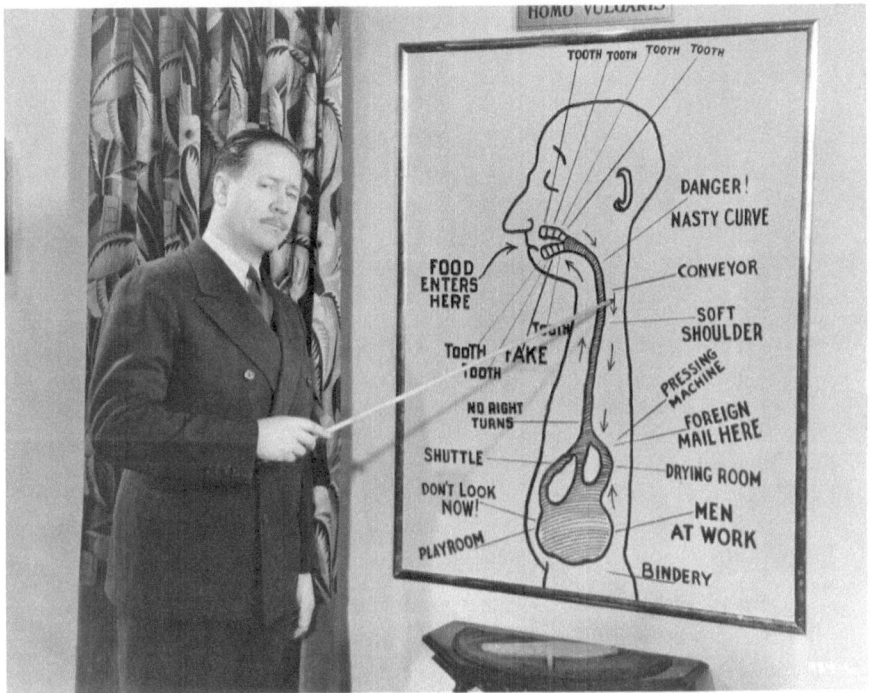

Robert Benchley in one of his short films, *The Romance of Digestion* (1937), which shows his professorial influence on Cuppy.

theory. Many humor writers, the newspaper reasoned, had worked past their prime. Both Benchley's retirement, and the tone of the *Tribune* editorial, would have played upon Cuppy's always-anxious mind. As early as a mid–1920s review of Benchley's *Pluck and Luck*, Cuppy had stated, "Many people in this world (such as it is) ... maintain that if Mr. Benchley is not the funniest humorist now going, or even coming, they are individually and collectively the last of the Mad Marches."[14]

However, these dark, end-of-the-line foreshadowing of the 1940s are getting ahead of the story. The chapter in hand addresses Cuppy in his 1930s prime. Yet, before exploring the importance of two additional friendships of note (especially a new illustrator named William Steig), one should examine some final facets of Cuppy's hermit nature and how they apply to travel and correspondence. Fittingly, he addressed the former subject in an early 1930s interview. Cuppy self-deprecatingly pushes beyond a simple discomfort-around-people excuse by offering this explanation:

> I do not travel. I think this is because I'm not much of an extrovert. I am not greatly interested in external objects, not even tall buildings and

mountains. Whether this is just plain dumbness or something more serious remains to be seen.[15]

While Cuppy was essentially embedded in amber as far as travel interests, friend Paterson had more mixed feelings upon the subject. In late 1929, shortly before *How to Be a Hermit* was published, she took a three-week trip to Europe, which appears to have focused upon Paris and the surrounding countryside. She affectionately shared the ups and downs of the visit with Cuppy via postcards and letters, and she gently lobbied for him to give travel a try:

> [We stopped] for dinner [at] a grand place [in Antwerp], better really I think if one must be a hermit than Jones Island; you should investigate it. We had a snifter of champagne and laughed so hard all evening about I forget what that we have been morose ever since.... I look forward to nothing but next Wednesday and the train out. All the same, Paris is grand. Believe it or not, I wished you were here. Kindly address me — respectfully of course — at Barclay's Bank, 168 ... Fenchurch Street, London Love to all.[16]

Frequently, Paterson's correspondence to Cuppy about this trip, or her later column comments on the vacation, make endearingly comic references/plugs to the humorist's recently published *Hermit* text. For instance, in a postcard she shares, "I have gained 6½ kilos and 19 grams [about 14⅓ pounds].... You couldn't write about food here — no time between meals."[17] Or, in one of Paterson's columns upon returning to New York, she once again entertainingly discusses the pros and cons of travel while plugging Cuppy's new book with a most appropriate analogy:

> We are working out a plan for motionless traveling, the idea being derived from Will Cuppy's chapter, in "How to Be a Hermit," on motionless housekeeping.... The technique will consist in getting to either Paris or London as rapidly and painlessly as possible, and then remainingly firmly there until the time is up.[18]

Of course, just because Cuppy had "bon voyage" issues did not negate his interest in reviewing a travel book if there were extenuating circumstances. A prime example occurred with his critique of the 1931 account *COCONUT OIL: June Triplett's Amazing Book Out of Darkest Africa! As Told by Corey Ford*. More importantly, Cuppy was drawn to a variation of his own special window into humor:

> [He has the ability to use] dozens of jokes which are almost certain to revive the lost art of blushing. Mr. Ford has accomplished some notable spade work in a field wherein the reviewer may boast that he is not a

total stranger, to wit, that of the lower animals. Among the critters discovered ... were the African lens louse, said to be closely related to the American publicity bug, the palooka, or punch-drunk boxing kangaroo ... the rare bulbawai or penguin bird, and the traffic warbler, something like a canary but much worse.[19]

Ultimately, Cuppy suggests that it is more fun, and less dangerous, to simply read about and/or research these subjects from the comforts of one's favorite armchair. Still, the humorist might have given a basic explanation for his bugaboos about skirting the globe in his dislike for the noisy "traffic warbler"—a creature which sounds very much like the boring tourist who babbles endlessly about his recent trip. Plus, Cuppy simply worshipped the quiet.

Why some people enjoy travel while others lobby against it remains one of life's mysteries ... unless the checking account is simply bare. But Cuppy's greater affluence (or at least comfort) in the 1930s would seem to nix that explanation. For Paterson and Cuppy, the question might simply come down to youthful norms. Paterson's childhood years were nomadic, and included living in Utah, followed by a pioneer-like prairie schooner adventure/migration to the Pacific Northwest, and eventually growing up on a cattle ranch in Alberta, Canada. And her early career included stops in Great Falls, Montana; Calgary, Alberta (Canada); Spokane, Washington, and Vancouver, British Columbia (Canada). Cuppy's life itinerary was much simpler—essentially Auburn (IN), Chicago, and New York City. Or, maybe a little Freudian clue is provided in the conclusion of an obscure and unusually autobiographical Cuppy essay, more whimsical than witty, which zeroes in on the pivotal reason he abhorred his dad—"Father travelled ... and was hardly ever home. Maybe it was for the best."[20] I am reminded of a line from Bud Schulberg's neglected masterpiece of an autobiographical novel, *The Disenchanted* (1950, inspired by his messy but fascinating screenwriting teaming with the self-destructive F. Scott Fitzgerald): "Shep [Schulberg] had been fascinated with Halliday's [Fitzgerald's] double sense of time. He did not go back to the past; he carried it with him."[21] As a travel-related addendum to Fitzgerald (1896–1940), no contemporary writer of Cuppy's era better represented how travel and excessive living keep an author from his or her life's work.

A second and final component of Cuppy's hermit nature, after his anti-travel agenda, involves his primary source of contact with the outside world—correspondence with a handful of profession-related friends. While this biography has provided a healthy examination of the humorist's letters to Isabel Paterson, it is also insightful to touch upon some of the entertaining correspondence he received from other friends as it can be as revealing as his own words. Moreover, it is important to underline the manifesto-like significance of meshing with an artistic community. What follows is a paraphrasing of another dark comedy Hoosier, Kurt Vonnegut (1922–2007), channeling one of his academic mentors, anthropologist James Sydney Slotkin:

> It was necessary for a creative person to belong to a school of practitioners who shared the same principles and ideals, because no one could amount to anything in the arts unless he or she embraced ... [common] ideology.[22]

Thus, Cuppy's letters from humorist Frank Sullivan (1910–1972) frequently offer the reader a mirror reflection of the eccentric comedian, à la Groucho looking at his Harpo "reflection" in the iconic mirror scene in *Duck Soup* (1933).

Sullivan, like Cuppy, was a high-profile humorist, defined by both his association with a New York newspaper (the *World*), and his free-lance essays for such magazines as *The New Yorker*. First, theirs was a mutual-admiration society. In a letter from late 1929, Sullivan's praise also includes some affectionate opening fun with Isabel "Pat" Paterson's name:

> I see by Pattabel Izzerson's column that your book is due shortly. I shall get a copy immediately. It ought to be swell and I hope it sells so many copies that Erich Remarque [whose classic anti-war novel, *All Quiet on the Western Front*, 1929, had just appeared] will have his nails bitten to the quick [over the competition].[23]

Second, like "Pattabel Izzerson," Sullivan went out of his way to promote his friend's work. In an undated letter (early 1930s), he wrote to Cuppy:

> My favorite line in a piece of matchless prose I have just turned in to "The New Yorker" is a reference to Winston Churchill as the author who wrote "The Inside of Will Cuppy." Maybe they'll cut it out on account of their aversion to having writers mention other New Yorker writers but I hope not.[24]

Third, like Cuppy, he was always suffering from some ailment, though Sullivan more often spoofed this tendency in himself ... and sometimes in his friend, too. Thus, in one Depression-era letter, he writes, "Excuse tardiness in answering your letter. I have been struggling against a combination of sloth, coryza [the common cold], misogamy, sinus and pessimism."[25] In a different letter from the period, he kids Cuppy, "How are you? Liver all right? Horace Liver all right? [the publisher, Liveright, of Cuppy's *How to Be a Hermit* and *How to Tell Your Friends from the Apes*]. Are your glands functioning? Mine have been garnished."[26]

Fourth, Cuppy and Sullivan both suffered from what contemporary *New Yorker* critic David Derby is wont to describe as "philosophical despair: the truth can never be known."[27] Sullivan's slant on depression, however, like his perspective on physical ailments, tended to be more self-deprecatingly funny than that of his friend. Ironically, the catalyst for one of Sullivan's most amusing takes on pessimism was inspired by a "portrait of you [Cuppy], gazing with innocent trusting eyes upon the world, your illusions unshattered [one assumes it was a picture of a *young* Cuppy]."[28] Sullivan then goes on to ask his friend:

> Are they still unshattered? Because if not, I have gone into the illusion shattering business as a sideline. Illusions shattered, twenty cents a dozen, estimates cheerfully given. Open all night. Mail enclosed card giving descriptions of illusions, and method of shattering desired.[29]

Fifth, despite Cuppy's talent for making and maintaining friendships with many of America's most gifted writers, he remained reclusive, even after his move to Greenwich Village. Consequently, Sullivan's letters to the humorist (like most of Cuppy's long-term correspondents) document their friend's inaccessibility. But, as with most things Sullivan, his description's potential remedies for the problem were invariably the most entertaining of Cuppy's confidants. In one letter, Sullivan claims to be working on

> my 176-page brochure on "The Sullivan Plan for Solving the Problem of Getting Hold of Cuppy." Barring interference by Tammany [the Democratic political machine in New York], and subject of course to the approval of the Archbishop, I think we have every reason to think it will go over big. It wouldn't cost you much. We serve an excellent dinner for $7. Girls are $5 extra. Boys are $10. Give my love to Pattabel Izzerson.[30]

Sullivan could also be surreally playful about Cuppy the ongoing hermit. Most prominent humorists of the era periodically flirted with fantasy, from Thorne Smith's (1892–1934) sexy ghosts in the *Topper* novels (1926, 1932, which later became a popular movie franchise), to James Thurber's short stories including "The Unicorn in the Garden" (from *Fables for Our Time,* 1940). Sullivan not only toyed with the subject, he used the genre to spin a hypothesis about the invisible Cuppy. In a 1937 letter "Dear Cup," he writes,

> I miss never seeing you but it is nice to feel that you are there. Are you there? Don't tell me that I have been nursing a delusion all these months, and that you aren't really there. This thought just occurred to

> me. It is alarming. Was it ectoplasm I saw having dinner ... at Blakes [restaurant] that night? Write immediately and reassure me in re this matter.[31]

Paradoxically, yet ever so appropriately, for a friend of Cuppy the recluse, Sullivan was also fond of lying low. This information is most entertainingly documented by Isabel Paterson, who periodically documented the phantom-like nature of Sullivan in her *Herald Tribune* column. An early example reads:

> Frank Sullivan did arrive ... [at the party], and his presence created a distinct stir, as he is very rare, almost unobtainable.... [Someone] asked us, in an excited stage whisper: "Can you point out Frank Sullivan?".... We said proudly we can catch him for you, having dragged him here personally, though he nearly got away in the elevator.[32]

Paterson's chronicling of Sullivan's hermit-like nature was second only to her similar references to professional recluse Cuppy. Thus, in another column, Paterson confessed that a friend:

> writes that Frank Sullivan can be captured by using any form of cooked cheese, or about a peck of tomato jelly.... Ah, yes but it would be necessary to discover his habitat first.[33]

A sixth link between Cuppy and Sullivan was their shared interest in keeping things simple in order to focus on writing—fueled by basic questions about life itself. For instance, in a letter from 1928, when Cuppy was still living in the most primitive circumstances on Jones Island, Sullivan wrote:

> I think it is good for me to be hard at work [writing]. I have also been looking for an apartment [in New York] and finding that you can't get anything but a pigsty for less than $100 or $125 [a month]. Living means so little and comforts mean so little that I hate like hell to spend $125 for a place to park at night.[34]

As previously suggested, the last quote notwithstanding, Sullivan tended to mask moroseness more than Cuppy. Still, both humorists had real doubts about the loyalty and intellectual level of their readers. In a letter to Cuppy from the late 1920s, Sullivan seems envious of Cuppy's island isolations and complains about editors pressuring him about how "essential" it is that the "dear public" constantly see something from him every day.[35] However, Sullivan went on to add, he knew that his editors "lie," because periodically he was away from his craft for extended periods, and upon returning the humorist found "the faces of the dear public shining through the dirt as usual, and bearing no traces whatsoever of the tears of suffering caused by scarcity of Sullivan."[36]

These shared links allowed Sullivan to get as close as anyone could to the self-proclaimed hermit. Yet, one of Sullivan's letters again underline Cuppy's apolitical nature, which was ultimately a major factor in Paterson later cutting ties with the former Hoosier (see chapter three). What makes this reference doubly interesting is that while Paterson was essentially a founding mother of the fiercely individualistic libertarian movement, and thus a mortal enemy of President Franklin Roosevelt's helping hand "New Deal," Sullivan was a longtime liberal Democrat. In a late-1930s letter to Cuppy, which includes kind words for the type of friends represented by Paterson and the humorist, Sullivan cannot resist closing with the confession: "I still have great affection for that wench [Paterson] despite the absurd political views she holds about my hero, Franklin Delano Roosevelt."[37] Obviously, this sentiment would not have been shared had Cuppy been anything more than politely respectful of Paterson's political perspective.

While Sullivan was a funny, kindred spirit, Cuppy's most supportive friend (after Paterson) was cartoonist/illustrator William Steig (1907–2003). Steig, the then-popular *New Yorker* cartoonist, and, later, an award-winning children's book author (and the creator of the character Shrek), had three special links to Cuppy. Most importantly, in the tradition of Paterson and Sullivan, he was forever supportive to the often morose Cuppy. Second, he would also enhance the humorist's work by illustrating *How to Become Extinct* and *The Decline and Fall of Practically Everybody*, becoming as important to Cuppy's comedy as illustrator Gluyas Williams was to Robert Benchley's essay collections. Third, Steig's extensive correspondence with Cuppy reveals an often kindred spirit as well as someone acknowledging the impact/influence of an older, artistically stimulating artist.

The Steig letters to the humorist cover the mid–1930s to the late 1940s. The correspondence perfectly complements the Paterson letters. More than anything else, they are comfortably full of the praise Cuppy required from his inner circle. The following letter excerpt is typical of how Steig constantly provided the insecure Cuppy with positive reinforcement:

> It is obvious from your letter that you are going crazy [from criticism] or you wouldn't talk about the general [lack of] appreciation of your work. No genuine talent, especially in the humor business is genuinely appreciated by more than 2 or 3 persons. You've got me and a couple of other intelligent guys.... Your wit has had such an impact on me that I find myself talking sometimes in your manner.... Dear Cuppy, please don't be unhappy — because I identify with you to such an extent that when you suffer I suffer.[38]

Fittingly, 1936 was also the year Steig started making his "symbolic drawings"—quick study line sketches of troubled souls, including such Cuppy-inspired characters as the "one who would like to be left alone."[39]

Steig was already sounding like Cuppy in an often comic letter from the previous year (1935). Living in the country for the summer, Steig immediately confesses to having "anxiety neurosis" but adds, "The country is nice, though. So quiet—it's possible at least to complete one worry and tackle another."[40] After an affectionately tongue-in-cheek diatribe about family, Steig adds, "They don't understand me. I'm sure you understand me, though. You're a nervous wreck like me."[41] ("Nervous wreck" was Cuppy's euphemism for "modern man.")

While Steig had more underlying hope than Cuppy, as with everyone in the humorist's small circle of friends, the two men shared a dark sense of humor. In an undated letter [circa 1941] Steig wrote:

> I agree with your remarks on humans [especially regarding their joint collaboration on *How to Become Extinct*].... My idea is to take these all [various villain types] & stick them in the state of Rhode Island, give them the equivalent of their wealth in consumer goods—4,000 bicycles, 9,000 tennis rackets, 80 bales of condoms, 8,000,000 cans of pimentos ... put a high wall around the place and let them fight it out. Then the rest of us could roam the earth like peaceful sheep.[42]

As Steig's letters suggest, here was yet another talented member of the Cuppy support system who had doubts about Homo sapiens. Indeed, when Steig's collection of drawings, *The Lonely Ones* (1942), was reissued in 1970, celebrated author William Saroyan's (1908–1981) new introduction included a telling memory: "When the book came out in 1942, I remember seeing in many reviews the drawing that seemed to be the immediate national favorite: 'People are no damn good.'"[43] That being said, unlike Isabel Paterson's general disregard for the less-than-capable masses, Steig had an innate sense as to why so many people "are no damn good." In a national profile of Steig published not long after *The Lonely Ones* first appeared, he said:

> Most people have reached a stage of embarrassment. They're stymied.... A person feels embarrassed when he doesn't respect what he's doing. He's all bottled up.... One of the most common feelings is rage—anger at the way things are being done, at the lack of grace, order, and honesty in the world.... Most people feel it and aren't aware of it.[44]

While Steig's empathy for even the "no damn good people" separated him from Paterson, it was closer to Sullivan's world view, and sometimes even Cuppy's—if one could get past the exterior curmudgeon. Regardless,

Paterson, Sullivan, and Steig were very protective of Cuppy. In the beginning, Paterson seemingly willed the Cuppy phenomenon to happen; Sullivan was one of many cheerleaders along the way, and Steig added to Cuppy's art with his evocative illustrations and a devotion which eventually had him replacing Paterson as Cuppy's most pivotal mentoring friend. Moreover, Cuppy helped give new direction to Steig's work. In fact, art curator Claudia Nahson's description of Steig's later drawings sounds like a Cuppy profile: "His world is full of curmudgeons, cranks, and complainers."[45] Of course, to return to the earlier Vonnegut reference, all of Cuppy's creative contacts/friends helped make the disgruntled former Hoosier's writing possible by being part of the same "school of [dark comedy] practitioners." Indeed, Steig's widow's description of her husband could double as a mini-biography of Cuppy:

> [Steig] hated pretension. He tended to dress as though he had gone into the closet and invited clothes to fall upon him.... His work was topical; it went deeper than that ... everybody looked foolish [in his work]. That's how a serious clown sees the world.... He walked with his head bent into the wind that he knew, committed worrier that he was, would come. He did have an endless supply of things to worry about, few of which made the least bit of sense to anyone. They were, in some way, like a comfort blanket.[46]

Cuppy, Paterson, Sullivan, and Steig all created their comic art fully cognizant of the sheer hopeless tragedy lurking just outside their creative frameworks. To focus upon Cuppy, however, he reversed the popular formula for the art of creating some comforting order out of the chaos of life. As Woody Allen is wont to say, "Art is where you get it right." In contrast, Cuppy anticipates Vonnegut's non-comfort-zone approach to writing:

> Let others bring order to chaos. I will bring chaos to order [our attempted daily schedules]. If all writers would do that, then perhaps everyone will understand that there is no order in the world around us, that we must adapt ourselves to the requirements of chaos instead.[47]

Naturally, Vonnegut hardly holds a patent on this theory; it is as old as satire itself. Yet, Vonnegut articulates the perspective at a time (the 1960s) when it was moving to post-modern center stage, ranging from his own anti-war masterpiece *Slaughterhouse-Five* (1968), to French New Wave films like Jean-Luc Godard's *Weekend* (1967). Again, Cuppy's dark comedy anticipates the shape of things to come. In fact, to play one final Vonnegut card, Cuppy's loopy "comfort blanket" worries are reminiscent of Vonnegut's most memorable literary figure, the frustrated and frustrating wise fool writer Kilgore Trout, who repeatedly surfaces in the novelist's work.

As Vonnegut once confessed, "Kilgore Trout is the lonesome and unappreciated writer I thought I might become."[48] Obviously, there is a little of the potentially self-destructive Kilgore in most creative types, but Cuppy was densely populated with Kilgores, or maybe one should say "Trout," given the frequency with which he wrote about lower life forms.

Cuppy's ultimate suicide makes one wish he had found the later safety valve of Jim Knipfel's darkly comic memoir *Quitting the Nairobi Trio* (2000). The title is a reference to pioneering TV comedian Ernie Kovacs's surreal slapstick sketch involving three violent characters in ape masks, trench coats, and derbies. The once-suicidal Knipfel, who had struggled through the most literal of personal challenges, now sees life metaphorically as an ongoing series of self-destructive slapstick sketches, à la the Nairobi Trio. The secret for survival is to recognize this fact, and then "figure out who — or what — [is putting you at risk]."[49] Consequently, safety is made possible by quitting your own Nairobi Trio. Like Cuppy and many others, Knipfel's greatest enemy was himself. Do not take anything too seriously; existence is simply a variation of the same pattern, and one's own dark side is frequently the source of what ails you. Seeing the connection and being able to laugh at it does not eliminate the problem, but the epiphany can make it more palatable. Ironically, Cuppy's aforementioned radio program was titled, *Just Relax*.

The following chapter examines Cuppy's productive 1930s more closely, and how his principal support group helped keep the humorist's self-destructive tendencies at bay — for a time.

SEVEN

Cuppy's Multifaceted 1930s

> "A gentleman is one who never hurts another's feelings unintentionally."—Oscar Wilde, from Henry Alford, *Would It Kill You to Stop Doing That? A Modern Guide to Manners*[1]

Ironically, Cuppy's 1930s heyday of dark comedy writing paralleled and/or butted heads with the last hurrah of theatre and film's "comedy of manners," those elegant high-society farces which might best be summed up by the name Noel Coward (1899–1973), from his quarreling stage lovers of *Private Lives* (1930), to the dueling wives (one dead, one living) in the medium/fantasy theatre world of *Blithe Spirit* (1941). At the same time Hollywood was conjuring up its own special brand of farce now known as "screwball comedy."[2] The prime time of this latter phenomenon might best be dated from Frank Capra's *It Happened One Night* (1934) to Preston Sturges's *The Palm Beach Story* (1942), with countless other examples of "caviar comedy," including Gregory LaCava's *My Man Godfrey* (1936), Leo McCarey's *The Awful Truth* (1937), and Howard Hawks's *Bringing Up Baby* (1938).[3] Thus, Cuppy was doing his best to tug to center stage a comedy genre of *non-*manner (black humor) in a comedy of manners era—no small task; though other dark comedy advocates (such as Groucho Marx) were out there tugging, too. As author William Gibson is alleged to have said many years later, "The future is already here. It's just not evenly distributed yet."[4]

One of Cuppy's proudest public moments actually acts as metaphor, of sorts, for this manners/non-manners comedy clash. In the early 1930s the humorist was acknowledged by a passing fan as he walked in Manhattan. This is especially significant, if one claimed, as was Cuppy's nature, that there was some shadowy "hate Cuppy" movement thwarting his every move. Yet, what makes the story significant is that Cuppy's companion was completely ignored—former heavyweight boxing champion Gene Tunney, whose famous "long count" defeat (1927) of Jack Dempsey remains

Frank Capra's *It Happened One Night* (1934), with Clark Gable and Claudette Colbert.

the sport's most controversial fight. The sidewalk scene seems emblematic of the change for which Cuppy was acting as a catalyst. Yet, it goes beyond the obvious — equating black humor with the visceral violence of the ring — and Cuppy having a relationship with the boxer. No, there is also the Tunney back story: the man who upset arguably the game's greatest champion, the man who remains the sport's most well-read boxer, the heavyweight fighter who quoted Shakespeare. By association, the intellectual champion elevates both Cuppy and his brand of comedy. Moreover, one could add a final paradoxical connection/twist between the two. Tunney never received the full recognition he deserved because of the "long count" controversy. In the seventh round Dempsey knocked him down for well over the ten count "you're out" norm, but Tunney was "gifted" with 18 seconds to recover because the champion did not immediately go to a neutral corner — delaying the beginning of the count.[5] Along similar lines, Cuppy and other dark comedy pioneers never received significant recognition for their accomplishments as the genre was long considered a lesser "sick comedy" style.[6]

Seven. Cuppy's Multifaceted 1930s

Regardless, as one more closely examines Cuppy's life in the 1930s, a good subtextual start would begin with Isabel Paterson's autobiographical novel *The Golden Vanity* (1934), the most entertaining character of which was inspired by Cuppy. As briefly noted earlier in this text, the Cuppy-based figure is an accountant-turned-playwright named Jake Van Buren. The relationship between Jake and the surrogate Paterson character (actress Mysie Brennan) more fully fleshes out their complex, real-life relationship. Given the critically well-received high-profile nature of the book, and the obvious links between Jake/Cuppy and Mysie/Paterson, the novel doubles as an insider's announcement of the humorist's arrival on the New York cultural scene. Keep in mind, period reviews (such as the *New York Herald Tribune* critique of October 21, 1934) openly discussed the autobiographical nature of Paterson's Mysie character.

The Golden Vanity follows the intersecting lives of three female cousins living in New York shortly before and after the stock market crash of 1929. Gina Fuller wants the Noel Cowardish caviar cavalcade life; Geraldine Wickes longs for a stable domestic setting; and Mysie is an loner whose passion/strength is her dripping-with-individualism reflectiveness. Jack is Mysie's best friend and the book's go-to comic relief. Given the then-recent success of *How to Tell Your Friends from the Apes*, a book whose ad campaign often had the humorist posing with toy monkeys and assuming a close-cropped haircut, which accented his somewhat simian appearance, Paterson's *Golden Vanity* description of Jake (Cuppy's nickname among friends) in the novel is hardly subtle:

> A young man who was distinctly handsome and yet rather resembled a monkey in features ... his eyes ... seemed shadowed by an abiding sorrow, as with the more intelligent of the simian tribe. It is the face of comedy.[7]

Not surprisingly, Paterson's ongoing real-life campaign to get Cuppy to drop his playwright aspirations finds its way into the novel as Jake comically articulates his issues with plot structure.

> I have a theory, that if I could see enough plays, I might discover what a play is, and thus be enabled to write one. It is a distinct handicap not to know. My dialogue is said to be too good; but I am informed that a plot is indispensable; I don't know why. It seems to me there should be a place for a pure dialogue play.[8]

Indeed, Cuppy could be comically confessional about struggling with a plot. In my only autographed copy of a Cuppy book, a first edition of *How to Become* Extinct, the humorist has written, "Dear Mr. Anderson: Well, I just thought I would [write], an[d] you are on my mind most of the time. Hopefully, you won't think I have muddled the plot — Cuppy." Paradoxically, even the positive reviews for *The Golden Vanity* suggests plot structure was also Paterson's Achilles' heel.⁹ Paterson, like Cuppy, seems to have been at her best when essentially playing herself and/or channeling a best friend. Thus, the *New York Times*'s positive review credits Jake's character as "amusing and even rather convincing," only topped by the "authentic" Mysie, the "proof of Mrs. Paterson's special talents."¹⁰

Jake's defense of a "pure dialogue play," however, stumbles into what Cuppy's satirical books did best — providing a platform to play a comic Socrates ... questioning and/or heckling society at every turn. Paterson's *Vanity* even describes Jake asking one of his questions "Socratically."¹¹ Along similar lines, the *Vanity* banter between Jake and Mysie is not unlike the comic "pure dialogue" patter actually credited to Cuppy and Paterson in the humorist's book *How to Be a Hermit*. Indeed, the duo's mutual friend and celebrated humorist Frank Sullivan had specifically praised that aspect of the *Hermit* text in an earlier letter to Cuppy: "I read ... the Socratic spinach dialogue with Pattabel [Isabel Paterson]. Boy, it's *swell*! ... You've *got* to do a lot of dialogue."¹² Since Jake/Cuppy references to the "pure dialogue" defense occur on more than one occasion in *Vanity*, one can assume that this was the humorist's real-life mantra on the subject. Certainly it was what Cuppy did best in his comic essays, and further explains his tendency to artificially engage various authority figures in quasi-dialogues — paper lions to satirically knock down as a contemporary comic Socrates. Since

A caricature of Isabel Paterson used to promote her "novel" *The Golden Vanity* (1934).

his "expert" targets were usually hoary historical icons, one might say Cuppy's living in the past was his dark comedy future.

Despite Cuppy's satirical gifts, his correspondence, particularly to Paterson, is heavy with self-doubt. He is, it seems, constantly in need of a dominating mother-like supporter. However, one of the many fascinating facets of *Vanity* is how Paterson herself reinforces/subtextually documents these facts by way of her characterizations of Jake and Mysie. The following excerpt showcases all these elements:

> "I might have known," said Jake, still amendable to [Mysie's] orders ... even if I did write a play [which he will call "Third String," an antiheroic title not unlike what Cuppy called the real play on which he was forever working, "Not That It Matters"], and it was accepted, it would go flooey at the last minute.... If the whole world is resolved that I shall die in the gutter, who am I to object."[13]

So what clues does *Vanity* provide as to the reasons Mysie/Paterson helps/encourages Sad Sack Jake/Cuppy beyond a sense of his innate talent? Mysie is fascinated by Jake's unpredictability (often comparing him to the weather), and the pure fun he can project:

> There was something uncanny about Jake, unclassifiable; he simply did not obey any of the rules; he seemed to but he didn't; so it was quite impossible either to judge or to predict him.... The world was entirely comic while one talked to Jake.[14]

Yet, the most poignant detail Paterson's *Vanity* reveals about Jake/Cuppy is a vulnerability borne of his proper, polite upbringing. This trait further explains another Cuppy connection with Sullivan, who once began a letter to the humorist with the admission:

> My delay in answering your letter has not been to lack of courtesy, for if I do say it my bringing-up was one of the best. Even now I curtsy whenever I am presented to my elders or to anyone who matters. Once in a while I lose my temper over this god damned typewriter but at those times such oaths and expletives as I admit are done in a nicely-modulated, aristocratic falsetto.[15]

Regardless, how did the politeness of Jake the loner sometimes get him (and, presumably, Cuppy) in trouble? Paterson's *Vanity* observes:

> Jake's long training with ... [a household of women] had perfected a natural talent for respectful dissimulation towards age and authority. He encountered bores with the same elaborate mendacity, a defense mechanism which sometimes defeated its own purpose, so that he spent much time evading invitations he had brought upon himself, to quiet dinners, spinsterish teas, and drunken parties, all of which bored him equally.[16]

(As a brief refresher, Cuppy's childhood was dominated by a strong-willed mother, grandmother, aunt and an idealized sister, whose influence was intensified by the general absence of the humorist's father.)

So what obsessed Jake, if he wanted to avoid every variety of social setting? Paterson's novel describes Cuppy, the writing hermit, right down to his voluminous notecard scribbling. Yet again, she provides poignantly comic details never mentioned in standard profiles of the humorist, from his obliviousness to anything but the research, to the sheer difficulty of keeping track of specific details among thousands of cards. With regard to the latter point, one is reminded of the old comic definition of a filing cabinet: "A place where one loses things alphabetically." Thus, what follows is Paterson's description of the working Jake/Cuppy:

> He did his writing in great discomfort with a bracket light glaring in his eyes [Cuppy wore strong glasses] and a litter of books and papers on the floor beside his chair; he made innumerable notes, and filed them, and couldn't find them again, and at intervals he spent whole nights going through the files.[17]

Earlier in this biography a strong case was made for Cuppy essentially being asexual, with his loner commitment to writing minimizing any sex drive. Though Paterson was briefly married once in real life, and in *Vanity* (to Jake, no less!), relationships also played a distant second to her writing, both in fact and fiction. Though *Vanity*'s Mysie/Paterson is talking about Jake/Cuppy, she might just as well have been describing herself: "Jake was absolutely inadaptable to ordinary human relations ... he's a born bachelor."[18] Indeed, sexuality just did not seem to play a major part in the Cuppy inner circle. For example, in an earlier letter the humorist received from fellow funnyman Sullivan, the latter casually shared, "Yesterday was my thirty-seventh birthday and the fourth anniversary of my impotence."[19] (Hemingway's similarly afflicted hero from the 1926 novel *The Sun Also Rises* could not have announced it more explicitly.) Fittingly, Cuppy's review of the James Thurber and E.B. White text *Is Sex Necessary?* was so positive, he closed the critique by reiterating, "I hope I have registered the fact that I like this book."[20]

Of course, this biography has already documented Cuppy's neediness as a relationship liability. Interestingly, Cuppy's family was rooting for him to marry the ever-so-supportive Paterson right to the late 1920s death of the humorist's mother. Another revealing *Vanity* gem occurs when Paterson quotes Jake's/Cuppy's mother's defense of Mysie's reasoning: "Who will get you out of your scrapes when I'm gone? I don't blame Mysie for declining the job."[21]

Paterson also gives Jake a platform upon which to discuss sex and/or its less-than-central role in most people's lives. In fact, Jake tells another *Vanity* supporting player that not only is it largely an asexual world, if one were to lock up two persons of the opposite gender, and then "at the end of a week open the sealed compartment, it will be found that they have spent the entire time doing a jigsaw puzzle."[22]

A final potential clue upon the Paterson/Cuppy anti-marriage position occurs in a later Paterson review of *Around the World in Eleven Years* (1936). This nonfiction book chronicles the vagabond's life of news photographer James E. Abbe, his wife Polly, and their children, Richard, Johnny, and Patience. Paterson's positive critique keys upon the views of the boys. (Plus, keep in mind, Cuppy and Paterson, like many East Coast-based writers of that age, were decidedly down on the perceived lowbrow nature of the movies, another basic component of *Vanity*.) Thus, Paterson's review highlights, in part:

> Richard is *never* going to get married. He says you have to work too hard when you are married ... he doesn't believe in love. He says all the cinemas always have love in it. Johnny hates love, too. He isn't so sure he will get married.[23]

Other obvious elements of the real Paterson and Cuppy embedded in *Vanity* would range from Jake owning a shabby little shack by the sea and doubling as a literary critic, to Mysie having strong political views on what would now pass for libertarianism. With regard to the latter subject, what follows is a typical example of Mysie/Paterson on her soapbox: "Why can't people be let alone ... between the blasted reformers and the earnest immoralists a pretty good country has been darned near ruined."[24] However, as the 1930s progressed, one can chart how Cuppy's increasingly apolitical nature would clash with Paterson's escalating libertarianism, the reason most often given for the 1940s break-up of their friendship. For instance, while Cuppy very rarely used contemporary politics as subject matter for his comic essays, one can find a rare early example (1931) in *How to Tell Your Friends from the Apes* (from a time when Paterson's influence on the humorist was at its apogee). One of Cuppy's *Apes* tag lines suggests modern man will never became extinct "if the [reforming] Democrats can help it."[25]

Yet, such specifics are atypical of Cuppy. One of his asides from a later (1936) review in his *New York Herald Tribune* "Mystery and Adventure" column provides a better barometer of his true thoughts on politics. Critiquing a novel entitled *Murder at 28:10*, Cuppy muses,

> The plot struck us as impressive, although it has lots to do with business and politics. Seems to show, too, that much brooding on these matters may unsettle the mind.[26]

In contrast, Paterson's "Turns With a Bookworm" column from the same *Herald Tribune* issue documents her increasing obsession with a pioneering libertarian political perspective:

> The Germans believe in Hitler, the Italians in Mussolini, and Americans in saving the world, the New Era, the New Deal ... anything offered.... [Some make excuses for the famines and executions under the great Soviet communist experiment.] We merely supposed that that was what was wrong under the [deposed Russian] Czar.... Since it continued on an even larger scale [under the reforming communists], it does not seem to us like a great improvement.[27]

(Such a flickering "newsreel" from the past still reads as very topical for the current libertarian movement.)

Though novels through the ages have drawn characters from real-life luminaries, one could argue that Paterson had an especially high-profile contemporary example to inspire her along these lines. *Vanity* was published late in 1934, while F. Scott Fitzgerald's last completed novel, the fascinatingly autobiographical *Tender Is the Night*, had appeared in January of that year. The latter book patterns its figures upon a litany of prominent figures in the arts, from the Cuppy and Paterson favorite, Robert Benchley, to humorist Dorothy Parker, to sometimes painter Gerald Murphy and his artistic community mentoring wife, Sara.

The next step, after *Vanity*, for a better understanding of Cuppy in the 1930s, would be to more systematically explore his *Tribune* column. While his freelance comedy essays had now begun to appear in various publications, much of Cuppy's Depression-era work has already been discussed herein via its collection in *How to Become Extinct*. While his 1930s comedy essays are examined later in the chapter, two pressing reasons necessitate now keying upon the columns. First, they are essentially neglected humor pieces, too. Second, the Cuppy columns constitute the most consistent and voluminous amount of published material the humorist would produce during his writing career.

In chapter five of the text in hand, it was first briefly posited that Cuppy's columns, like the theatre criticism of his comedy hero Robert Benchley, were most valuable as humor essays.[28] A more thorough examination of Cuppy's "Mystery and Theory" pieces reveals several key points. First, let there be no question that the joy of reading the column came from his comic asides. For instance, in a Cuppy "review" of Helen Reilly's *Mr. Smith's Hat*, which involves a zoo setting, the simian-related critic notes:

> Miss Reilly provides no diagrams [at the setting]. She may feel, as we do, that if you need a diagram to understand the layout of a monkey house you'd better be resting up instead of reading a book.[29]

In Cuppy's critique of Rufus King's *Murder in the Willett Family* he opines:

> To any and all who have ever felt just a bit fed up with their families, we heartily recommend a reading of Mr. King's latest. If the wild Willette don't make you count your blessings, nothing will. Besides, you will get a swift story of slaughter in several forms.... If you ask us, it [the murderer] might be any member of the family, for they are all fairly mad.[30]

Second, as the last quotation suggests, much of Cuppy's column comedy is tied to black humor, a natural extension of reviewing murder mysteries. The dark comedy suddenly surfaces in brief jabs, ranging from, "We hope this author keeps on slaughtering people right, left and sideways," to another review opening with the observation, "Wealthy miser blown to pieces in his bedroom (goody! goody!)...."[31] Though our focus here is the 1930s, the black-humor asides were a staple throughout the 20-plus-year run of "Mystery and Adventure." For example, here are some observations from a 1929 column:

> The tale should appeal to lovers of the exotic, macabre, ghostly and that sort of thing. Perhaps the leading critical question raised by the story is, "Who's loony now?" ... (Fans may as well know that nicotine "is not well suited to murder because it is difficult to administer." You have to hold them down.)[32]

Flash forward to a Cuppy review from 1949, in which he writes:

> When Frank came home, Alice said, "We've got to get rid of him [her husband]" ... and it seemed like a good idea at the time.... [The author] tells how they went about it ... and what happened next. Those who can bring comparison with them [the killers] should be able to work up more excitement in this simple cautionary tale of critters who took the wrong turning any number of times.[33]

Third, as the "critters" crack suggests, Cuppy's satirical dicing of lowbrow humanity sometimes continued in the columns, too. Thus, returning to our 1930s focus, in Cuppy's critique of *The Rose of Death*, he dishes, "Its peculiar style ... must be an acquired taste that we haven't acquired."[34] Yet, here's the rub: his fickle phenomenon is greatly toned down in the "Mystery and Adventure" pieces. To illustrate, the previous quote immediately pivots 180 degrees in tone by adding, We're [still] recommending this mostly to those who have enjoyed ... [author] Masterman's other tales."[35] This surprising politeness might be an extension of his aforementioned lack of respect for murder mysteries in general. Thus, Cuppy's criticism could simply coast through the pleasure of merely reporting on, in his mind, vacuous novels pleasantly knocking off the illiterate bourgeois or "booboisie" (to borrow the similarly minded perspective of Cuppy contemporary H.L. Mencken). Consequently, unlike the humorist's need to build into his straight satirical essays a pithy argument on just why Darwin might have been wrong (have we really evolved that far?), Cuppy's mystery critiques were based upon a genre dependent upon the short shelf life of their interchangeably expendable casts. I am reminded of a much later comment by another celebrated essayist, William H. Gass, who, like Cuppy, used certain focused pieces as a refuge from his contempt for humanity. Gass wrote, "I was once asked by a French newspaper to state, in a word, why I wrote. I replied in a sentence suitable for a courtroom. I write to indict mankind."[36]

The fourth Cuppy column component represents the clearest break with his comedy essays — the "Mystery and Adventure" pieces frequently have him assuming an antiheroic position. For example, in his review of *The Feather Cloak Murders*, Cuppy says of the novel's amateur sleuth, "[He's] a teeny bit feeble-minded and weakens our faith in his giant intellect. (Note to author: Pay no attention to this, I'm probably wrong.)"[37] In his critique of *Vive Le Roy*, Cuppy alibies that

> our author's [Ford Madox Ford] celebrated narrative method, upon which we are not competent to lecture ... seems a dizzy sort of runaround.... [But] Don't pass up this unusual item just because it is written by a [good] writer.[38]

At times Cuppy comically showcases a broader antiheroic nature in his short notices, such as the amusing self-effacement he brings to his closing comments on J.M. Walsh's *Exit Simeon Hex*: "Mr. Walsh [only recently] took to writing ... and has already published fifty novels. His books may also be had in French, German, Hungarian and Swedish. Such is life."[39]

In contrast to Cuppy the antiheroic critic, this whole book has documented a scholarly satirist whose slashing style has targeted seemingly every authority figure in Western civilization, starting with Aristotle. Even in Cuppy's early *How to Become a Hermit*, which has some generic antiheroic elements, the overriding thrust of the text is a dark spoof of Henry David Thoreau's *Walden*. Paradoxically, in Cuppy's columns he is more apt to actually quote experts! For instance, in his review of the anthology *3 Star Omnibus*, he recycles the praise of mystery scholar Dorothy L. Sayers on a particular story, "Trent's Lost Case," included in the text: "'It is the one detective story of the present century which I am certain will go on to posterity as a classic.'"[40]

So why the switch by Cuppy from pit bull to pussycat? The answer is multi-faceted. First, he has merely retreated to some fifth columnist satire in his genuflecting to experts in the column. In the just-noted quote, Cuppy cannot resist the sarcastic add-on,

> Would you want to miss such an opus? No, it is your duty as a decent American citizen to peruse ... [this volume] and find out the meaning of "masterpiece," "classic," and other critical terms used by great authors.[41]

Cuppy plays the same satirical subterfuge in his critique of Carolyn Wells's *Murder In the Bookshop*, with Sayers again subtextually taking one for the mystery team:

> Miss Wells ... [is also] the author of "The Technique of the Mystery Story," one of the slickest tomes on that subject extant, if not the slickest. (Oh sure, Miss Wells is darned near as intellectual as Dorothy L. Sayers, if it comes to that. Only, it doesn't show on her a great deal.)[42]

Second, Cuppy dialed down the satire for the same reason he was more polite in "Mysteries and Adventure": the humorist did not need a soapbox to aggressively shish kebab a genre he found second-rate. This freed him to devote more left-handed research time to his life's work, like his anthropomorphic satire of citizens ... by way of dodos and wombats. Third, Cuppy's column was a job he needed and which the humorist professionally executed with an entertainingly comic flair. Because he did not wish to lose this position, which still kept him both in the public eye and allowed him to practice a modicum of merriment, the column represented a gentler Cuppy, with few pans. Fourth, even when he gave a rare raspberry to a novel, like *Murder at Elstree*, or *Mr. Thurtell and His Dog*, he frequently included something winningly comic from the text: "'A note in the front states: "Some readers may think that a passage at the end of Chapter 1 bears a resemblance to a passage in Borrow's 'Lavengro.' It does. It is that passage.'"[43] Fifth, on other occasions, Cuppy simply found ways to comically describe basic plot points. In his review of *The Rubber Band*, he describes a murder suspect as "a British diplomat, croquet expert and pumpkin pie connoisseur."[44]

Of course, the general lack of "Mystery and Adventure" pans can also be "read" as a form of reaffirmation parody, what is sometimes called the mockumentary.[45] That is, Cuppy sometimes praises novels yet includes quotes from the focus text which suggest a negative verdict, such as his recycled closing summation of *The Silver Peril*, from a character named Jane: "'Cyril—oh Cyril, I suppose it had to end this way'"[46] Cuppy also casually praises another novel, *Shell of Death*, via a hermit character (of all things): "He talks like this, maybe for fun: 'So if any of yez hears an ululation tonight ye'll know I'm in it for ut.' Naturally, he is murdered in his hermit's hut."[47] Damning something by way of an author's own words might best be summarized by a quote from period performer Tallulah Bankhead, which author/personality Alexander Woollcott cited, aptly enough, in an essay entitled "Capsule Criticism." Listening with Woollcott to some rather poor dialogue during a play under review, she comically twisted an old axiom when she whispered to Woollcott, "There is less in this than meets the eye."[48]

Moving beyond the new antiheroic nature Cuppy brings to his "Mystery and Adventure" pieces, a fifth and final component of the column is a comically personal tone which again links these capsule reviews to his freelance articles. Ironically, Cuppy the murder mystery critic also periodically confesses he does not like gory stories. For instance, in discussing *Ring Around a Murder*, he shares, "[The author] would do well to avoid offensive images of one sort and another, as some of us cannot take it — sensitive, you know."[49] Plus, Cuppy's columns are brimming with his comic traits and/or pet peeves, which most often surface when he is describing various characters under review. In *The Silver Scale Mystery* he says of the heroine's brother, "He quotes Scriptures — watch him," while in his *Second Key* critique he reveals that a certain Mrs. Lowndes has not "contributed a lot to the anatomy of jealousy (our favorite passion)."[50] Moreover, as much as he publicly tried to avoid biting the genre hand which fed him, occasionally the column would be comically honest. For example, when praising Raymond Holden's *Penthouse Murders*, he credits the author with having "a gift for human dialogue as opposed to the bookish conversation offered in most mysteries and other bad books."[51]

The general lack of memorable/quality titles being reviewed by Cuppy reinforces his negative perspective on "Mystery and Adventure." Yet, occasionally, the column will provide a window into literary material the humorist admires, and even the musings of a *fan*. To illustrate, in his critique of Edgar Wallace's crime novel, *On the Spot*, Cuppy comically quakes at the publisher's notion that this is "'the greatest story ever written of America's gangland,' by saying, "it isn't even a patch on Mr. W.R. Burnett's 'Little Caesar' [the source of the celebrated 1930 gangster film of the same title]."[52] Still, Cuppy feels that *On the Spot*'s gangland "atmosphere is authentic" and that he "had the pleasure of shaking Mr. Wallace's hand just after he had come from Chicago."[53]

One genuine pleasure, however, which seems to be demonstrated by perusing many Cuppy columns, is his fondness for various mystery anthologies. The most obvious explanation is simply the overall upgrade in content quality. Yet, the always-frugal humorist forever notes the bargain nature of purchasing multiple classics between two covers. Not surprisingly, the humorist/critic himself will later edit several mystery anthologies in the 1940s (see the following chapter). Still, for the moment, the subject of anthologies provides an excellent transition to this chapter's third 1930s period focus — Cuppy's freelance comedy essays — following the "reading" of the major character he inspired in *The Golden Vanity*, and the unacknowledged humor nature of his "Mystery and Adventure" column.

Since much has already been written in this text about Cuppy's 1930s comedy essays, by way of those collected in the later *How to Become Extinct*, I will simply focus upon three of his most superlatively representative pieces from the decade, as chosen by humor scholar Louis Untermeyer for his anthology, *A Treasure of Laughter* (1946). The Cuppy essays are "The Goldfish," "The Pterodactyl," and "The Plesiosaur" (the latter two being now-extinct primitive reptiles). As a footnote to the selection of "The Plesiosaur," Cuppy had earlier received the highest private kudos for this essay from his friend, the acclaimed cartoonist William Steig. In a late-1930s letter to the humorist, Steig credited the piece as being the best Cuppy essay with which he was familiar.[54]

Numerous commonalities link these three essays with most of Cuppy's freelance comedy articles. First, unlike the reined-in "Mystery and Adventure" critiques, these pivotal pieces are savagely satirical attacks on the human race, masked as exercises in naturalism — "pessimistic naturalism."[55] For example, in "The Goldfish" he manages a satirical trifecta, by first indirectly suggesting even the best of mankind are doomed, followed by their institutions, and then — the pièce de resistance — he combines both perspectives by a shish kebab of Britain's royal family:

> Goldfish come of a very old family but it seems to do them no good.... They have been cultivated so long that they are now useless.... Queen Victoria had a Goldfish.... This statement is offered without documentation. It is based upon the self-evident truth that if Queen Victoria did *not* have a Goldfish, then history has no meaning and might as well stop.[56]

Second, if his comic doomsday perspective is not clear enough — history "might as well stop" — when applied to still-extant species (like the goldfish), why not expand the point further by examining extinct creatures such as in "The Pterodactyl" and "The Plesiosaur"? As one of Cuppy's publishers suggested, "If the reader wishes to become extinct and is willing to take the trouble, he has merely to read about the Dinosaur and the Pterodactyl, and act accordingly."[57] Humor historian Norris W. Yates has summed up, in part, Cuppy's dark comedy philosophy as, "Man is a concentration of the worst aspects of a meaningless universe."[58] This is bleak stuff— another reason Cuppy used the lower-animal subterfuge as more palatable comic puppets for his propaganda.

Third, these trios of essays are also emblematic of Cuppy's straight essay credo of, to butcher an old axiom, "Damn the experts, full speed ahead!" There is no velvet-gloved hand treatment of authority figures, à la his "Mystery and Adventure" columns. Cuppy the dissident dismantles the academics in multiple ways. First, he simply casts comic aspersions upon their procedures. Thus, with regard to "The Plesiosaur":

> They tried to get along with gizzards instead of stomachs, swallowing pebbles after each meal to grind their food. At least, pebbles have been found near fossil Plesiosaurs, and to a scientist that means the Plesiosaurs had a gizzard.[59]

Cuppy also had fun mocking evolution and, by extension, man's own chance to survive. This can be found in the following footnote from "The Pterodactyl": "In those days animals thought nothing of growing a new limb or organ to adapt themselves to conditions. We seem to have lost the knack."[60] Along similar lines, the same essay states: "He [the pterodactyl] had no teeth and no tail and may be regarded [by experts] as an improvement. If you call the lack of one's teeth and tail an improvement."[61] Finally, Cuppy is capable of flat-out negating the experts. For instance, in another footnote he observes, "Some scientists say the Pterodactyls merely glided and never attained true flight. As a matter of fact, they flew."[62]

As the last quote suggests, however, Cuppy occasionally plays at being a wise fool,—assuming the professorial stance, only to slide into silly and/or unverifiable facts. Here is one such example:

> Goldfish are fond of nibbling at a bit of Anarcharis, also called Waterfeed or Ditchmoss or Babington's Curse. Mr. Babington had a really frightful time with it. There are nine kinds ... in the United States. You don't need all of them.[63]

His wise-fool mask can also surface at the conclusion of a quasi-scientific statement as he suddenly lapses into anything but technical jargon, "Rhamphorhynchus, an early Pterodactyl, had pointed jaws full of teeth, a long tail with a membranous tip, and a somewhat half-witted expression."[64] Yet, Cuppy's cynical narrator in all his satirical pieces is invariably more nihilistically wise than fool, when one takes the time to read between the lines. Consider the footnote in which he allegedly compares the pterodactyl to a "critter" still in existence: "Bats [humans] are going to flop [become extinct], too, and everybody knows it except the Bats [people] themselves. Well, that's always the way."[65]

Of course, Cuppy's increasing goal over time was to erase the anthropomorphic cover he used for his satire. Indeed, he first started his frontal-attack opus upon human history, what would later be published posthumously as *The Decline and Fall of Practically Everybody* (1950, edited by Fred Feldkamp) in the early 1930s. Plus, as the aforementioned link between the useless goldfish and Queen Victoria suggests, this increasingly less veiled hostility was bursting out in short pieces long before the appearance of *Decline and Fall*. Even the early *How to Tell Your Friends from the Apes* had forays into comic studies of man's (especially primitive man's) limitations. But Cuppy still plugged along with what he liked to call his "animal books" throughout the 1940s. In fact, even the last text he prepared for production, the also posthumously published *How to Attract the Wombat* (1949), was, as the title suggests, yet another fifth columnist satirical attack under the guise of an animal menagerie. Yet, as previously noted, in his blistering *Wombat* introduction, Cuppy dropped any cover-up pretenses with acidic comments like:

> Why do you suppose I did that [outrageously anthropomorphic treatment of animals] unless it was to get in all those dirty cracks about the human race, a form of life I suppose I am a little too much inclined to look down upon.[66]

One is tempted to ponder if his frustration over whether the *Decline and Fall* text would ever be published, tempered with the open bitterness he revealed at the beginning of the *Wombat* text, contributed to his suicide shortly before the latter book's publication. While the ultimate answer is lost to time, there is no doubting the frustration Cuppy felt over his "animal" stories being more palatable to period audiences. For instance, what follows, in part, is a 1937 *New Yorker* rejection letter, a publication in which many of the animal pieces for 1941s *How to Become Extinct* first appeared, giving a thumbs-down verdict to some biting essays on historic figures, two of which would later appear in *Decline and Fall*:

> No matter how funny a piece may be, [chief editor and *New Yorker* founder Harold] Ross says, people are sick to death of Godiva and her hair and her horse, and don't want to hear any more about them. I suppose the same thing goes for Cleopatra and Aspasia.... I'm [Wolcott Gibbs, editor/humorist] afraid that I'm inclined to agree with the rest of the boys and girls.[67]

As Cuppy's age, health issues (real and imagined), and general fears/frustrations grew over the years, I am reminded of an old axiom associated with a cynic's last days. A rough paraphrasing would read as follows:

> When you are younger, you think there's a wise man behind that door [of the future] with a white beard, and you can see him and he'll tell you the answers. But that man is not there.

Beyond this mere speculation on what contributed to Cuppy's ultimate suicide are the comments, ironically, of a much later *New Yorker* writer, whose description of a character not unlike the humorist remind me of the arbitrary deadlines/pressures many creative figures place upon themselves: "[There is both danger and] pathos of over-cerebration, the endless, self-feeding excitement of a terrific mind that can't stop spinning."[68]

Regardless of such conjecture about Cuppy's dark close to the 1940s, the 1930s humorist was sometimes as close as he ever got to the elusively proverbial glass being half full. One might best note that upbeat tone by quoting a final antiheroically funny balancing act to a review column from 1934. Cuppy's critique of *Hearken to the Evidence* opens with the most amusingly even of playing fields:

> When this department differs critically from other judges, we believe in giving full publicity to the other side — shows we're just bristling with justice and complete fairness.[69]

Thus, besides his mounting success as a humorist, columnist, and a literary figure who inspired a character in a novel which Stanford literature professor/critic Albert Guerard stated might have been written by a celebrated author like Jane Austin or Edith Wharton, not to mention Paterson's ongoing sprinkling of Cuppy's name in her influential *Tribune* column, Cuppy managed to make his public presence known in an assortment of other ways.[70] For instance, in 1933 NBC gave Cuppy a 15-minute weekly radio program, *Just Relax*, in which he and actress Jeanne Owen discussed an unlimited supply of personal pet peeves. The content, written entirely by Cuppy, was a series of rambling dialogues — really more monologues — covering everything from Cuppy critters to hermiting. Even though he now spent the majority of his time in his Greenwich Village apartment, he would forever after be known as the eccentric "Hermit of Jones' Island.")[71] Unfortunately, NBC made the situation worse by switching the program's time slot several times, preventing Cuppy from building a regular fan base. Consequently, he was canceled after less than a year.[72] Still, Cuppy was ahead of his time in the dark-comedy department, and one can get a sense of the program in some material he wrote during the 1930s for another radio humorist and future television personality, the curmudgeonly Henry Morgan. What follows is one of several potential riffs in what Cuppy describes as his "persecution complex" style:

> Why is it that I never get a seat on the subway? Not that I want a seat but if I wanted one I couldn't get it. I have noticed this over a period of years. If there are say fifteen seats on one side of the car, I am the sixteenth person, and so forth. I can walk the length of the train and never

see a seat. The only reason I walk through is to see if there IS a seat just for the hell of it, to check. There never is. It seems uncanny, that's why I mention it. Is it that way with other people? Do YOU ever find a seat? The fact is, I'd rather stand. I'm so used to it now. I just wondered WHY. One reason is because I would hate to be like the people who rush to get a seat. They can't be very nice people.... I would not run after a seat if I never sat down in all my life, because I think it is extremely ungraceful and mean.[73]

Cuppy was also in the public eye during the 1930s by way of a book he did not author. Yet, unlike Paterson's *The Golden Vanity*, with which one had to be in the literary know to realize the character of Jake was based upon Cuppy, the humorist was front and center in the English comedy text *Garden Rubbish, and Other Country Bumps*, by the writing team of W.C. Seller and R. J. Yeatman (1937). Cuppy was responsible for the tongue-in-cheek footnotes in this critically acclaimed humor book, which the *New York Times* called:

> a masterpiece in its own way. Certainly it overflows with such a buoyant spirit of ... ribaldry as must delight the heart of every one who has ever looked upon a garden with love or loathing.[74]

The same review, as was typical of the other period critiques, also lavished praise upon Cuppy: "Will Cuppy's notes, we must add, bring an American touch to these British-born pages, and enchant us by having, in general, nothing to do with the case."[75]

The Scottish Seller and the Portugal-born Yeatman had met while both were at England's Oxford College, and eventually established their comedy credentials while writing for Britain's watershed comic magazine, *Punch*. Their greatest joint claim to fame was a humor book, which anticipated Cuppy's *Decline and Fall* by 20 years: *1066 and All That* (1930), a twisted guide to all the history you could possibly remember. Though the duo took joint authorship of their books (like the later Beatle songwriting team of John Lennon and Paul McCartney), one humorist often did the brunt of the work on each project. Fittingly, Seller, a Cuppy-like character, was the primary author of *Garden Rubbish*. Sellar was also somewhat shy and introverted, often wrote in a melancholy tone, and yet was quite capable of coming across as a free spirit in the occasional social setting. Thus, it is easy to see how such collaboration was born. The book's success also further enhanced Cuppy's popularity in Britain.

Regardless, as suggested by the *Times* review, Cuppy's inspired *Garden Rubbish* footnotes rarely have anything to do with the subject at hand. For instance, a section of the book on mulching has the following note:

> When a child is born among the Dyaks of Landak and Tajan, in Borneo, the natives plant a fruit tree and carefully watch its growth to see whether the baby will be tall or short, straight or crooked. It would of course be simpler to watch the baby.[76]

Along similar surreal lines, another section of the text discussing broken flowerpots cuts to the Cuppy note, "I don't like cold weather myself. Otherwise, I have no suggestions to make."[77] In Cuppy's own humor books the footnotes are more pointedly attached to the main body of the work, a pattern which only rarely occurs in *Garden Rubbish*. Fittingly, Cuppy only flirts with a connection in his follow-up to some Seller and Yeatman thoughts on weather and weeding: "You often hear that the English climate has had a profound influence upon the English temperament. I don't believe it. I believe they were always like that."[78]

Fittingly, for two humorists borne of *Punch* magazine, the decision to juxtapose their material with Cuppy's in an often nonsensical manner connects the American's work even more with the comedy writing (often referenced as "dementia praecox") nature of his hero, Robert Benchley.[79] In fact, Benchley's late essays would be so sufficiently imbued with this phenomenon that when he reluctantly retired from writing (1943), he designated his crazy comedy successor to be the even loopier S. J. Perelman.[80] Ironically, in one of Benchley's last films, the posthumously released *Road to Utopia* (1945), the humorist seems to borrow a page from Cuppy's collaboration on *Garden Rubbish*. In *Utopia*, arguably the best of the Bob Hope and Bing Crosby "Road" pictures, Benchley's supporting contribution adds cinematic footnotes to the comedy proceedings. To illustrate, Benchley periodically appears in the corner of the screen and shares a bit of comic wisdom, such as, "This is a device known as a flashback," or "Did you ever stop to think of one of those dog teams? [The movie is set in the far north.] The lead dog is the only one that ever gets a change of scenery." Though such examples are in line with the Cuppy norm of a direct link between the text and the funny footnote, Benchley's on-camera prologue to *Utopia* anchors the proceedings in the aforementioned "dementia praecox":

> The motion picture which you are about to see is not very clear in spots. As a matter of fact it was made to demonstrate how not to make a motion picture and at the same time win an Academy Award. Now someone in what is known as the [studio] front office has thought an occasional word from me might help clarify the plot and other vague portions of the film. [chuckling] Personally, I doubt it.[81]

Regardless, Cuppy's 1930s persona was also briefly showcased on the comic lecture circuit, another period venue pioneered by Benchley and his acclaimed late 1920s humor "lecture," "The Treasurer's Report," which was eventually both recycled as a pioneering 1928 sound film short subject of the same title, and the later headline essay in the Benchley collection, *The Treasurer's Report and Other Aspects of Community Singing* (1930).[82] This talking Benchley breakout, initially staged in a Broadway revue, led to a celebrated second career as a movie character actor and radio personality. Unfortunately, Cuppy's foray into the lecture circuit was not so fortuitous. Yet, he had a very successful run of several weeks at New York's tony Rockefeller Center's Rainbow Room nightclub. However, in a subsequent speaking date for a Rochester, New York, ad club, he became so nervous that the resulting "talk" was such a failure he refused a fee. Like his seemingly congenial nature when forced into a social setting, it would seem that too much public interaction, either with friends and/or paying customers, was more than this self-proclaimed hermit could comfortably sustain. Still, his brief 1930s adventures in radio and public speaking merely added more merry mystique to his comedy personae. Of course, there is a certain irony involved in the fact that Cuppy's increased prominence paralleled a decade (the 1930s) in which his essays assumed a darker hue (see chapter five). Yet, it was not so much that he was biting the hand that fed him. More success merely allowed Cuppy to reveal more of his nihilistic nature. In addition, a more prosperous Cuppy was still an enemy of budgets and savings plans, as he comically chronicled in the essay "I'm Not the Budget Type" (1937). The humorist observed, in part:

> Veteran budgeters tell me that I confuse what I need with what I want. To me there's a difference, because what I want I practically have to have.... As for saving for what I want, what I want is more money. How would you budget that?... The Cuppy Plan of Getting Along [is] Borrowing.... "My purpose in life is to borrow a thousand dollars." ... An acquaintance of mine more than hinted, recently, that persons who borrow constantly are lacking in character. I think she was wrong. What I lack is not character. It's money.[83]

Be that as it may, the best window into Cuppy's briefly improved 1930s mindset occurs in one of his extended "guest appearances" in Paterson's "Turn with a Bookworm" column. He feels good about several writing projects, including a reference to what will eventually be published as *The Decline and Fall of Practically Everybody*. Though the piece dovetails into dark comedy, Cuppy allows more hope to shine through than was often his then in-print norm ... even if he is admittedly playing mindgames:

> Anyway, it [the writing] really makes me feel good for the time being, and you know that poor Uncle Will [Cuppy] needs to be happy if possible, even if it involves a little tinkering with the facts of life as we

know it. I mean, what if it is all as awful as you are practically sure it is? What else does life consist of but these little self-bafflings? Answer me that![84]

Even a 1930s failure like Cuppy's *Just Relax* radio program had its joys, from countless literary fans, to humorous critics like *The Forum*'s Cyrus Fisher. Most importantly, Fisher not only called *Just Relax* the best program on radio in October of 1933, he chronicled a humorist happily determined to do it his way, come what may:

> [Cuppy is] deliberately avoiding the facts of life, confounding honest radio fans with fifteen minutes of shameful nonsense. But some of us will refuse to believe we are being cozened; it will not disturb us to learn that Mr. Cuppy's investigations into the effects of spinach on the love life of Norwegians are grossly fraudulent. And if you are one of those in that minority, you will look forward every Friday to ... Cuppy's quiet but florescent meanderings.[85]

Of course, arguably the goofiest example of Cuppy free-spiritedness during the Depression involved, of all people, aviator Amelia Earhart (1897–1937). On the eve of her famed trans–Atlantic flight he sent her the following Western Union Cablegram (May 22, 1932), "God bless you[.] You cute thing[.] Your adoring Will Cuppy."[86] Since this is the only piece of Cuppy correspondence in Earhart's private papers at Purdue University (West Lafayette, Indiana), it is obvious that the humorist was merely playing at being a groupie, possibly emboldened by some of that random bootlegger booze which occasionally washed up on his Jones Island beach.

Cuppy scholar Thomas Maeder also suggests that the 1930s might have been even more of a moon shot decade for the humorist had he not been such a professional curmudgeon about perceived slights, including the so-called "hate Cuppy" movement.[87] Regardless, the humorist had definitely made his major pet peeve presence known in 1930s comedy circles. Indeed, one could rewrite Thoreau's aforementioned mantra of "most men lead lives of quiet desperation" to better define Cuppy's now-emerging cynically angry voice thusly: "His was a life of comically *loud* desperation."

EIGHT

Here Come Cuppy's Mystery Anthologies of the 1940s

"We both sincerely trust that you may find in these [*World's Great Detective Stories*] pages much that is worth your while and nothing to make you sorry that the Chinese invented printing."— Editor Will Cuppy's introduction to his second mystery anthology (1943).[1]

As in all things for Cuppy, even in an introduction to a murder mystery anthology, comedy was front and center. While this text has already devoted a great deal of attention to Cuppy's comedy-oriented *New York Herald Tribune* review column, "Mystery and Adventure," in the 1940s, the humorist's association with the genre further escalated when he edited three popular mystery anthologies: *World's Great Mystery Stories*, *World's Great Detective Stories* (both 1943), and *Murder Without Tears* (1946).

During the 1940s Cuppy continued to write his freelance comedy essays, which now frequently surfaced in the *Saturday Evening Post*. However, due to the massive research Cuppy applied to his brief satirical pieces, the last of his humor books to appear during his lifetime, *How to Become Extinct* (1941), predated his onslaught of murder mystery anthologies. Couple this with the ongoing weekly mystery column, and the pedestrian public might assume that Cuppy comedy had now assumed a back-burner position. Certainly one sees this reflected in the later opening of his 1949 *New York Times* obituary, "Will Cuppy, author, critic and humorist...."[2]

Yet, just as the dissection of his columns revealed their inherent dark-comedy tendencies, a closer examination of editor Cuppy's anthologies also reveals an often-multi-faceted black humor and/or theatre-of-the-absurd foundation to his murder-mystery selections. The Cuppy introductions to each of his anthologies could easily double as straight comedy essays, as this chapter's epigraph illustrates. However, just as humorist Cuppy saved the most bitingly revealing insights about his satire for the introduction to his last personally prepared comedy text, the posthumously published *How to Attract the Wombat* (1949), editor Cuppy followed a similar pattern with the anthologies. Only in the introduction to *Murder Without Tears*, the final text of his mystery trilogy, does he baldly state what has been apparent from a reading of all the anthologies. Cuppy's catalyst for this confession is his fondness for the book's dark-comedy moniker:

> A lovely title, you must agree, but what does it mean? Simply that this collection ... [includes] pieces which may make you smile for one reason or another ... crime experts who are either unwilling or unable to lighten their gruesome material ... even a smile or two — are incomplete specimens. Some small portion of the cerebral cortex is probably missing or in a rudimentary state.[3]

This admission goes beyond a public embracing of dark comedy in *all* aspects of his writing and editing. The statement also represents a modest defense against hypocrisy. That is, though he was not a fan of a genre he reviewed for years, he sometimes found it tolerable if peppered with macabre and absurd humor. While Cuppy's columns allowed him to interject those very embellishments into his own critiques, with few fouls to the work being reviewed (since critical pans were rare), Cuppy's anthology selections generally demonstrated the same macabre merriment.

Paradoxically, the dark comedy inherent to the new 1940s movie mystery genre now known as film noir, and demonstrated by titles like *Murder My Sweet* (1943) and *The Big Sleep* (1946), were starting to catch up with Cuppy's groundbreaking black humor. Fittingly, Cuppy intuitively sensed the movement years before it was officially recognized by film scholars. For instance, he anthologizes two short stories from arguably noir's founding father, Dashiell Hammett, whose novel *The Maltese Falcon* was the basis for the groundbreaking 1941 noir classic of the same name, with a breakout performance by Humphrey Bogart as the soon-to-be iconic private eye Sam Spade. Thus, Cuppy includes Hammett's "A Man Called Spade" in the *World's Great Detective Stories*, and another Spade story, "They Can Only Hang You Once," in *Murder Without Tears*.

Like Cuppy, Hammett also believed in mixing murder with merriment, a fact demonstrated by all his Spade stories, as well as his *Thin Man* novel, which spawned filmland's most successful "A"-picture franchise until the James Bond series. The original *Thin Man* movie appeared in 1934; starring William Powell and Myrna Loy, it was a critical and commercial smash, and inspired five sequels. Hammett's novel, and the Powell/

Loy movies which followed, were as much screwball comedies as murder mysteries, and more fully demonstrate the humor tendency which this drew this author to Cuppy.[4] Ironically, given the increased visibility/popularity of mixing humor with homicide during the 1940s, either in the various writing modes of Cuppy, or in the important emerging genre of film noir, polite society still had issues with the development. Note the condescending tone included in the aforementioned Cuppy *New York Times* obituary: "His writing had a dry, contemplative flavor that made him popular with persons who thought that murder could sometimes be funny."[5] Along related lines, while the *Times* reviewed all of Cuppy's comedy books, it chose to give only the most cursory critique to his final murder-mystery anthology.

Of course, off the record, Cuppy himself could be rather condescending about the mystery genre, if one divorced it from *comedy embellishments*. Paradoxically, he was very open about these feelings in his correspondence with noted professor and author/critic John T. Frederick shortly before he started editing his anthologies. Earlier in this text it was noted that Cuppy appeared on Frederick's CBS radio program *Of Men and Books* in 1942, in order to discuss mystery novels. In their preliminary correspondence, Cuppy boldly confessed:

> I am afraid I would not willingly read a mystery story if it were not my job to do so.... I am only lukewarm in my enthusiasm for all this trash [mysteries].... A mystery can't be wonderful, because it just doesn't have anything to do with the human spirit and man's heights and depths.... It is only about a tiny little matter and the most unimportant of all matters at that — who don [*sic*] it.[6]

While these were not new revelations to Cuppy's inner circle — similar comments have already been cited in this text from his 1920s correspondence with Isabel Paterson — to share them with such a tony literary figure at this particular time is startling. Maybe one explains it as another basic component of the dark comedy he so enjoyed — the ability to shock. More disturbing, however, is the ease with which Cuppy promises to say whatever it takes to put the program over. That is, at another point in the previously quoted lengthy letter (a Cuppy specialty), the humorist counsels Frederick about his negative attitude toward mysteries:

> Don't let it frighten you. I am an experienced publicity hound and know how to handle such problems — for instance, I am able to pretend that I just adore going to bed with a ghastly little piece of mystery tripe.[7]

Without justifying such duplicity, several explanations come to mind. First, Cuppy did find mystery more palatable — if comedy was involved.

Will Cuppy at one of his periodic appearances on CBS radio (circa 1942).

Second, the humorist liked to operate under the delusion that a "hate Cuppy" movement was always derailing his work. Thus, one could easily see the humorist justifying his love-of-mystery cover as pure self-defense — Cuppy's variation upon Darwin's Theory of Evolution, which was always lurking between the lines of his satire. Third, Cuppy frequently included himself in his disappointment over man's lack of meaningful evolutionary progress. That is, humans were racing towards extinction like so many of the other creatures about which he wrote. So what was the harm in an occasional lie here and there? After all, he had obviously played the needy lie game for much of his adult life, from constantly depending upon the physical assistance of the Jones Island Coast Guard, to the ongoing psychological cheerleading of Paterson. Fifth, with tongue firmly in cheek, one could claim Cuppy anticipated a comic-multiple-personality Sybil; he occasionally claimed to so hate doing the mystery column that he somehow morphed into another character when writing the reviews. Cuppy even christened this alter-ego critic "Oswald Terwilliger" and thought of him as only marginally intelligent (the very opinion he held regarding the average murder mystery fan).

Whatever one's "reading" of Cuppy's duplicity on the subject of mystery, his anthologies reveal several truisms about the humorist on literature. First, Cuppy was a champion of great writers, and while his mystery collections include many predictable author choices, such as Agatha Christie, Sir Arthur Conan Doyle, and the aforementioned Hammett, editor Cuppy draws many selections from literary giants not normally associated with the genre. This latter group would include William Faulkner, F. Scott Fitzgerald, and Aldous Huxley.

Indeed, Cuppy's first selection for his first anthology is Faulkner's macabre tale with the black-humor conclusion — "A Rose for Emily." The ending even references a variation of Cuppy's desire for murder with a smile. The bedroom of an elderly, aristocratic, unmarried lady — Emily by name — has been opened after her death. No one has entered the tomblike chamber for 40 years. The bed contains the corpse of a lover Emily poisoned four decades before — after he refused to marry her:

> The man [lay] ... with a fleshless grin. The body had apparently once lain in an attitude of an embrace but now the long sleep that out lasts love, that conquers even the grimace of love, had cuckolded him ... had become inextricable from the bed in which he lay.[8]

Yet Faulkner tops this fusion of horror and humor with his final revelation about this wannabe bride who committed the murder: "[The investigators] noticed that in the second pillow was the indentation of a head. One of us lifted something from it, and leaning forward ... we saw a long strand of iron-gray hair."[9]

Faulkner's "Emily" tale is a perfect companion piece for another of Cuppy's *World's Great Mystery Stories*—Ambrose Bierce's "The Boarded Window." Bierce, sometimes seen as a darkly comic precursor to Cuppy,[10] and a satirist in the grand tradition of Swift, is also not normally associated with mystery. Yet, as with Faulkner's otherwise conventional tale, both writers jolt the reader with their theatre-of-the-absurd surprise endings, sort of O. Henry meets the Grateful Dead. Bierce's story chronicles a struggling Ohio pioneer whose wife suddenly takes ill. Try as he might to nurse her along, she dies. In shock but ever caring, he prepares his beloved for burial, including binding her wrists with a ribbon. However, it has grown late by the time this dreadful duty is completed. Exhausted, he decides burial must wait until morning, and he falls asleep in a chair by the table upon which he has placed her.

Hours later something awakens him in the pitch-black cabin. Then the table shakes and he hears a light step upon the floor. His terror grows when an unseen force brutally pushes the table against him, and he hears something fall violently to the floor, followed by scuffling. Bierce then writes, "There is a point at which terror may turn to madness, and madness incites to action."[11] Somehow the pioneer gets to his rifle and fires blindly into the darkness. Though he does not hit anything, the weapon's discharge briefly illuminates the room, and reveals an enormous panther dragging his wife's body by the neck towards a window.

The settler passes out and does not regain consciousness until the following day. His wife lies near the window, apparently dropped by the panther after the firing. The woman's throat is dreadfully lacerated, and the cabin is awash with blood. For a lesser writer, this offbeat thriller might have thus ended. But Bierce, like Faulkner, takes the finale to a more twisted level with his close, "[His wife's] hands were tightly clenched. Between the teeth [of his spouse] was a fragment of the animal's ear."[12] The antihero of "The Boarded Window" has sadly failed his wife *twice*, with his loving ribbon binding actually contributing to her death. This anticipates film noir's black-humor fatalism, in which acts of kindness invariably make things worse. Faulkner and Bierce stories such as these constitute more bizarre background horrors for what passes as the human comedy. In a similar vein, Hitchcock invariably referred to his neo-noir *Psycho* (1960) as a dark comedy, or simply a "humorous film."[13]

Indeed, like Cuppy, Hitchcock was not overly fond of mysteries. What he most enjoyed was the black humor chronicling of the story itself.

A second Cuppy truism showcased in his anthologies is the inherent black humor (often at the expense of the masses) to be found even in his selections from the more signature mystery writers. For instance, Agatha Christie's "The Adventure of the Egyptian Tomb," included in *World's Great Detective Stories*, has a narrative in which a bemusedly cynical investigator lectures:

> I believe in the terrific force of superstition. Once it gets firmly established that a series of deaths are supernatural, and you might almost stab a man in broad daylight, and it would still be put down to the curse, so strongly is the instinct of the supernatural implanted in the human race.[14]

The masses take another metaphorical shot to the jaw in Cuppy's *Murder Without Tears* inclusion of Hammett's "They Can Only Hang You Once." A payoff reading of a will becomes an exercise on why a seemingly wealthy man chooses to leave nothing to his conniving family: "Lastly [they deserve not a scrap] because their painful lack of any decent sense of humor will keep them from ever seeing how funny this has all been"—laughter from the dead about the pettiness of the living.[15] Of course, any Sam Spade story is also richly anchored in sarcastic banter befitting a character

Hammett described in "A Man Called Spade" (included in *World's Great Detective Stories*) as, "The amusement twitching Spade's face accented his likeness to a blond Satan."¹⁶ For example, the same essay has a classic Spade comeback to a baiting antagonist:

> "Let's stick to what we know," he growled. "Sure," Sam agreed. "What is it?"¹⁷

Of greater surprise, concerning Cuppy's recycling of mainstream mystery writers, is how a selection like Dorothy L. Sayers's "The Abominable History of the Man With the Copper Fingers" from the *World's Great Detective Stories*, blends so easily with the macabre Kafka-on-wheels nature of the Faulkner and Bierce pieces. The crux of the story concerns an artist perversely honoring a former lover by creating a large settee with a base like a Roman couch of oak, with a silver inlay, topped (the actual seat) by a "great silver figure of a nude woman, fully life-size, lying with her head back and her arms extended along the sides of the couch. [Seeing the artist] sprawling over it ... gave me ... a shock. He seemed very much attached to it, though."¹⁸

Cuppy sometimes affectionately kidded Sayers in his "Mystery and Adventure" review column (see previous chapter). Yet, the humorist's inherent respect for her went beyond Sayers's ability, as in the passage just quoted, to essentially view humans as a moral leper colony. He also admired the range of her writing, from essayist and novelist, to playwright and translator. (Sayers considered her greatest accomplishment to be a translation of Dante's *Divina Commedia*.) Of course, since Cuppy damned all mystery which was devoid of comedy, Sayers's primary fictional sleuth, Lord Peter Wimsey (who headlines ten of her novels), was a character he could appreciate, especially when one factors in Sayers's frequent description of Wimsey — a mixture of Fred Astaire and P.G. Wodehouse's Bertie Wooster. But if one wanted to dig deeper for an additional Sayers plus in the world according to Cuppy, the humorist would have appreciated how her later biographers suggested Sayers's mysteries as being inherently parodies of the genre.¹⁹

Certainly Cuppy best documents his own case for Sayers's spoofing nature by including a parody-oriented Lord Wimsey story, "In the Teeth of the Evidence," in *Murder Without Tears*. Besides its obvious kidding of the detective trade, the most pleasant surprise about the tale is how much Wimsey sounds like a British version of Cuppy, a man curmudgeonly comic about the most basic of pet peeves. The story opens with Wimsey at his dentist complaining about how an upper grinder went to bits after only eating an omelet, without even a thought of cracking nuts. But a more blistering tipping point occurs when his dentist asks if the drilling is causing any pain. Wimsey replies, "No *pain*, unless you count a sharp edge fit to saw your tongue off. Point is, why should it [my tooth] go pop like that? I wasn't doing anything to it."[20] The short story also trashes two subjects about which Cuppy was decidedly trepidatious — children and relationships. For instance, when the authorities are considering whether a Dr. Prendergast's death was an accident or a suicide, one character observes, "If you ask me, I should say Mrs. P. was the biggest argument we have for suicide."[21]

Before the obvious twist which will naturally turn Sayers's tale into a murder mystery, "In the Teeth of Evidence" is layered with both parody and comedy, exactly what one would expect of such a punning title, or of an author whose signature sleuth is named Wimsey. Easily the tale's funniest line, however, is another bit of black humor. Prendergast had just filled his automobile with gas prior to the alleged accident, when possibly a lit cigarette ignited the petrol fumes and caused his fiery death. An investigator notes that the victim seems to have mistakenly left the ignition on: "The proper thing ... is to switch off the petrol and leave the engine running so as to empty the carburetor but you don't always think straight when you're being burnt alive."[22]

A third Cuppy fundamental to be found in his mystery anthologies — and a natural transition from the parody component noted in Sayers' work — is that the humorist/critic simply adored mystery material which broadly spoofed the genre. For this similarly inclined biographer, the most entertaining Cuppy anthology choices are these over-the-top parodies, such as his inclusion of Mark Twain's "The Stolen White Elephant" in *World's Great Detective Stories.* The premise is that a royal white elephant of Siam is to be given as a gift to Great Britain, but the animal has disappeared in transit. A famous New York detective, Inspector Blunt, is placed upon the case, and the tale quickly morphs to inspired spoofing of standard murder-mystery procedure, including missing-person basics — for an elephant. For example, Blunt asks for Jumbo's place of birth, if his parents are living, his height, weight, length of tail, and type of footprint, the latter resembling the mark left when one up-ends a barrel in the snow."[23]

Twain also uses his elephant story as a vehicle for his own litany on what he scornfully enjoyed calling the "damned human race." Thus, his tale eventually includes a series of news reports about the delicious destruction caused by what is ultimately a runaway pachyderm:

> Elephant arrived here from the south, dispersing a funeral on the way, and diminishing the mourners by two.... I have just learned that nothing of that funeral is now left but ... there is an abundance of material

for another ... [said beast has now] broke up a revivial, striking down and damaging many who were on the point of entering upon a better life.[24]

Laced throughout Twain's essay is an ongoing parody of all things detective, from the incompetent Blunt and his even more dimwittedly supportive Watson-like client, to a broader in-story backlash against inspectors (which even includes various minstrel shows), spoofing detectives unable to find a missing elephant. Yet, beyond the parody and dark comedy, the real reason Cuppy selected the essay might just be that it begins with a comic footnote! With tongue firmly in cheek, the note claims the story was left out of Twain's *A Tramp Abroad* (1880) because it was "feared that some of the particulars had been exaggerated, and that others were not true. Before these suspicions had been proven groundless, the book had gone to press."[25]

Cuppy also anthologizes broad mystery parodies by other noted humorists, such as Stephen Leacock and Irvin S. Cobb. The two Leacock selections, "Who Do You Think Did It? or, The Mixed-Up Murder Mystery" (in *World's Great Mystery Stories*), and "Maddened by Mystery or The Defective Detective" (in *Murder Without Tears*), are, as their titles suggest, as entertainingly loopy as the Twain essay. Cuppy also gives them the singular honor of closing each of these anthologies, just as "The Stolen White Elephant" is the final piece in *World's Great Detective Stories*. The clear implication is that Cuppy wishes the reader's last lingering perspective of his anthologies be one defining mysteries as the silliest of all genres.

"Who Do You Think Did It?" is simply a textbook example of what parody studies label "creative criticism."[26] To create an effective spoof, one must be thoroughly versed in the subject under attack. Thus, parody can be the most palatable of *critical approaches*, offering insights through laughter. The "creative criticism" significance of the genre is important, given that parody has often been considered a lesser parasite on true works of artistic and/or pop culture significance. Yet it takes just as much creative talent to both perceive a given structure and then effectively spoof the target as it does to create a structure in the first place. Parody is simultaneously something old and something new: kid a traditional structure, have fresh fun with the content.

In "Who Do You Think Did It?" Leacock effectively dismantles Sir Arthur Conan Doyle's legendary Sherlock Holmes. The key to Holmes's success as an investigator is his unparalleled power of deduction, in which a simple observation produces volumes of alleged fact. One of Leacock's most imaginative skewerings of such deduction is in the following conversation between detective Transome Kent and the Inspector, who speaks first:

"These are the tracks of a man with a wooden leg"—Kent nodded—"in all probability a sailor, newly landed from Java, carrying a Singapore walking stick, and with a tin whistle tied around the belt." "Yes, I can see that," said Kent thoughtfully. "The weight of the whistle weighs him down a little on the right side."[27]

Holmes's godlike status gives him almost carte blanche power in his special world of mystery. Leacock also spoofs this status when the investigating Kent moves about Grand Central Station harassing assorted travelers by peering into their faces. When a train official asks him to stop, Kent curtly replies, "I am unraveling a mystery...." "I beg your pardon, sir," said the man, "I didn't know."[28] Plus, it would not be a Cuppy selection if said short story was devoid of dark comedy. Thus, one of the newspapers reporting on the case states this is the third club man (gentleman) killed in the past two weeks: "While not taking an alarmist view, the paper felt that the killing of club men had got to stop. There was a limit, a reasonable limit, to everything."[29]

Leacock's "Defective Detective," as the title suggests, is an even more direct bludgeoning burlesque of Holmes, from calling his "Defective" character the "Great Detective" (a moniker sometimes applied to Holmes), to noting early that a "half bucket of cocaine [a Holmes vice] and a [drug] dipper stood on a chair at his elbow."[30] Conan Doyle was also adept at suggesting that apocalyptic events would occur if Holmes did not immediately solve the mystery. Consequently, when a client comes to Leacock's "Defective Detective," his title character observes, "I suppose ... it [the case] is connected ... with the highest diplomatic consequences, so that if we fail to solve it England will be at war with the whole world in sixteen minutes."[31] The answer is a quick affirmative.

Cuppy's *World's Great Mystery Stories* also includes a parody from a most unlikely source, given his aforementioned displeasure with the populist writing of Will Rogers. The selection in question, by Rogers's friend and fellow populist, Irvin S. Cobb (1876–1944), is a courtroom mystery entitled "A Bird in the Hand." Also like Rogers, Cobb was involved in films during the 1930s, appearing as a supporting player in John Ford's *Steamboat 'Round the Bend* (1935, a pivotal Rogers picture), while Cobbs's "Judge Priest" short stories were the basis for two other Ford films, *Judge Priest* (1934, another signature Rogers/Ford movie), and *The Sun Shines Bright* (1953). Yet while Rogers was the iconic persona of the era, Cobb was the more versatile and prolific author. He was a longtime journalist, especially for the *New York World*, as well as a later war correspondent for the *Saturday Evening Post*. Though Cobb's focus was usually on humor, his writing range extended from musical comedy to mystery and horror.

Read today, "A Bird in Hand," with its central crackerbarrel Southern lawyer protecting law in Manhattan, one is reminded of Andy Griffith's 1980s television series *Matlock*, where he also plays a folksy small town attorney in the big time. But just as *Matlock* gave Griffith a serious role, with the populism toned down from his *Andy Griffith Show* comedy, Cobb's story reins in the broad humor. Of course, as there is invariably a residue of comedy simply in the casting of Griffith in any part, Cobb's description of his central "A Bird in Hand" character, Colonel K. Blue, might have been an amusing Cobb self-portrait:

> In a small town he would have been ... [considered] a type and a character.... You thought of stiffened lava when you looked him in the face.... He was just a homely, awkward, dependable-looking individual with a South Carolina tidewater accent and a fine gift for remaining silent unless and until he had something to say.[32]

Regardless, the tale begins as a straightforward recounting of an apparent domestic murder. A tenement woman is found dead — hanging with bound hands from a rafter in her flat — after an alleged fight with her common-law

Will Rogers (left) buttonholes Irvin S. Cobb in *Steamboat 'Round the Bend* (1935).

husband. This man, the accused murderer, was found passed out drunk when the police broke down the appartment door.

The first darkly comic twist occurs, however, when the prosecutor anchors his case upon the repeated refrain of the couple's parrot at the time the victim was discovered: "Oh, Daddy, please don't do that to me!"[33] The attorney also builds up the significance of this testimony as providential, as if God Himself had brought back the pleading voice of this poor woman.

The second black-humor bomb of Cobb's story occurs when his Colonel Blue trumps the prosecution by calling their star witness, Laura the parrot, to the stand. Naturally, there are objections from the defense, but since the bird is the cornerstone of the case, and the judge is as curious as the next gallery member about such a defense ploy, he allows this most unusual procedure. Well, Colonel Blue simply feeds that parrot a few bites of banana and, in short order, teaches Laura to say, "Tell the police to go find Ramon Gaza! Tell the police to go find Ramon Gaza!"[34] Ultimately, this was pure gamesmanship by Blue, to introduce evidence which proved that the victim's former jealous lover, Ramon Gaza, had stumbled upon a suicide and framed his rival.

With Cobb's dark-comedy touches and that punning title, "A Bird in the Hand," it was obviously a Cuppy kind of mystery. Yet, one wonders if editor Cuppy was attracted to the story for possibly two additional reasons. First, populist or not, Cobb, like Cuppy, had real issues with both organized religion and any individuals claiming to have a direct pipeline to God. Thus, Colonel Blue's put-down of the prosecutor's sanctimoniousness would undoubtedly have scored points with Cuppy. Second, through Cobb's pivotal use of an innately comic type of bird, and a story-ending revelation that Blue is an amateur archaeologist, one has a character not that far removed from Cuppy the comic naturalist. While history has not recorded whether these two hypotheses were additional factors in Cuppy's selection of Cobb's essay, it does provide a segue to a related topic concerning the humorist's mystery anthologies. A reading of the three short story collections reveals that an inordinately large number of the most entertaining selections, especially from mystery works by authors best known for their use of humor, often use animals as characters.

Cobb's story use of the parrot reflects yet another author (Twain) satirically railing against sanctimony via the runaway pachyderm taking out a revival meeting. Yet Cuppy's signature use of so-called lower animals as a vehicle for his dark humor is reflected in numerous other selections from his anthologies, ranging from Bierce's macabre introduction of a panther in "The Boarded Window," to Leacock's wonderfully outrageous eventual revelation in "Maddened by Mystery or the Defective Detective," that

England's prominent missing prince is really a Dachshund dog (also a possible jab about an inbreeding royal gene pool producing less-than-bright Brits?).

The most ironically fascinating use of an animal in a Cuppy murder-mystery selection, however, has to be his inclusion of Poe's "The Murders in the Rue Morgue" in *World's Great Detective Stories*. In fact, the selection feels as if Cuppy added the piece, despite the story's legendary legitimacy to be in such an anthology, as a personal in-joke. After all, what animal is most synonymous with Cuppy's comedy? Obviously the title creature from his career-making *How to Tell Your Friends from the Apes*. Poe's story culminates with a razor-wielding ape slicing some lovely human throats in a finale that anticipates the Georgy Dibdin-Pitt play *Sweeney Todd*. Appropriately, Cuppy's philosophy about the interchangeably of man as beast is also suggested by Poe's ape initially picking up a razor in order to mimic the shaving technique of his master.

Of course, including a Poe story in a mystery anthology is a natural, given that he is universally credited with being the father of the modern detective story. What is sadly neglected, though, is that Poe is also one of the pioneering authors of American dark comedy.[35] The latter lack of recognition occurs because Poe, like Cuppy, believed in mixing humor with horror, but in the past the macabre mystery elements of Poe's stories tended to overshadow the comedy, or even veil it to the shocked period reader. Consequently, one has a made-to-order tale for Cuppy's take on mystery, even down to the surprise killer being the humorist's signature beast of choice. Sometimes a humorist-turned-editor can make darkly comic jokes (divinely personal jokes) without even writing a word. (As a Cuppy/Poe addendum, both authors passionately felt the best literature was the short essay/story, one that could be read at a single setting.)

Even when creatures, per se, are not at the heart of the Cuppy selected stories, animal imagery abounds. For example, in F. Scott Fitzgerald's "A Short Trip Home," from Cuppy's *World's Great Mystery Stories*, one gets an alternate take on the humorist's down-on-humanity story. That is, so much of Cuppy's work satirizes by way of demonstrating animals acting as senselessly idiotic as humans; with Fitzgerald's tale, people are frequently described as animal-like. To illustrate, Fitzgerald's villain, a realistic ghost of a gangster, too stubborn to know he is dead, is painted as having the "eyes of an animal, sleepy and quiescent in the presence of another species [living humans]."[36] His victim, like many Fitzgerald women, is a beautiful but vacuous girl, of whom he observes when a true friend attempts to rescue her, "Her lovely eyes narrowed and her face took on a look of dumb-animal-like resistance."[37]

In James Thurber's "A Sort of Genius," from the "Murder in Real Life" section of *Murder Without Tears*, he keys upon two characters, Mrs. Jane "the pig woman" Gibson, the chief witness for the state investigation of a murdered minister and his mistress, and one Willie Stevens, a pivotal witness for the defense. Like the "pig woman," Stevens is considered the town oddity, and has "been compared inferentially to an animal."[38] In addition to again demonstrating the hypocrisy inherent to organized religion (the *unfaithful* murdered minister), Thurber's essay falls in line with Cuppy's less-than-idealized perspective on both humans and animals. Of course, if there had been a Thurber pooch involved, an exception would have been noted. In Thurber's drawings and writings he had a soft spot for man's best friend, an animal he felt was victimized by its long association with man. Thurber once said, "[Dogs] tried patiently at all times to understand Man's [senseless] way of life ... a sound creature in a crazy world."[39]

The aforementioned *Murder Without Traces* section in which Thurber's story appears, "Murder in Real Life," helps designate this volume (including that provocative title) as the most macabre of Cuppy's mystery anthologies—since these are true tales. *The* overtly comic essay herein is Edmund Pearson's "Rules for Murderesses," which offers some general guidelines based upon actual cases. The most winning lesson is the first:

> If you decide to murder your husband you must never act in concert with a lover.... Plain murder is often forgiven by a jury. But murder combined with a love-affair is almost always disapproved. The feeling is that somebody has been having too much fun.[40]

Fittingly, for an essay selected by a Hoosier editor, Pearson's short piece devotes space to Indiana's infamous Mrs. Gunness's "murder farm," a matrimonial killing field where countless immigrant Americans were tempted to visit with a male dowry in hand—only to never be heard of again. There is much to attract Cuppy to the case.

Yet, the most thorough retelling of Gunness's perverse case occurs in another essay in this comically grizzly section of Cuppy's anthology— Steward H. Holbrook's "Belle of Indiana." However, before further fleshing out Holbrook's account of a Hoosier killer who makes Lizzie Borden seem like a misdemeanor case, one must add that the "Belle of Indiana" has a number of comic footnotes which sound suspiciously like the work of editor Cuppy. For instance, Mrs. Gunness periodically cared for children, and the note attached to this information states, "I dislike to use the term 'care for' in connection with *anything* in which Mrs. Gunness was concerned, but it must suffice for the present."[41] Another more lengthy footnote, only quoted in part, addresses the type of matrimonial journals Gunness used to attract her prey, closing with the following aside:

Eight. Here Come Cuppy's Mystery Anthologies of the 1940s

> I once knew a lumberjack who got a very good wife by mail order. I also knew a farm hand who got a frightful witch in the same manner and was forced to strangle her to regain his peace of mind.[42]

Besides these dark-comedy notes, and a setting in the humorist's home state, the murder revelations began to hit the world media (1908) at an impressionable time in Cuppy's youth — his years at the University of Chicago. Add to this Cuppy connection the humorist's propensity for selecting tales with animal-related elements: husky farmer Belle used her elaborate hog-killing apparatus both to kill and more easily disperse her army of victims. Finally, Cuppy was a great fan of all kinds of music, and Holbrook's take upon the mass-murdering Belle includes a popular period ballad not unlike the earthy comic tunes favored by Isabel Paterson's rendition of the Cuppy-inspired Jake in her *Golden Vanity* novel. Consequently, here are the final verses of a Belle song, chronicled by Holbrook:

> There's red upon the Hoosier moon For Belle was strong and full of doom; And think of all them Norska men Who'll never see St. Paul again.[43]

Though hardly even passable lyrics, they bring genuine historically accurate dark-comedy relief to the murder-mystery genre.

Cuppy's focus on improving mysteries via comedy is further accented by the high ratio of humorists included as anthology contributors, such as Ambrose Bierce, James Thurber, Irvin S. Cobb, and Stephen Leacock. Moreover, even his more traditional mystery-writer selections, such as a "hardboiled" Dashiell Hammett or a "softboiled" Agatha Christie, are famous for bringing a comic touch to their whodunits.

While Cuppy's selection of the Poe piece is *the* inspired comic in-joke of his mystery trilogy (for reasons already noted), the credit for the most atypically poignant anthologized story, as it relates to Cuppy, would be his inclusion of H.G. Wells's "The Door in the Wall" in *World's Great Mystery Stories*. Once again there are animals and a twisted conclusion, yet it plays out differently. A famous statesman is forever haunted by an enchanted garden he once stumbled upon as a child of five or six. Playing by himself in the country, he encounters a bright white wall, with an odd green door. Once through the opening he is in a fantasy land of fountains and friends and tame exotic animals, with his most persistent later memory of this surreal world being two exquisite panthers. For reasons still unclear to him, he is abruptly escorted from this place, though this Eden never leaves his thoughts. In subsequent years he seemingly has brief opportunities to revisit this paradise but other distractions keep him from acting upon what are fleeting chances. His bittersweet later revelation is the tragedy of youth: "Of course I didn't know then that it wouldn't always be there."[44]

Still, as an adult, a rare chance or two to revisit the enchanted garden occurs. But now, like Wendy in *Peter Pan*, he allows grown-up responsibilities to take precedence over the joyful escape of youth. Late in life, he shares his sad tale with an old friend. He wistfully declares that if he were to be granted one last chance at this heavenly garden, he would not hesitate to seize the day. Soon after this declaration the man is found dead in a construction site excavation, the victim of a long fall, after entering a small door in a work area wall meant to protect the general public. The tragedy occurred on a late-night walk, when security lights may have made the blockade resemble a white fence. Had the elder statesman somehow taken the opening as his long-lost green door to his childhood magical mystery garden?

One could also "read" this ending with a certain degree of black humor — the door to paradise is really a ticket to death. Yet, in terms of the story's big picture, I am reminded of Cuppy's lifelong fond memories of his grandmother's Indiana farm (see chapter one), and how his childhood experiences there accented sentimentality over satire, in relationship to animals, for the first and last time in his life. Seemingly, every story selected by Cuppy for his anthologies had some sort of potential subtextual code. Regardless, Cuppy was all about keeping it real, and there is nothing more real than the ambiguity which shrouds so many of the mysteries he picked.

Touching as the interpretation of the Wells tale might be, Cuppy's specialty is still sideswiping mysteries. Such a task would not be complete without including his mentoring friend Isabel Paterson's negative perspective on the genre. Thus, he quotes a variation of a Paterson crack he enjoyed writing about in private (see earlier chapters on his fellow *Tribune* columnist) in his introduction to the *World's Great Detective Stories*. Pretending to be a fan of the genre, he states several alleged murder mystery positives to a never-identified doubting "lady novelist," culminating with:

> "But, my dear woman, they rest your mind!" To which she calmly rejoined, "Sure they do, if you have that kind of mind." [While in private Cuppy would then second this verdict, here his agreement comes by default.] Though I can't see that the lady proved anything by this wisecrack.... I intend to omit all mention of the mind from future debates on detective reading, at least until we get some scientific data showing what actually happens up there when one is pursuing "The Fatal Goulash" or similar volume.[45]

At least in private, as previously noted, Cuppy on mysteries could be as lacerating as the later public remarks of another dark-comedy artist, Edward Albee, on what he perceived to be lesser writing:

> If you write plays because you just want them to be liked, you have to lie too much. People like theatre that is safe, generally speaking — things that are easy, that are not too deeply troubling. In other words, people want to go to the theatre and waste their time.[46]

(As a footnote, Albee, like Cuppy, was adept at using animals or animal-like behavior in his satirical attacks on mankind, such as his award-winning plays *Who's Afraid of Virginia Woolf?* and *The Goat, or Who Is Sylvia?*).

Yet, as this chapter demonstrates, if there was any mystery wiggle room for Cuppy, it involved humor. One might best close with an insight from a critique of a book by Cuppy's friend and sometimes-illustrator William Steig. Fittingly, the *New York Herald Tribune* review of *The Lonely Ones* is from 1943 — the same year Cuppy's first two mystery anthologies appeared. The observation about Steig's volume applies equally to the murder mystery material best tolerated by Cuppy: "The distance between funny and frightening is often extremely short.... That is why [such material is] ... so cruel and so frightening and so funny."[47]

NINE

The Years Leading to Suicide — Literally, *How to Become Extinct*, and Still *Attract the Wombat*

> "[Isabel Paterson] says, if she is known a hundred years from now, it will only [be] because she appears as a footnote in 'How to Tell Your Friends from the Apes,' for when Will Cuppy is recognized by posterity as one of the great humorists of the age, scholars will have a lot of fun trying to find out who Isabel Paterson was."—A 1933 profile of Paterson.[1]

The opening Isabel Paterson quote is there to both underline her ongoing mentorship/promotion of Cuppy (to the point of big-picture posterity), and to suggest that her *New York Herald Tribune* column, "Turns with a Bookworm," remains the best gateway starting point into Cuppy's final years. As noted earlier in the text, her column often represented a showcase/mouthpiece for his thoughts on a myriad of subjects, as well as a device for which Paterson might launch her latest riff upon an assortment of Cuppy-related topics. The humorist underscored the personal importance of his "Bookworm" appearances by the fact that he saved many of the columns.[2]

After all, the "Bookworm" was where Cuppy first announced (1933, see chapter 7) his pride at being recognized when his Manhattan strolling partner was none other than former heavyweight boxing champion Gene Tunney: "[Cuppy] feels he might as well die to avoid anti-climax."[3] However, the bonus of a closer scrutiny of this Paterson column further brings out the sometimes-couple nature of Cuppy and Paterson. No other citation of the Tunney-Cuppy story reveals that Paterson was also a member of this

Manhattan walk. Yet, immediately after the "Bookworm" documentation of Cuppy's big moment, Paterson adds:

> We also feel that we have become a famous author; Mr. Tunney has read our novel.... No, he didn't just say so out of politeness; he proved it, because there was an anecdote of him in it but without his name.... And he found the passage.[4]

There are, of course, several other pivotal 1930s notations of Cuppy in "Bookworm" which set the tone for the importance of his later relationship with Paterson — and how their late 1940s split undoubtedly contributed to Cuppy's suicide. Ironically, one such citation even deals with an erroneous report (1936) of his death, brought on by his ongoing reclusiveness. Again, Cuppy chose "Bookworm" to first address the rumor. There is an added bonus to this particular example of Paterson setting the record straight — it once again demonstrates her unacknowledged abilities as a humorist:

> Will Cuppy has been pondering how to refute a recent report that he is dead.... He says so many [other] people have denied being dead that nobody believes the denials any more.... Personally, we should not believe it on a doctor's certificate.... We know we'll be dead first.[5]

In another Paterson column from the 1930s, she grants her humorist friend a sort of oracle status:

> Why is it, we demanded bitterly of Will Cuppy, that over the weekend the only time we feel like writing is Sunday night, which means tottering through a long day Monday with no sleep, and at the end of the week, when we ought to write this stuff bright and early, or, anyhow, early ... we don't even begin till the shades of eve are falling? "There is a name for that," said William, with a sapient air. "Yes, yes, what is it?" "It is called LIFE," he said.[6]

Indeed, the best prelude/insight to the ongoing Cuppy-Paterson odd couple relationship of the 1940s can be found in two "Bookworm" columns from late 1939. In both cases the duo sound like an old married couple. The first involves Cuppy constantly interrupting Paterson during lunch in order to answer crossword puzzle questions:

> William would demand: On whom did Melchisedec [New Testament, Hebrews] bestow a blessing.... What was the name of the Scandinavian tree of life.... Is there such an animal as a jerboa? [desert rodent].... When replying in due order, we [Paterson] simply could not remember the name of cole slaw, which was there before our eyes.... [The ultimate question is] "Have you strong emotional feelings about things that have nothing to do with your own affairs?" If anyone says "no" to that, he must either be mistaken, or live in a diving bell.[7]

(As a paradoxical footnote to Cuppy's obsession with crossword puzzles, despite his general disregard for murder mysteries as literature, he sometimes referred to them as "puzzle books.")[8]

The second 1939 "Bookworm" story which helps set the table for a better understanding of the Cuppy-Paterson relationship in the 1940s involves another of his special interests — music. In a lengthy anecdote, to which much of her column is devoted, she shares, in part:

> For years it has been our habit to carry on long arguments with Will Cuppy about his musical preference [for Wagner over Bach, Brahms, and Beethoven], with the full understanding that we have no idea what we are talking about.... The object is to show that words and music have practically nothing in common.... [My mocking stance] is wholly irrelevant ... especially to a tone-deaf arguer [Paterson].... [Ultimately, with the support of a mutual musical friend, Paterson said to Cuppy:] "Haven't we always told you that the Wagnerian operate characters are stuffed ... [like] Central Park swanboats...."
>
> William was subdued.... He brooded in silence for some time, and then went out.... But at the door he turned back sadly and said: I suppose you know that the swan is stuffed too."... The next day the argument started again from scratch.... It is, as we stated above, a purely vocal exercise; but differs slightly from most debates carried on today, in that we both know it doesn't mean anything.[9]

As this text has previously documented, Cuppy was an accomplished amateur student of music, while Paterson enjoyed kidding her own "tone-deaf" nature. For instance, in another late 1930s column, she confessed that accomplished writer/violinist Catherine Drinker Bowen "still thinks she could develop some latent musical aptitude in us."[10]

Both of these Paterson-Cuppy anecdotes (on puzzles and music) are consistent with earlier comparisons of their friendship to a dualing intellectual vaudeville team. But these two stories further suggest an affectionately combative mutual-curmudgeon society. While previous examinations of the duo in this text have chronicled Paterson as a combination cheerleader/creative catalyst for Cuppy the evolving humorist, these two 1939 windows into their combat-zone couplehood dynamic are yet more evidence of how exasperating he could be, as well as how she might occasionally enjoy baiting him (as in the case of Cuppy's love of Wagner). Essentially, Cuppy was an alienated man at odds with himself. Still, Paterson's mentoring job in this friendship was ultimately as a stabilizing witness to Cuppy as he struggled with being himself. Sadly, at some point, the job aspect of the friendship took precedent, resulting in a metaphorical divorce. Undoubtedly, it contributed to his eventual suicide.

Thornton Wilder once said, "It's possible to make books of a certain fascination, if you scrupulously leave out the essential."¹¹ When writing a biography one need not be so scrupulous about the proverbial *missing pages* of any attempt at a reconstructed life — absolute truths are never a given. As noted earlier, what biographers attempt is the "best truth possible." There remains no definitive reason Cuppy and Paterson finally ended their friendship, beyond the humorist's ongoing neediness, and Paterson's increasing political agenda, versus Cuppy's largely apolitical nature. Yet, as biographer Robert K. Massie suggests, when writers set out to profile personages of the past, they must move beyond dates and places. In order to "reassemble the dust," the biographer must become "invisible daily to the subject's elbow, listening to the subject's conversations, observing smiles and frowns, then using the advantage of hindsight to judge [as fairly as possible]."¹²

Paterson's "Bookworm" column is just the "elbow" at which to stand for Cuppy information. Yet, these late columns are best framed by three dates: 1943, 1947, and 1949. Paterson's most influential book, the nonfiction text *The God in the Machine* drew a great deal of controversy upon its publication in 1943. This text, and her mentoring of Ayn Rand, jumpstarted the Libertarian movement, and forever transitioned Paterson from being known as just a witty columnist and sometime novelist, to a major conservative voice in the volatile 1940s. Second, among Cuppy's papers at the University of Chicago, the humorist's saved references to himself in Paterson's "Bookworm" column stop after 1947.¹³ Whether or not 1948 is the date the actual break occurred, an apparent chill had set in. Third, Paterson left the *New York Herald Tribune* just prior to Cuppy's September 1949 suicide. Possibly, this exit exacerbated the depression which resulted is his death.

What follows is a closer look at Paterson's Cuppy-related columns from the 1940s. First, one notes that Cuppy is much less of a "Bookworm" presence than in the 1930s. Granted, there is still strong support early in the decade. For example, a December 1941 column strongly supports the humorist's recently published *How to Become Extinct*:

> We named it first [on our recommended Christmas list] after a complicated ethical argument with ourself.... We thought it might look like bias ... [but] we decided that it would certainly be a very weakminded concession to count influence not to name it first.... Truth will prevail.... *Extinct* stays at the head of our list.¹⁴

That being said, Paterson's column does not become the one-woman band for Cuppy's book which had been the case with the humorist's earlier *How to Become a Hermit* and *How to Tell Your Friends from the Apes*. Indeed, Cuppy's work and/or the humorist himself is now more likely to be used as a segue for an attack against the political left. For instance, in another late 1941 column Paterson wrote:

> Now we've taken home our copy of *Extinct*, and can't quote exactly a passage in which the author says that by the law of averages it is almost impossible to be wrong all the time.... We wanted to ask William to reconsider this statement ... the thing is possible, by side-stepping the law of averages to the [political] left.[15]

Not surprisingly, Cuppy did not save this particular column in his private papers. Along similar lines that same year (1941), Paterson's column used a previously noted Cuppy quote to derail the writing of a specific liberal:

> Will Cuppy summed up the problem of the writer in one sentence.... He said he would like to write a book ... but he couldn't think up the words. Worse than that, when one sets about writing a book, one thinks of far too many other words. Miss [Gertrude] Stein's [1874–1946] books appear to us to be composed entirely of those other words.[16]

A display of Cuppy's ***How to Become Extinct*** (1941) in a New York City bookstore window.

It was as if Cuppy had gone from the co-star of a Punch and Judy show to simply being part of a punch line.

In the years between 1941–1947, there were still affectionately "Bookworm" Cuppy mentions. For instance, in a 1944 column she again allows him to play a comic sage, on the subject of great authors being difficult in private:

> Will Cuppy once wrote: "Virtue is our dearest desire, and we achieve it even if we have to make our own definitions." Also even if we have [to] impose it posthumously on someone else.[17]

Of course, maybe the real message here are the spaces between Paterson's added words—might she have thought of a Cuppy quote because he instinctively came to mind as a gifted author who was also a challenge? Interestingly, this same Paterson column closes with a comment which could be "read" as a Cuppy dig. She is sarcastically writing about an author, Samuel Shellabarger, who sounds suspiciously like the humorist, a former college professor, who feels "uncannily at home anywhere in southern Europe between the years 1460 and 1540."[18] At this time, the professor-like Cuppy had been working on his history-derailing *The Decline and Fall of Practically Everybody* for over a decade, though it would only be published posthumously through the efforts of his editor/friend Fred Feldkamp. While Shellabarger's historical window to the past was narrower than that of Cuppy's, both former academic authors were happiest when writing about the distant past. Yet Paterson bitingly suggests that, for such men, a passion for history is not enough: "Only one more qualification would be necessary—that he should be a novelist to begin with [demanding a narrative skill neither man possessed]."[19]

That being said, my favorite late "Bookworm" Cuppy references includes an affectionate plug for the humorist's book of reprinted material, *The Great Bustard and Other People* (1944), and a self-deprecating explanation Cuppy gave for not always using his own name at book signings:

> He autographed copies of "How to Tell Your Friends From the Apes" with the signature "Button Gwinnett" [one of the 50 members of Congress who signed the Declaration of Independence] because, he said, it was so much more valuable to collect than his own name.[20]

Regardless, such mentions had faded out by late 1948, after she had had a falling out with Cuppy and Ayn Rand. Thus, in a "Bookworm" from December 8, 1948, Paterson complains:

> Though there are said to be authors who enjoy writing, they don't act as if they did—their tempers are on edge, and while they have no scruples about boring their friends or family into a coma by talking about the

work in hand, or reading portions of it aloud, unless they meet with organized resistance.[21]

Not surprisingly, neither this quote nor the following Paterson column quip made Cuppy's private papers. The latter cryptic comment occurs in one of her last "Bookworm" pieces. Again, there are no specific name(s) involved, but a Cuppy inference is certainly present: "As for nipping authors in the bud probably the only effective course would be to provide them with ample means and leisure."[22] Again, this comes after years of encouragement over Cuppy's *Decline* text, both privatively and in her column (as early as a "Bookworm" from February 16, 1936[23]). (Rand also needed a great deal of Paterson cheerleading.)

These seemingly veiled Cuppy negatives, occurring at a time when there had been a verified break in their friendship, are a far cry from the humorist's warm comments about Paterson in a 1942 letter to the academic/critic/broadcaster John Towner Frederick:

Though this Isabel Paterson photograph is from an earlier era, its no nonsense starkness seems to harmonize with someone who could and did walk away from relationships.

Well, anyway, Isabel Paterson, God Bless Her, says in [the] Sunday "Tribune" that *Extinct* was the best non-fiction of the year [1941]. I think she really means it. Anyway, it was a good thing to tell Harry Scherman, of the Book of the Month Club, as she did.[24]

As Paterson's praise suggests, the decade of Cuppy's tragic demise opened positively with the publication of the *Extinct* text. Cuppy briefly summarized the early commercial success of the book in another letter (Christmas 1941) to Frederick, but he quickly slid into his standard black cloud/bad luck mentality with regard to the publication of his books:

P.S. The book [*Extinct*] seems to be going very well, for me. [It] has sold out the first printing and cut into the second. What the war [the December 7, 1941, bombing of Pearl Harbor put us into World War II] will do to books, I dunno. My first [*sic*] book [*How to Be a Hermit*] was published on Black Monday [October 29, 1929 — the Wall Street crash; actually shortly before this date], my second [*How to Tell Your Friends from the Apes*] on Blue Wednesday [Cuppy's euphemism for 1931, the worst year of the Depression], and now this war [coincides with the appearance of *Extinct*].[25]

What this dyed-in-the-wool pessimist could not deny, however, were the great notices *Extinct* received. Arguably, Cuppy's favorite all-time review of anything he had written came from zoological expert Raymond Ditmars' (1876–1942) critique of *Extinct* in *Tomorrow* magazine. Ditmars's many books range from *The Reptile Book* (1907), to *Snakes of the World* (1931), and *Field Book of North American Snakes* (1939). These credits are noted merely to set up the joy Cuppy shared in his letter to an academic friend (New York University English professor Warren Bower) over Ditmars's praise of *Extinct*:

> If I am an authority on snakes, it's only because I have read the complete works of Dr. Raymond L. Ditmars, who knows all about it. I meant to get in touch with Dr. Ditmars last summer ... ask his permission to mention him but he was out of town. I do mention him several times in the book, in none too serious fashion, as where I state: "When you hunt Rattlesnakes, be sure to take along some high shoes, a pair of leather puttees and, if possible, Dr. Ditmars." Well, just last week, Dr. Ditmars himself reviewed ... *Extinct* ... and he wasn't annoyed at all. He even says ... I hope the present generation of young scientists will not be quite so stuffy and cantankerous as a fair portion of their elders have been."[26]

The zoological scholar also wrote of the *Extinct* text:

> In these days of serious book preponderance [on World War II], it is refreshing to come upon the work of an author who has a high sense of humor and keeps a boisterous pitch from start to finish.... This book ... is a swell way to take one's mind from blitzes, spearheads, encirclements, strikes, and taxes.... I suggest that a check-list be kept, in order that not a single page be missed.[27]

In the same letter to Bower, Cuppy also expresses great pleasure over another expert's critical hosannas for *Extinct*. In fact, in the world of scholarly science, the book's endorsement by naturalist/entomologist/marine biologist/author/explorer William Beebe (1877–1962) was an even bigger coup. In the years before television, Beebe was America's most famous naturalist. Still, Cuppy's correspondence acknowledgment of Beebe's *Extinct* praise is equally humble: "Dr. William Beebe, who is tops in fish [research], seemed to feel the same way [as Ditmars] ... in his review.... They can take it. [There's] nothing stuffy about either of these scientists, is there?"[28] The publication in which Beebe's review appears is not noted in Cuppy's letter. Happily for the humorist, the critique is in Cuppy's home newspaper — the *New York Herald Tribune*. Beebe's lengthy, glowing review has an opening which must have gone a long way towards healing some of Cuppy's longstanding graduate-school gripes:

> When a scientist begins to read Will Cuppy's "How to Become Extinct," it doesn't seem as funny as he thought it would be because so much of it is scientifically correct. Then something happens and he begins to laugh and then says "Lissen" to anyone within hearing and reads the page all over again aloud. The scientist reader sort of comes to and realizes that Will Cuppy is saying what he always wanted to in class but never dared. I have seen ... each type of reader, a scientist and a non-or layman, both laughing their heads off.[29]

Given Cuppy's relentless satirical shellacking of Aristotle's vaunted reputation, the high point of the critique was both Beebe's agreement upon that score, and the review title itself: "Great Truths of Natural History: Even Aristotle Sometimes Guessed — but Cuppy? Ah, Cuppy!"[30]

Such high praise from the naturalist community was quite a paradox for the academically iconoclastic Cuppy. Did this response weaken, even for a second, Cuppy's protective shell of cynicism, his angry defense against the often inherent falseness of that brand known as *all–American optimism*, a product which leads to so many broken dreams? One hopes, at least briefly, that in Cuppy's own private purgatory of cantankerousness, he secretly allowed himself a moment of exuberance similar to actress Sally Field's second Oscar acceptance speech, during which she bubbled, "You like me, you *really* like me!" Yet, for the decidedly unbubbly Cuppy, this seems unlikely. Regardless, the irony did not stop there. The bastion of New York papers, the *Times*, devoted *two* positive reviews to this scholarly satirist. The first, from Charles Poore (1902–1971), just settling into a long and distinguished career with his punningly entitled "Books of the Times" column, has insightful fun describing Cuppy's multi-faceted deadpan attack mode:

> Mr. Cuppy's solemnly hilarious style ... [can] persuade you that he really does know something about the dinosaurs, the tortoises ... dodos, three-spined sticklebacks ... woolly mammoths ... [and so on] ... but he frequently insists on heckling you [by way of the footnote] as you read

along.... Cuppy campaigns tirelessly against people who say that such and such a species has become extinct, and then reveals how he himself became extinct just about a century after Darwin went for that ride on that time-struck turtle.[31]

This high-profile review (December 6, 1941) might also have been responsible for the esteemed Raymond Ditmars's critique the following February, given that just after Poore affectionately suggests Cuppy might be channeling Groucho Marx, he asks, "What would Dr. Ditmars say?"[32]

The second *New York Times* review, Edward Frank Allen's amusingly entitled, "Mr. Cuppy's Primer to Extinction," plays at being both a positive tongue-in-cheek critique and a comic essay itself: "The book is, by and large (mostly by, as Mr. Cuppy might say) something to enlist the interest of anyone who is in the slightest degree viviparous."[33] Yet Allen is more effective with the straight-degree praise component of the piece, such as quoting arguably the book's best dark-comedy footnote: "Three million alligators were killed in Florida between 1880 and 1900. Goody!"[34] Still, Allen's attempt to play humorist in his review is an important signal that Cuppy had reached a level of comedy recognition/repute that no longer made it necessary for the critic to make a case for the artist under glass. The fact that this phenomenon was now occurring in the *New York Times* simply added to Cuppy's kudos.

However, given that Cuppy remained a glass-half-empty sort of fellow, he privately expressed displeasure that the *Saturday Review* had not chosen to critique *Extinct*, and that the *New Yorker* (a publication in which many of the volume's original essays had appeared) was not featuring the text in its end of the year (1941) lists of recommended books.[35] Paradoxically, given all this discussion of which publications were or were not critiquing *Extinct*, a review from this period which had nothing specifically to do with Cuppy's books now seems prophetic. *PM*, one of New York city's most left-wing newspapers, printed a combination review/publication overview entitled, "There's War on the List, Good Americana and Anthologies," on one of history's game-changing days — December 7, 1941.[36] The piece documented the ongoing popularity of the murder mystery, and, more importantly, observed:

> Obsessed with the war and distressed by shortages and the prospect of prices heading up, the book publishers nevertheless gave us above-the-average measure ... in the field of the anthology.[37]

Naturally, every statement in the previous quote was immediately maximized in the days, weeks, months, and years to follow that infamous date and the United States' entry into World War II. Thus, it should come as no surprise that murder-mystery reviewer Cuppy should soon turn editor and have an anthology of the genre in print by January of 1943, *World's Great Mystery Stories*. Another would follow by late that year, *World's Great Detective Stories*, and a final collection would be out in 1946, *Murder Without Tears* (see previous chapter).

Once again, here was a Cuppy irony to match the naturalist establishment's praise for *Extinct*. The humorist's belief in some nebulous "Hate Cuppy" movement forever out to derail his writing career was certainly not preventing him from using his mystery critic credentials to cash in on this war boom for mystery anthologies, and compendiums in general. However, that Cuppy was at this time also able to edit these books, sign off on an anthology of his own previously published essays (*Bustard*), continue his weekly *New York Herald Tribune* column, and write new freelance essays (now most frequently for the *Saturday Evening Post*), merely underlines the advantages of leading a hermit-like existence. Moreover, just as Paterson could once occasionally lure Cuppy out of his Jones Beach and/or the Greenwich Village apartment hideaways for some professionally related socializing, the humorist could still play nice if it served his purposes. For example, what follows is an excerpt from a thank-you letter from one of his publishers (Farrar & Rinehart) and partial owner/editors (Stanley M. Rinehart, Jr.), for Cuppy's promotion of the *Bustard* book:

> I have been hearing all sorts of nice things about your appearances at the book fairs in Philadelphia and Boston, and I think the time and effort required were very much worthwhile. You seem to have made many new friends in both cities. A check for the balance of your expenses is in the works and will be along in a few days.[38]

In this five-year period (1941–1946) Cuppy was responsible for four published anthologies and the *Extinct* text. He also continued to work on such projects as his serious play and his satirical *Decline and Fall* history text. In Cuppy's three final years, between the publication of *Murder Without Tears* and his 1949 suicide, he focused on *How to Attract the Wombat* collection of 1940s essays — which hit bookstores two months *after* his death. The intensity of all this work is caught in a later essay, "More About Wombats," which Cuppy specifically wrote for the *Wombat* book. In it he describes the completion of a manuscript as "roughly comparable to release from a long jail rap into the sunlight and freedom."[39] So what happened? Should not the approaching "sunlight and freedom" have led to anything but suicide, especially when any such eloquent sampler of magazine essays literally represents writing "rescued from the dust of past periodicals."[40] One might better argue that the lingering "jail rap" of the still-unfinished materials was just too much pressure. In fact, the research comedy notecards Cuppy left behind were so voluminous (roughly two hundred thousand in number), that editor Feldkamp even managed to produce another posthumous text the humorist had planned — the satirical datebook, *How to Get from January to December* (1951). Indeed, this adds yet another paradox to Cuppy's career, in terms of humor book totals; he was as prolific in death (thanks to the devoted Feldkamp) as he was in life.

Perhaps the best course for getting some final insights into Cuppy's demise is to mimic his day job — a murder mystery critic, closely reading a text for clues. Consequently, a dissection of the last book Cuppy personally prepared for publication, the *Wombat* text, might prove helpful. After all, as Feldkamp's *January to December* introduction suggests, the work is Cuppy's, since he did "painstaking research endlessly on all [subjects], an occupation which ruled out the possibility of any kind of active social life."[41]

For starters, *Wombat* shows no decline in Cuppy's wit. Moreover, as is his norm, whatever the topic, mankind is normally the satirical target. For instance, in his essay on wart hogs being the ugliest of animals, he notes that couples often "do not live together much. Love is blind but not that blind. Sometimes they meet in the forest where the light is more flattering."[42] Yet, after Cuppy's rather bludgeoning previously cited opening to the text, wherein he expresses amazement that most readers still do not recognize his subtextual satirization of humanity, the humorist's tone seems softer in what he calls his "third animal book."[43] Of course, as with Cuppy's curmudgeon squared opening in which he does not want to pull his satirical punch, the humorist refuses to hide behind the so-called lower life forms. For example, in an essay on fly swatting, he provides the following tongue-in-cheek pep talk about the human challenges of the task:

> [Remember] you can ... look at television, and go to the movies. You can read mystery stories and try to guess who done it. Keep your chin up and always remember that if you are not the fly's superior in every single respect ... you are at least his equal, mentally.[44]

Cuppy's *Wombat* text continues the humorist's tradition of questioning the experts, such as the following footnote in his piece on the kiwi: "The scientific name of this bird is the Apteryx, meaning that he has no wings whatever. He has so."[45] In one of Cuppy's insect essays he notes that "Lepidopterists, or Butterfly professors" tell readers that the

> brilliant coloring of certain Butterflies is warning to insectivorous animals that they are not good to eat and should be left strictly alone. But sometimes a Butterfly meets an animal that has never heard of the theory of conspicuous coloration. Then he is out of luck.[46]

Yet, even in Cuppy's ongoing war against experts, his *Wombat* jabs can assume a softer intonation, especially when it involves a scholar he admires and/or from whom he has received positive research feedback. A perfect combination of old school iconoclastic Cuppy and the gentler new brand occurs when the subject is the humorist's favorite punching bag expert from antiquity—Aristotle. In a piece on the nautilus, a type of sea mollusk, Cuppy acknowledges the wisdom of the aforementioned Dr. William Beebe on the subject, but the humorist cannot resist adding that while this scientist is a "rabid" Aristotle fan, even Beebe "confesses that his hero is cockeyed on the animal's [the nautilus's] sailing propensities."[47]

Finally, one has always been able to mine Cuppy's humor books for amusingly offbeat insights about his life, and *Wombat* is no exception. Consider the revelation that his Aunt Atta's only flaw in the art of swatting flies was being too concerned about incidental breakage of "her bric-a-brac."[48] The newest evolving component to surface in Cuppy's quiver of personal asides is an increased whimsical note that occasionally confesses, "I'm just an anti-hero, too." An earlier example of this vulnerability can be found in the aforementioned Cuppy article from 1943, "Certainly, I Play the Piano," in which he is poignantly open about his absentee father.[49] The tendency toward vulnerability seems increasingly prevalent in *Wombat*. To illustrate, in discussing the octopus, Cuppy suggests that the creature's formidable appearance makes people overlook such matters as character and inner worth. He then admits, "I have a slight tendency to do this myself but I'm trying to get over it [though the statement's footnote immediately rebounds to his normal brash tone]. I'll let you know how I make out."[50] Regardless, Cuppy is at his most whimsical when he addresses why he added more wombat material to the text. An unnamed source, about whom Cuppy allegedly knows very little, has told him that any manuscript with "wombat" in the title needs more wordage on that creature before publication. Cuppy's only background on this anonymous advisor is that, despite a "heavy glass bowl of Goldfish ... [falling] on his head when he was two ... he survived to become a power in the [New York] literary world."[51] Modestly amusing on the surface, the real humor comes from the inside joke—Cuppy is writing about himself. Yet, it is a bittersweet game at best, since Cuppy's goldfish-bowl incident was unknown to the general public, and his being a literary power player was pure self-mockery, given that Cuppy's unique status as a satirist did not occur until the posthumous publication of *Decline and Fall*.

Consequently, these gentle tweaks to Cuppy's style have the feel of someone letting go, or at least looking for ways to still amuse himself. Granted, the "voice" of *Decline and Fall* returns to Cuppy's earlier, more biting style. Of course, there are a myriad of explanations for that, including the fact that the book was composed over a 16-year period, and it completely drops any façade of using lesser life forms as a cover for satire about humanity. There is even an intriguing longshot explanation. Maybe Cuppy was now uncomfortable about returning to his more visceral approach, and/or possibly after the gentler *Wombat* he no longer even felt at one with the material. After all, the unpublished work left behind by many authors often reveals variations or changes in the public's expectations. For instance, Hemingway's posthumously published *Islands in the Stream* (1970) bares a sexually ambiguous central male, far removed from the novelist's macho big-game hunter persona. Sometimes there are reasons why authors do not publish everything they write.

Though open to varying interpretations, period correspondence with Cuppy best suggests he was caught between being a perfectionist and having lingering concerns about the marketability of the ever-evolving *Decline and Fall* manuscript. Mid-1940s letters from William Steig, the artist who essentially replaced Paterson as Cuppy's handholding cheerleader, often read as missives from a pep-talk mentor. Consider the following excerpt:

> You're right to perfect the [*Decline and Fall*] history — though everything in it seems perfect to me already (except the pictures which I wish could have given more leisure to). It's unquestionably your masterpiece & ought to make sure to have no regrets afterward. I think it should be a tremendous success with the cognoscente & and popularly [*sic*] as well (50,000 [sold] at least). It should be a welcome relief from all the jumble of histrionics being written — & people are history conscious now.[52]

Less than two weeks later Steig wrote Cuppy again, and his letter sounded like the *Decline and Fall* was a done deal — a position on which the book's illustrator should have inside information.

> I hope you're finishing the history [*Decline and Fall*] easily. You ought to make F&R [Farrar and Rinehart publishers] advertise a lot. They tell me agents can get publishers to advertise — so why can't a writer do the same?[53]

In still another Steig letter from this time (July–August 1944), the illustrator acknowledges a Cuppy kindness:

> Many thanks for the nice book — it's exactly what we needed up here [Steig and family had moved to the country, just outside New York City.].... And to go to all this trouble in the heat & while working on your book. You're one of the few civilized people left & a good example for me, who am in danger of developing the wrong way.[54]

(As a footnote to this letter, and so much correspondence examined for this text, summer heat in a pre-air conditioned era, was a constantly noted bane to creative types. It further explains why a cooler place outside the city, be it the country, or a hovel by the sea, was yet another plus for these writers.)

Steig's support even surpassed that of Paterson, given the illustrator's appreciation for how much the humorist had impacted his own career. In the mid–1940s Steig's drawings took on a new direction. A pivotal catalyst in this transition was brought to Steig's attention by Cuppy. What follows, in part, is yet another Steig letter from that fertile correspondence period of summer 1944, in which he expresses his great admiration for what Cuppy's insightful thoughtfulness has meant to him:

> I'm bowled over. God bless you. I don't think you know how much that [picture you sent] means to me. It has clues for a whole new way of working & of seeing reality — [it] might change the course of my life, for the better. I mean it. I'm your slave from now on.[55]

These Steig thank-you letters would not seem inconsistent with the softer tone often found in the *Wombat* text. Though Cuppy represented a lifelong study in neediness and ongoing support, he could also be the thoughtful, quirky friend. His generosity might range from a game-changing gift (e.g., the Steig picture) to a Christmas card — in July, to be interpreted as having been sent by the agnostic-sounding Cuppy incredibly late, or early. While random acts of Cuppy kindness can be found throughout his life, they seemed more prevalent in the final years. Still, the humorist did not make himself any more accessible. For instance, in a Steig letter from 1945, the illustrator warmly analyzes Cuppy's handwriting, only to close with a poignant comment about their minimal number of get-togethers — a paradoxical revelation given the genuine friendship oozing from Steig's correspondence: "I did give your handwriting a going over a long time ago. I remember quickly coming to the conclusion that you are one of God's chosen. My intuition was confirmed by reading your work, and by our too few meetings."[56] Making the comment sadder is the same letter's open invitation for Cuppy to "drop in" anytime on the illustrator and his family, adding, "It really isn't a long trip — about a half hour or so, all told."[57]

However, the most gut-wrenching Steig letter to Cuppy is one which is postmarked shortly *after* the humorist's death. The irony of the opening, "All these weeks your letter has been lying [unanswered] on my desk," morphs to the tragic by the concluding paragraph:

> Are you writing any more history [*Decline and Fall*]? I'm surprised at myself for remaining interested so long. The other day a visitor looked

through [my copy of] your [*How to Become a*] *Hermit* book & nearly died laughing. You ought to stay away from how to spots [*How to Attract the Wombat* was about to be published] & do some work [on *Decline and Fall*].... Forgive me for neglecting you so long.[58]

The 65-year-old Cuppy died at St. Vincent's Hospital on September 19, 1949. Fittingly, for a nighthawk, the time was 12:35 A.M.[59] He had been found unconscious in his Greenwich Village apartment over a week earlier, and never regained consciousness. Most of his obituaries explained his death along the lines of the *Chicago Tribune*'s comment, "His health had been failing for several years."[60] So what were these problems? The reclusive Cuppy had high blood pressure, early symptoms of diabetes, depression, was overweight, and had a poor diet — consisting largely of the ironically named "Lucky Strike" cigarettes, hamburgers, and massive amounts of coffee. Sharing these details with a psychiatrist/physician friend, I asked what additional health issues Cuppy might have been facing. The answer was even more hypertension, lack of energy, and an increased risk of emphysema.[61] Given Cuppy's already rundown condition, it must have been especially daunting for an author whose writing routine was at its apex. Here is how a much younger Cuppy described the grueling process of moving information from his massive 3 × 5 notecard collection to the printed page: "I look these [facts] up ... piece them together in ways too diverse and fatiguing to describe.... This makes life about seventeen times more complicated."[62] That Cuppy greatly admired prolific authors cannot be contested. His "Mystery and Adventure" newspaper column included innumerable favorable mentions of such writers, suggesting the humorist put undue pressure upon himself to follow suit. Moreover, Cuppy's depression had recently spiked over approaching eviction from his book-laden safehouse of an apartment where he had lived for 20 years. Though the newspaper coverage never mentioned the word "suicide," the humorist who often threatened to take his life had done just that. Given Cuppy's penchant for dark comedy and frequent forewarnings of self-destructive behavior, his friends later affectionately kidded, he probably felt that taking his own life was easier than moving. Still, given his long history of depression, including the more recent twist that he felt as if a World War II bomb had already killed him, Cuppy's case was a macabre variation of the boy who called "wolf" once too often. His death by an overdose of sleeping pills was clinically described as "coronary arteriosclerosis."[63]

The humorist's belief that there was always some "Hate Cuppy" movement afoot to sabotage his brief moments in the spotlight might have been given some final credence when his home newspaper, the *Herald Tribune*, initially ran the wrong photograph with his obituary![64] Yet, one could reframe this unbelievable error as an offbeat gift to the husky writer with the rosy-hued complexion — Cuppy always wanted a pale, thin, Hamletish appearance; this perfectly matched the photograph which accompanied his obituary.

Of course, it would not have seemed Cuppy-like if there had not been other in-depth ironies surrounding his demise. The brief *New York Sun* and *New York Daily News* obituaries mistakenly had him completing his doctoral thesis at the University of Chicago — thus making him more scholarly in death.[65] The equally short notice in the *New York Journal America* noted many of his book titles but closed with the rather disquietingly misleading statement, "In addition, he wrote many animal stories for magazines"— underlining, yet again, Cuppy's constant complaint that the masses just did not get his satire.[66] Among the other New York daily newspapers, only the *Times* and the *Herald Tribune* (whose Sunday book review sections were tops in the city) gave him the lengthy obituaries befitting his status as a major writer. Yet, as referenced in the previous chapter, the *Times* article tone was condescending towards Cuppy's dark-comedy métier: "His writing had a dry, contemplative flavor that made him popular with persons who thought that murder could sometimes be funny."[67] In contrast, the *Herald Tribune*'s piece was exhaustingly spot-on, except for that little detail of the wrong photograph for such a longtime employee ... though one might claim it was Cuppy's crowning achievement as a professional hermit.[68]

More ironies can be found in the remembrances which surfaced during the weeks following his death. Perhaps the most poignant appeared in the *Saturday Review of Literature*, the tony publication whose lack of interest in reviewing Cuppy's *Extinct* text had so upset the humorist. Still, the piece was sensitive and attempted to celebrate his dark sense of humor by assuming a most provocative perspective:

> He had something that poets have, the harassment of "wonder," though in him it took fantastic prose form ... his own particular kind of humor ... may have been a bit nearer to an imagined God's than that of most people! For the Creator has certainly presented us with some extraordinary phenomena, mixtures of the esthetic and the sadistic that mere Man could never have conceived ... a super-human mischief that often seems quite unfunny to humans? ... If life comes after this, Will is wandering about in it with a somewhat diffident exploratory expression upon his face.... He had the haunted look of the true humorist.[69]

With a final paradox, Cuppy could not even be a headliner in death. The passing of arguably's New York's most fiery popular former mayor, Fiorella LaGuardia, paralleled the humorist's, thus stealing front-page headlines. In addition, beloved character actor Frank Morgan (most synonymous with his title role in *The Wizard of Oz*, 1939) also died that day, dominating the obituary section of most newspapers. Indeed, the placement of Morgan's picture in several dailies, such as the *New York Journal American*, often appeared above and/or so near Cuppy's death notice, a cursory reader might have assumed it was the humorist's photograph. If there is laughter beyond life, Cuppy was undoubtedly howling.

TEN

Enhancing a Legacy by Way of Posthumous Publications

In the middle of Arthur Miller's *Death of a Salesman* (1949), the title character's wife, the vigilant watchdog of his life, erupts with anger at his unappreciative sons: "Attention must be paid. He's not to be allowed to fall into his grave like an old dog. Attention ... must be finally paid."[1] Will Cuppy's posthumous work necessitates a similar demand.

The movingly surreal "movie" which passed for Cuppy's life became an even more surreal feature with the posthumous publication of three more Cuppy books: *How to Attract the Wombat* (1949) *The Decline and Fall of Practically Everybody* (1950), and *How to Get from January to December* (1951). One might even draw promotional material for said "movie" from the autobiographical film *American Splendor* (2003), about the underground-comic-book curmudgeon Harvey Lawrence Pekar (1939–2010). The Cuppy-related line to lift from *Splendor* would be, "If you're the kind of person looking for romance ... or some sort of fantasy figure to save the day ... guess what? You've got the wrong movie." Regardless, F. Scott Fitzgerald once said American lives have no second acts, but Cuppy had one — in death. Tellers of biographical tales are often comically disparaged by non-profilers, such as novelist Vladimir Nabokov's crack, "Remember that what you are told is really threefold: shaped by the teller, reshaped by the listener [reader], and concealed from both by the dead man of the tale."[2] While these wry observations are anchored in the legitimate multi-faceted "angles of vision" (interpretations) all thinking individuals bring to any artistic endeavor (biography or otherwise), Cuppy's popular posthumous trilogy is amazingly instrumental in the validation of his legacy.

Before addressing these works, however, further reference must be made to the text from which the chapter opening "attention must be made" quote is taken — Arthur Miller's *Death of a Salesman*. These lines would resonate as a rallying cry for Cuppy, regardless of when they were written. Yet, the fact this award-winning Broadway play opened (February 10, 1949) only months before Cuppy's suicide death and also featured an underappreciated, similarly aged New Yorker (Willy Loman) who takes his own life, too, gives the words an eerily appropriate link to the humorist. Though Loman was constantly amidst the people as a salesman, and Cuppy was a reclusive writer, Arthur Miller's memoir describes Willy's profession as something closer to the humorist:

> These men lived like artists ... whose product is first of all themselves, forever imagining triumphs in a world that either ignores them or denies their presence altogether. But just often enough to keep the game going one of them makes it and swings to the moon on a thread of dreams unwinding out of himself.[3]

Certainly, Cuppy had more success in life than the fictional Loman. Yet, in the end, both figures, as is often the case in one's latter years, seemed to have their eyes trained more on life's rearview mirror. While Willy was haunted by a lyrical, ghostly, idealized past (a character drowning in his own delusions), Cuppy's memories were bitingly clear, such as a previously noted reference the humorist made about being glad an uncaring father was seldom home. Still, in neither Cuppy's nor Loman's mind had the classic American success story seemingly been fulfilled. Sadly, in a society so driven by the nebulous nature of success, anything perceived as less can threaten one's identity. Though "attention must be paid" to both characters, Cuppy is the more tragic figure, beyond being drawn from reality. Tragedy is anchored in the central figure ultimately knowing who he is and recognizing an Achilles' heel. Loman is at a loss on both counts. To satirize his profession à la Cuppy, Willy is the traveling salesman who never arrives. That is, Willy boasted to his family about being "well liked," and emphasized the importance of that trait to his sons. However, no one comes to his funeral.

That pitiful send-off is also a warning about today's explosion in social media, where being "well liked" has become "practically a profession itself. [Facebook *friends* and Twitter *followers* encourage people to measure] their worth by the rise or fall of [such] numbers."[4] Be it the 1940s or today, by overplaying the "well liked" card, one risks building a sense of self-worth upon sand. In contrast, cynical Cuppy was a card-carrying misanthrope. Granted, he appreciated — indeed, within his tiny circle of friends, he could demand — a show of affection. An unguarded Cuppy could even flirt with the aforementioned attitude about humanity of another curmudgeon, Oscar Levant: "Well, you know I hate 'em 'till they say hello to me."[5] Still, Cuppy's dark comedy damned being "well liked," and his ongoing attempts at "how to tell your friends from the apes" suggest a mindset closer to that of Joseph Conrad's *Heart of Darkness* (1902), in which the signature character's death mantra, "The horror, the horror," is a chilling commentary on the hypocrisy of humankind.

Loman's suicide was a final example of his neither understanding himself nor comprehending the continued ludicrousness of trying to push a failed American dream upon his eldest son (the insurance death money was to set up an already-botched business opportunity for Willy's boy, Biff). Cuppy's quiet, noteless suicide, on the other hand, has more the tired disguised feel of "the horror, the horror." After all, the humorist had been chronicling the satirical abyss for years. One might say Cuppy was finally making good on all his "how to become extinct" research. Unlike his fictional Willy Loman, if Cuppy had written a suicide note it would have reflected the similar satirical sentiments of the later George Carlin, who never tired of explaining a pet peeve shared with Cuppy: "You know why they call it the America dream? [pause] Because you have to be fucking asleep to believe it!" As a final footnote to all this talk of tragedy, it bears noting, Cuppy was fond of stating, "I'm billed as a humorist, but of course I am a tragedian at heart."[6] Though intended playfully by the satirist, as this text has documented, the observation is essentially true.

Regardless, one could aptly paraphrase a Humphrey Bogart crack about James Dean's passing and apply it to Will Cuppy: "He died at the right time. It was a good career move."[7] Like Dean's *Rebel Without a Cause* (1955), Cuppy's unexpected death occurred just before his latest work (*Wombat*) appeared. Call it a perverse twist of pop culture, but posthumous works frequently generate added interest from the public. Of course, the phenomenon can sometimes be less dependable in cinema. For every box-office hit like *Rebel*, there is a posthumous picture which the star's untimely death, such as Clark Gable and *The Misfits* (1961), can keep normally loyal fans away. That being said, literary circles are more likely to be posthumous-proof. Cuppy's *Wombat* book generated a great deal of affectionate critical praise, and the reviews often read like upbeat obituaries — just two months after the real ones had occurred. The most moving critique came from his old friend, humorist Frank Sullivan. Reviewing *Wombat* for Cuppy's *New York Herald Tribune* he wrote, in part:

> I bring a bias to this report of Will Cuppy's book, for I not only had a tremendous amount of fun from his wry, cool, wise, laconic humor during the last twenty-five years, but I also had the stimulating pleasure

of knowing him. He was not a gregarious man ... [instead he] chose to live the life of a hermit ... he accepted the universe ... but he did not accept it gleefully.... This colored his outlook.⁸

In Sullivan's essay, he fortuitously mentions a parallel between Cuppy's writing and the work of humorist Robert Benchley: "The birds and beasts baffled Will as much as they baffled and alarmed his contemporary, Robert Benchley."⁹ Of course, while Benchley's antiheroic alter ego fled from these feathered creatures, Cuppy invariably embraced a darkly comic attack mode. Consider, for example, his footnote about the canary: "A hardened cynic was once heard to mutter, 'The more I hear of Canaries the better I like Cats.'"¹⁰ (Though it is unlikely either Cuppy or Benchley would have been fans of Emily Dickinson's famous poem, "'Hope' is the thing with feathers," both antiheroic humorists would undoubtedly have appreciated Woody Allen's later sardonic use of the poem in the title to his darkly comic essay collection, *Without Feathers*, 1975.)

Sullivan's Cuppy-Benchley link merits some additional commentary, because the duo's previously noted parallels (ranging from being professorially antiheroic humorists, to doubling as critics whose reviews still put the accent on comedy), continue with the events leading up to their deaths. This is no small detail, given the lengths to which this text has gone to document the high regard in which Cuppy held Benchley, as well as the influence Benchley had on all humorists of that era.

Like Cuppy, Benchley had grown unhappy with the direction (or misdirection) his career had taken toward the end of his life. Officially retired from writing, and discontented with the quality of films in which he was being cast, his drinking problem had resulted in his being diagnosed with cirrhosis of the liver. Coincidently, just as Cuppy forever regretted never completing his serious play, Benchley felt equal bitterness for not writing his long-researched history book on the humorists of the Queen Anne period.

Technically, Benchley died of a cerebral hemorrhage in 1945. Yet, when I interviewed his daughter-in-law (Marjorie Benchley) for my biography of the humorist, she shared a most telling revelation. When Marjorie told her husband (Nathaniel) of his father's death (Nat was returning to New York on a troop train and initially no one had been able to contact him), the young man "didn't seem surprised; distressed but not surprised. So I think Bench [Nathaniel] felt he [Robert] was rather giving up."¹¹

The following summary of how Benchley reached this state sounds a great deal like the unhappy medicated final days of Cuppy: by the early 1940s Benchley needed sleeping pills at night and Benzedrine in the morning. According to Nathaniel, near the end his father had assumed a darkly comic philosophy on quitting the Benzedrine ritual — Benchley no longer felt the need to be awake! Suicide, after all, comes in many forms. Benchley's death, and the sad manner in which Cuppy's comedy hero slowly gave up, could arguably be counted as one more Benchley influence on the scholar of "how to become extinct."

Interestingly, one might make a final Benchley-Cuppy-Sullivan connection by noting the first posthumous collection of Benchley essays, *Chips Off the Old Benchley* (1949), appeared the same year as *Wombat*—with Sullivan doing the introduction. (Along paradoxically macabre lines, *Chips*'s publication coincided with Cuppy's passing. For instance, the *New York Times*' review appeared just the day before the humorist death, September 19, 1949). Regardless, as in Sullivan's *Wombat* review, he movingly mixed mirth with insight about a gifted friend. For example, Sullivan wrote:

> When he [Benchley] died ... he left friends in all the known walks of life and in a number of special walks invented to accommodate friends of his who did not fit into any of the conventional walks.... Everyone ... wanted to be Mr. Benchley's close friend.[12]

Everyone wanted to be close with Robert Benchley.

Though none of the many *Wombat* rave reviews topped Sullivan's poignantly personal touch, the *New York Times*' take on the book was the most novel — an affectionately tongue-in-cheek poem profile of the humorist. Entitled "Of Wombats and Such," the opening stanza sets the tone:

> Of mice and men, of
>   God and guppy,
> Here sings Keraunophobia [fearful of
>   lightning & thunder]
>   Cuppy.
> A mind of cheerful love
>   and knowledge, he
> Evolves his own unique
>   zoology.[13]

Of course, if Cuppy the curmudgeon could have

commented on this offbeat tribute, he would have summoned up another persecution reference to his imagined "hate Cuppy" movement — since he disliked poetry! In his early correspondence with Isabel Paterson, the two sparred about the merits of verse almost as much as they did about Cuppy's obsession with writing a serious play. Cuppy's continued distrust of poetry could also appear entertainingly in the oddest places, such as his review of E.B. White's *Quo Vadimus? Or, the Case for the Bicycle* (1939). Cuppy's favorite portion of this text involves White's own kidding of verse in "'How to Tell a Major Poet from a Minor Poet,' which contains that impossibly perfect gag, 'All poets named Edna St. Vincent Millay are major.'"[14]

Even if *Wombat* had been the last Cuppy text to appear, one knows that old axiom would still have applied: "No cry is so far that we can't hear the echo." Luckily, given the devotion of Cuppy friend and editor Fred Feldkamp, an even bigger "cry" was yet to come — at least in terms of a bona fide best seller: *The Decline and Fall of Practically Everybody* appeared almost exactly a year (1950) after both Cuppy's death and *Wombat*'s publication. The headline for the *Decline* review from the humorist's home newspaper, the *New York Herald Tribune*, went so far as to say: "Will Cuppy's Last and Best Compendium" (October 22, 1950). Once again, as with the *Wombat* reviews, the critique reads both as high praise for the text and as yet another surrogate obituary/historical overview of the humorist. Though not noted in the *Tribune* review, these added Cuppy insights came courtesy of Feldkamp's informative "Introduction" to *Decline*. (To honor the centennial of Cuppy's birth, the 1984 reprinting of the text was further bolstered by the addition of Thomas Maeder's updated "Afterword.") Such bonus material merits highlighting because it so affectionately and poignantly celebrates a delightfully eccentric humorist — underlining again, for new generations of readers, Cuppy's scholarly attention to detail, even while satirically sideswiping the very academic world from which he drew his subjects. Obviously, the best-seller status of *Decline* is anchored in Cuppy-inspired satire, his transition to a direct attack upon humanity (instead of his usual lampooning via lower life forms), William Steig's amusing caricatures of history's characters, and pop culture's perversely eternal fascination with an artist's work — *after* s/he had died. Yet, the sensitively entertaining biographical nature of the original "Introduction," and the later anniversary "Afterword," were boons to both *Decline*'s initial and subsequent critical and commercial successes. Regardless, the *Tribune* review offered an excellent summation of both the book and its author:

> Here, told in the unique Cuppy manner, with copious side comments, are the stories of a diverse company.... From Plutarch to Toynbee, there has never been an historian quite like Cuppy ... distinguished not only

by a curious turn of mind ... but he was also a sound historian, a scrupulous digger for facts, and a debunker of great gift ... it is good to be reminded of rare Will Cuppy again.[15]

The *Tribune* tribute/critique of *Decline* was further enhanced by the reproduction of several Steig illustrations. Even the sometimes- reluctant *Saturday Review* wrapped its praise of *Decline* around some reproductions of Steig:

> [Cuppy's] style of humor is unique and, like the taste of an avocado, a little hard to describe. For one thing, he was a man of immense and staggering scholarships; but, more important, his erudition is part of the warp and woof of his humor ... you'll never get as painless and pleasurable a history lesson as you'll get in "The Decline and Fall of Practically Everybody."[16]

Consistent with such praise, the *New York Times* showcased two separate hosannas to *Decline*. The first was a mini-critique, which opened with unadulterated praise: "Will Cuppy's cheerful [note card] files go marching on in 'The Decline and Fall of Practically Everybody,' a studiously irreverent Plutarchingtonian view of such characters as Cheops, Charlemagne ... Christopher Columbus ... [and so on]"—followed by the *Times*' extensive favorite quotations from the text.[17] The newspaper's traditional full-fledged critique followed a few days later. Amusingly entitled, "A Footnote Covers Lady Godiva," it is yet another sublime profile of the humorist, masquerading as a review. However, unlike the *Tribune*'s effective applications of Feldkamp's "Introduction" information in their review, *Times* critic C.B. Palmer also had his own bittersweet personal Cuppy material from which to draw:

> This reviewer had occasion to transact some business with him a little over a year ago [shortly before Cuppy's suicide], trying to persuade him to write a certain article for *The [London] Times*. Mr. Cuppy loved the subject but warned that he was a very slow worker and wasn't too sure that people liked his kind of stuff anymore. He was pleased to pinkness by reassurance that certain people, at least, thought him among the funniest men writing in English.[18]

Despite Palmer's report of Cuppy being "pleased to pinkness," the critic had inadvertently honed in on the humorist's late-in-life fearful mantra—he was a victim of a slowing pace and a shrinking audience. Like a commentary on many creatively self-destructive types—whose *work-work* mode has always been that of a whirling dervish—Cuppy's sacrificial life begs the question: how far are we willing to go to make art? The pace, and/or the inability to maintain that pace, has driven many artists over the proverbial edge. For Cuppy, one might also define his end as an emotional martyrdom — the humorist fulfilling his long-standing suicide threats.

Palmer's review also addressed the more traditional conjecture expected of a critic:

> It [*Decline*] is in a sense his "big" book, his answer to those who complained that he wrote only about animals.... [Cuppy's] manner was simple enough: a dead-pan statement of impeccable fact, then a caustic or plaintive or astonished footnote.... [With] the chapter on Catherine the Great ... surely one of the funniest things written in years.[19]

As with many of the *Decline* reviews, Palmer also seconds some wishful thinking from Feldkamp's foreword — if only this book had been available in past history classes![20]

Of *Decline*'s universal acclaim, however, the wittiest kudos were from *Chicago Tribune* critic Richard Blakesley, whose best quip, fittingly enough, included recycling a publicity footnote about the text: "'Footloose in the footnotes of history' is the best description of this hilarious hike thru the ages with ... Will Cuppy. It took him 16 years to dig up this additional lowdown on the highups."[21] With a critique carrying the affectionately ironic title, "Will Cuppy's Last Laugh Is His Best," Blakesley also briefly expands upon the paradox inherent to this best seller: "The only serious note to the undertaking is that he did not live to enjoy the praise and the profit his best work deserves."[22]

Back in Cuppy's rarely visited Hoosier homeland, there were also positive *Decline* notices, best exemplified by an *Indianapolis News* review with yet another comic title, "Everyone Is Covered (Even Godiva) by Cuppy":

> Born and reared at Auburn [Indiana], [he] worked ... years on this book ... which may disillusion those boobs who think such easy reading is simple to write.... You haven't really met these historical personages until Cuppy introduces them.... It's guaranteed to make you laugh.[23]

Still, there is a touch of Thomas Wolfe's *You Can't Go Home Again* in the *Indianapolis News* critique. That is, after saying such positive things about *Decline*, the anonymous reviewer felt compelled to add, "Although Cuppy was recognized as an excellent book critic (he reviewed an estimated 4,000 books for his New York paper) he had no far-reaching acclaim as a humorist."[24]

What prompted such a petty closing jab, especially after another wise, glowing review? Was this a case of home-state sour grapes? After all, it *was* an anonymous critique. Another explanation could be catch-all provincialism. The critic knew enough to essentially say nice generic things about the book, e.g., "'Decline' will be on excellent addition to any bookshelf," because reviewers for prestigious presses like the *New York Times* had confessed to experiencing "hilarious enjoyment of the whole blessed thing."[25] After protecting himself, this argument would suggest the *Indianapolis News* writer simply could not appreciate the significance of Cuppy's work, either in the past and/or the 1950 present.

The *Indianapolis News* review is reminiscent of the critical reaction to other groundbreaking black-humor artists, such as Charlie Chaplin and his watershed film *The Great Dictator* (1940). The critiques for this movie often featured the same odd mix of praise followed by qualifiers.[26] More specifically, even the most positive *Dictator* reviews had a split-personality nature to them. Consider this line from a period article in the *Los Angeles Times*: "[Many] critics panned Chaplin's picture for its [dark] thematic content, while paying great tribute to the comedian's personal performance."[27] *Decline* appeared over a decade after *Dictator*, and black humor now played more effectively with a mass urban audience. Still, heartland values at the time remained more anchored in the polar opposite populism of a feel-good Hoosier humorist like Cuppy contemporary Emily Kimbrough (1899–1989). Indeed, the Muncie-born author's then most recent book, *Innocents from Indiana* (1950, praised in its *Indianapolis Star* review), paradoxically paralleled the publication of *Decline*.[28]

Of course, Kimbrough remains most identified with her nostalgic best seller *Our Hearts Were Young and Gay* (1942, co-authored with Cornelia Otis Skinner, as was *Innocents*). *Hearts* was also a critical and commercial success when adapted to the screen in 1944. A Cuppy-Kimbrough comparison is made easier when one applies an old art axiom spouted by an army of teachers: "It's all in the title." That is, nothing contrasts the conflicting genres of the darkly comic Cuppy with the Capraesque Kimbrough like the dueling monikers of the simultaneously published *Decline and Fall of Practically Everybody* and *Innocents from Indiana*, or *Our Hearts Were Young and Gay* appearing just one year after Cuppy's *How to Become Extinct* (1941). Even today, populism plays to a broader audience than dark comedy.[29]

Interestingly, Cuppy's final posthumous work — thus far —*How to Get from January to December*, published the year after *Decline*, showcases a somewhat gentler humorist. While the satirical bite remains (miles of black humor still separate him from Kimbrough), the format of Cuppy's crazy quilt almanac allowed the humorist to draw from such a broad range of topics that the reader feels a more casually cozy close-up emerging. Though not remotely close to a memoir, the text rivals his first humor book, *How to Become a Hermit*, in its revelation of fun Cuppy facts. Fittingly, the

Cuppy origins for a comic almanac seemingly date from a period shortly after the publication of *Hermit*. During 1934 a monthly Cuppy column called "Ye Housewife's Almanack" appeared in the *South Whitley Tribune* (Indiana) newspaper. The duration and possible limited syndication of said column is unclear. (Please see the bibliography.) Regardless, editor

Charlie Chaplin's title character satire of Hitler in *The Great Dictator* (1940).

Fred Feldkamp has done an excellent job in giving the Cuppy enthusiast a fitting, personal finale to the humorist's work.

While a *January to December* almanac would leave one to expect a brief Cuppy satirical sortie for each blasted day in the year, the premise is only a point of departure for whatever topic moves him. Granted, since editor Feldkamp was working with an unfinished manuscript, one could argue a scattergun scenario was a product of necessity — filling in literary holes (empty calendar dates) from Cuppy notecards. Yet, because the humorist himself so frequently wanders from the alleged specific topic of countless dates, any poetic license Feldkamp might have taken seems consistent with Cuppy's eclectic style. For example, though Cuppy's reference for November 7 begins with that date being the anniversary of General Henry Harrison winning the Battle of Tippecanoe (1811), the humorist immediately segues to a childhood memory about the general's grandson, President Benjamin Harrison. It seems that the Hoosier leader had visited Cuppy's Auburn hometown during his re-election campaign of 1892, and the humorist felt his mother's musical selections (as part of the local Ladies' Glee Club) for the occasion had directly contributed to Harrison being badly defeated![30] (The musically inclined Cuppy would have been eight years old at the time.)

One might break down the best of *January to December* into several categories. First would be Cuppy staying on topic, directly addressing a date. For instance, United States Navy Commodore Stephen Decatur, author of the line, "My country, right or wrong," was born on *January 5 (1779)*. Liberal Cuppy cannot help taking issue with such jingoism by quoting a rebuttal from G.K. Chesterton,

"'My country, right or wrong,' is a thing that no patriot would think of saying.... It is like saying, 'My mother, drunk or sober.'"[31] Moreover, on *October 8 (1871)* Mrs. O'Leary's cow kicked over a lamp and started the Great Chicago Fire. Cuppy, after a long tenure at the University of Chicago, is especially fond of that fact. Yet, he feels compelled to report that the O'Leary family (and others) later contested this statement. For Cuppy, historian or not, this feels like courting chaos:

> If Mrs. O'Leary's cow did not kick over that lamp, what *can* we be sure of? ... [The cow] has now become a part of my general outlook and I'd find it pretty hard to change. I can see the O'Learys' side of it but what about me?[32]

Second, like any good almanac, going back to Benjamin Franklin's watershed *Poor Richard's Almanack* (sometimes *Almanac*), Cuppy's *January to December* also includes bits of advice. However, being a satirist, Cuppy's text doubles as a skewering of crackerbarrel common sense tips, be they anonymous or from Will Rogers the earlier noted populist he loved to hate. To illustrate, for the *October 14* entry, Cuppy randomly addresses the belief that eating fish is good for the brain: "[It depends] partly upon the brain involved. Some people could eat fish from now till Doomsday and be little the wiser. The Trobriand Islanders, for instance, live almost entirely upon fish and they can't even speak English."[33] Along related lines, Cuppy's *January 13* entry tackles the culinary question as to whether certain foods make people feel amorous: "don't get your hopes up. I've been eating the items in question ... oysters and other shellfish for years, and I feel about as usual.... [Instead] you could try amassing a great deal of money. That works fine."[34]

Third, no Cuppy compendium would be complete without some zoological-inspired satire. He manages to work alligators into his *June 12* ramblings: "A few alligators are naturally of the vicious type and inclined to resent it when you prod them with a stick. You can find out which ones are by prodding them."[35] The catalyst for Cuppy's *February 26* notation is allegedly the Iowa birth of Buffalo Bill Cody (1896), but he then has some fun with why the bison was once threatened with extinction (one of his favorite topics): "What really happened to the buffalos is just what you might expect if you've ever seen one in a zoo. The moths got into them."[36] *New York Times* critic Charles Poore's championing of the book was particularly fond of the following Cuppy animal observation: "Most armadillos are restricted to a low grunt. Armadillos make affectionate pets, if you need affection that much."[37]

Fourth, the iconoclastic Cuppy loves to dismantle scholars, and *January to December* frequently showcases this tendency. Moreover, being a former college literature major, he especially enjoys hamstringing the so-called authorities who question whether Shakespeare authored his plays. Cuppy's *April 9* entry opines, "You can't spot these people at sight. Only an expert can tell that anything [is] — uh — unusual about them — that is, in their lucid intervals."[38] For Cuppy's *August 29* citation he discounts scientists that claim the gemsbok, a South African antelope, never drinks water: "This simply means that these scientists have never happened to see a gemsbok drinking water. I always use my own judgment in problems pertaining to gemsbok."[39]

Fifth, if questionable scholarship were not enough, human antics in general drove Cuppy to satirical distraction. His *March 9* citation, marking the birth of phrenology founder Franz Joseph Gall (1758), targeted a practice that claimed you could tell a person's disposition, character and special talents by feeling the bumps on one's head: "As this was obviously ridiculous from any point of view, a great many people believed it, until they lost interest and took up something else."[40] Contrastingly, Cuppy's *February 24* citation begins with a seemingly softer take upon humanity's inherent idiocy, then dovetails to a darker prognosis: "Just when you're beginning to think pretty well of people, you run across somebody who puts sugar on sliced tomatoes ... there are people you wouldn't believe."[41]

Regardless, among *January to December*'s unofficial Cuppy summing ups, one receives final merry peaks at countless other favorite topics and/or targets. His coffee drinking "like a fiend" is addressed *June 9*.[42] He trumpets the importance of the Yankees — the most significant thing to *ever* happen on *July 28* was a Babe Ruth led victory over the St. Louis Browns. He further mocks the "nonsense" for which Aristotle is credited (*April 17*), and provides additional evidence for *not* traveling: Socrates "never left Athens" (*June 7*).[43] He asserts that hamburger trumps all other foods — including desserts! (*September 8*). He goes on to disparage those who find figures in star patterns, like the Big Dipper. The scientific name for the Dipper, he points out, means "Greater Bear," but maybe "long ago ... bears looked

Publicity shot of Yankee icon Babe Ruth (mid–1920s).

more like dippers than they do today" (*February 15*).⁴⁴ His essentially nihilistic view of life comes out yet again in a (*June 15*) acknowledgment of the day Benjamin Franklin did his kite flying electricity experiment during a thunderstorm (1752) — with Cuppy then crediting this Renaissance man with being the first American "to realize that life is often pretty drab for most of us."⁴⁵

The best argument for *January to December* being the ultimate Cuppy compendium comes from the inclusion of a rare tongue-in-cheek tip on mystery criticism. The example is drawn from one of the text's many advice entries. Cuppy is allegedly responding to an anonymous question about why the humorist dislikes mystery characters staring off into space. Cuppy explains that this staring business is the genre's "worst cliché I have encountered in a long and checkered career.... What's wrong with the verb 'to look.'"⁴⁶ Then, with his signature passion, he amusingly cites Webster upon the necessity of a prolonged gaze, à la staring, necessitating looking upon some fixed object. Yet, as his comic diatribe winds down, he warns the reader to temper any similar feelings or risk being bagged by that "man with the net ... [who] might not understand."⁴⁷

My only modest tweaking to Feldkamp's masterly editing of *January to December* would have involved the date *September 17*. Given Cuppy's godly regard for Robert Benchley, it would have made sense to commemorate the date upon which Cuppy received the funniest of fan letters from his comic hero. Said correspondence reads, in part:

> I have been a Cuppy fan ever since you gave me the first intelligent *favorable* review I ever got. I have had some mighty intelligent *un*favorable ones but it takes a good man to make sense while giving me a boost.⁴⁸

Predictably, as with *Decline*, the reviews for *January to December* were superlative. The *New York Times*' Charles Poore stated, "It belongs in the classic American humorous tradition of irrelevance, where four and four are always adding up to two.... It takes all kinds of worlds to supply Will Cuppy's people."⁴⁹ The *Chicago Tribune* critic enthused:

> How to get from January to December is a problem that has plagued humanity since the beginning of time.... But it took Will Cuppy to smooth the way with a device that man has always possessed — laughter.... If you're a Will Cuppy fan you'll find this book the brightest star in his constellation of comedy; if not, get the book anyway and you'll probably haunt the bookstores looking for its predecessors.⁵⁰

The *New York Herald Tribune*'s review noted, "One of Cuppy's unique qualities as a humorist was his zeal for research, with critic Herbert

Kupferberg being most fond of Cuppy correcting the misconception that famed novelist Honoré de Balzac (1799–1850) had died of drinking too much coffee; it was overwork, since coffee never killed anybody, but "overwork has slain millions."[51] Kupferberg's preference for this modestly amusing insight in a book of big laughs reveals an insider's knowledge of Cuppy, for the humorist went beyond a fiend-like love of coffee. As if borrowing the work habits of Balzac, Cuppy also rose at midnight and wrote slowly but with incredible focus all night—fueled by innumerable cups of black coffee. Indeed, in honor of Cuppy the mystery critic, one might posit more circumstantial evidence for a Cuppy-Kupferberg connection by the fact that Kupferberg's normal reviewing specialty was music, the humorist's favorite subject after satire ... and maybe coffee.

Whether or not Cuppy and Kupferberg were acquaintances, or the latter critic simply had privileged information by also being of the *Herald Tribune* tribe, it is easy for Cuppy fans to empathize with the humorist. For example, as his first book-length biographer, and an avowed admirer of his work, it is second nature for me to see an undercurrent to much of his life and art. Draw a random subject at hand from any of the aforementioned Cuppy bugaboos, and bingo, a sort of profiler's channeling is at hand. To illustrate, take his dislike of traveling and I hear the curmudgeon explaining, "People think that going somewhere new is going to change them, forgetting that they take themselves along, too." Like so much in life, Cuppy is a wonder of contradictions—a satirical Socrates bravely attacking assorted icons (including Socrates!), while masking a mass of personal insecurities with a hermit's lifestyle. Though Cuppy neither had nor liked children, one could still liken him to that favored comic uncle you adored as a youngster—the one who only occasionally made the odd family gatherings, yet always enlivened them when he did. While never seated at the kids' table, he did not connect with adults, either—sort of like the suicidal Seymour Glass of J.D. Salinger's seminal darkly comic story "A Perfect Day for Bananafish" (from *Nine Stories*, 1953). Interestingly, like Miller's *Death of a Salesman*, Salinger's "Bananafish" also first appeared in the New York literary scene shortly before Cuppy's suicide.[52]

The close proximity of such famous fictional suicides to that of Cuppy's own personal Armageddon are undoubtedly coincidental. Yet, as humor scholar Norris W. Yates has suggested, "The depth of Cuppy's pessimism rivaled [Ring] Lardner's; he stressed that nothing worked well in alleviating *la condition humaine*. He could see only one final solution: ... 'becoming extinct'...."[53] One is also reminded of Alexandra Styron's description of her father's (Pulitzer Prize-winning novelist William Styron) ongoing balancing act between his depression and an obsession with writing. "Like that of a marathoner running in the dark, my father's path was sometimes as murky as it was long."[54] Let one just say, that Cuppy (and a number of driven writers like himself) passed his own metaphorical night in Gethsemane, and then some. Even an undated [mid–1940s] Cuppy note to the person hired to maintain the humorist's clipping files/scrapbooks has the chilling aforementioned Benchley depressed air of an individual who has given up, "This is the lot [of articles to be pasted on] 47 animals. I am up at 5 [P.M.? Cuppy wrote at night] again, taking medicine. I believe the more medicine you take the better you feel."[55] Consequently, Cuppy's posthumous trilogy, appearing so closely together (1949–1951), after a career in which his satirical texts had surfaced only intermittently, during a lifetime of frequent depression, both underlined his presence as an important humorist and signaled that Cuppy's questioning dark world view— particularly with *The Decline and Fall of Practically Everybody*— had never been more timely. For good or bad, his black-humor legacy remains even more topical today. Indeed, I am reminded of a Cuppy-like line from what is arguably Woody Allen's funniest film, *Love and Death* (1975), "You know, if it turns out that there is a God, I don't think that he's evil. I think that, that the worst you could say about him is that basically he's an underachiever."

Afterword: Comparing Cuppy to Some of His Comic Contemporaries

> Only old Benjamin [the donkey] professed to remember every detail of his long life and to know that things never had been, nor ever could be much better or much worse — hunger, hardship, and disappointment being, so he said, the unalterable law of life.— George Orwell's *Animal Farm* (1945).[1]

George Orwell's (1903–1950) Swiftian satiric fable about the Stalinist Soviet Union, *Animal Farm*, anthropomorphically chronicles a barnyard revolution against tyranny (Mr. Jones of Manor Farm), leading to an equally terrible totalitarianism. Freed of evil farmer Jones, the animals gradually allow Napoleon the pig to attain Stalinist-dictator status. Among the animal masses, only Benjamin the donkey anticipates the ultimate commandment of the domain: "All animals are equal but some animals are more equal than others."[2]

There is no documented link between Cuppy's view and Orwell's application of the same principles to *Animal Farm*, with or without highlighting Benjamin the donkey. Of course, the humorist was also popular in Britain during this period, and Orwell often drew inspirations for his work from pop culture. For example, the catalyst for the "Big Brother is watching you" telescreens in Orwell's renowned novel *1984* (1949) came from the strategically placed large monitors in Charlie Chaplin's *Modern Times* (1936).[3] Regardless, while Orwell takes one on a deeper satirical journey, Cuppy's sarcastic observations on the absurdity in the world frequently demonstrates that the *seemingly* trivial can sometimes assume the same intellectual/emotional significance of what traitor time designates an important event. In either case, the critter criticisms of society by both artists demonstrate that facts do not contain any more truth than moral fables.

Ironically, while Isabel Paterson did not review *Animal Farm* in her "Turns with a Bookworm" column, her biting comments therein — hardly surprising, given her libertarian beliefs (versus socialist Orwell) — are reminiscent of misogamist Cuppy's primitive hermit days on Jones Island: "He [Orwell] lives on a Scotch island [the then-isolated Isle of Jura, off the west coast of Scotland] to get away from the common man."[4] Except, Paterson's crack was meant sarcastically, because while she and Cuppy were forever questioning the merits of Homo sapiens, Paterson was suspicious of Orwell's common-man causes. Regardless, this particular Paterson column (August 18, 1946) is full of other references which bring Cuppy to mind, ranging from a new book on apes, to an aside about Cuppy's favorite cartoon character, Krazy Kat.[5]

Nonetheless, the main point in making a Cuppy connection with Orwell is to underline how *Animal Farm*'s dazzling critical and commercial success (Paterson notwithstanding), was yet another 1940s example of the world catching up with Cuppy's ongoing career of satirizing humanity, via anthropomorphic means. Indeed, the title of the volume with which Cuppy kicked off the decade could not have been more succinct — *How to Become Extinct*. Moreover, like all satirists, both men insisted upon telling people exactly what they did *not* want to hear. Though Orwell, like Isabel Paterson, was much more politically inclined, each man had doubts about mankind's ability (whatever the "ism") to remain forever vigilant *after* any and all alleged "power to the people" transitions. Though *Animal Farm* was inspired by Stalin's usurping of the proletariat and fellow Lenin disciple Leon Trotsky ("Snowball" in Orwell's novel) following the Russian Revolution, the fable's warning about the inherent gullibility of people could just as well be applied to *anything Cuppy*, or any major uprising. In fact, Orwell seems to footnote the historical link by calling *Animal Farm*'s ultimate dictator pig "Napoleon" — the general/emperor of the French following their revolution to eliminate a ruling class. Both Cuppy and Orwell, especially under the guise of the wise fool, Benjamin the donkey, suggest there is little long-term hope for humanity. As critic Orville Prescott seems to summarize for them, the ancient cycle of revolution follows an old formula: "First brotherhood, then organization and then tyranny."[6] Cuppy and Orwell would be quick to add that the course of human events is so ridiculous that only a company of idealists could have conceived it.

While the humor inherent to Orwell's fable was something new to his writing, it had been the stock-in-trade for Cuppy's oeuvre since the beginning. Interestingly, a cover blurb for a 1962 reissuing of *How to Get from January to December* suggested his comedy was a cross between James Thurber (1894–1961) and S.J. Perelman (1904–1979).[7] While that is not exactly the case, the first humor book from each of the trio appeared the same year (1929): Cuppy's *How to Be a Hermit*, Thurber's (with E. B. White) *Is Sex Necessary?*, and Perelman's *Dawn Ginsbergh's Revenge*.

Though Cuppy has much more in common with Robert Benchley, who rates one final pass in this text, a brief comparison of Cuppy to Thurber and Perelman merits fleshing out, too. As in film, where first-time comedy directors often go the parody route, such as Buster Keaton's *Three Ages* (1923), or Woody Allen's *Take the Money and Run* (1969), these initial book outings by Cuppy, Thurber, and Perelman were also spoofs. Each volume kidded the multi-faceted popularity of that era's self-help manuals. The works by Thurber and Perelman particularly parodied love. While the Thurber/White title, *Is Sex Necessary?*, makes that point obvious, one should note the most ambitious essay in Perelman's text also provides spoofing tips on "How to Make Love." In marked contrast to these satirical sideswipings of relationship advice, Cuppy's *How to Be a Hermit* comically keyed upon going it alone. His parody target was the *House Beautiful*–type magazine then coming into vogue—so different from his eyesore-of-a-bachelor-shack on Jones Island.

While Cuppy, Thurber, and Perelman all write from the perspective of what comedy historian Norris W. Yates would describe as the 20th century's "little man,"[8] each of their takes on this antihero is markedly different. A brief tutorial on the subject might best start with the aforementioned topic of sex. A noticeable thread from their starter books would be that, while women often surface in the later writing of Thurber and Perelman, they would continue being a no-show for Cuppy—beyond the historical personages of *The Decline and Fall of Practically Everybody*, or the occasional intellectual vaudeville-like sketches inspired by Isabel Paterson in *How to Be a Hermit*. Thurber's and Perelman's perspective on the subject could not be more different. Thurber would elevate the frustrations inherent in relationships to high art with two *New Yorker* short stories from 1939: "The Life of Walter Mitty," and "A Unicorn in the Garden."[9] Yet, the potential for the battle of the sexes is forever lurking in his work, starting with the milquetoast male of the "Mr. and Mrs. Monroe" stories collected in his book *The Owl in the Attic* (1931).

By contrast, if Perelman pieces reference women, they are more likely to play sexual-innuendo games, like the following observation from the story "Nothing But the Tooth," from his celebrated collection, *Crazy Like a Fox* (1944):

> Before I could learn whether it was a bite or just a gentle hug the editor recommended, out popped Miss Inchbald with lipstick on her nose, giggling, "The Doctor is free now." "Free" indeed — "running amok" would be a better way to put it.[10]

Indeed, Perelman's perspective in *Dawn Ginsbergh's Revenge* is often that of a sexy girl/woman, half child (but not the half that shows). For instance, the narrator of the book's first story, "Puppets of Passion," describes the title character thus:

> She [Dawn] looked around at the immense room that was her bedroom. It was, she reflected, large enough for the whole Sixty-ninth Regiment. To tell the truth, the Sixty-ninth *was* in the room, in undress uniform. Dawn was like that, unconventional.[11]

In the text's "What it Means to Be a Professional Beauty," the narrator observes of a central character forever in bed, "with Constance it was always her own bed, and it was probably spending so much time in bed that laid the [sexual] foundation for her later success."[12] Yet, in *Dawn Ginsbergh's Revenge* pieces like "The Pitfalls of the Stage," Perelman is just as likely to assume the spoofing "voice" of the alleged innocent woman child, "Unsophisticated country girl that I was...."[13] However, Perelman's proclivity for sexually provocative comic writing, or at least surreally romantic storytelling, is best showcased in his film work, from co-scripting the similarly oversexed Marx Brothers classics *Monkey Business* (1931) and *Horse Feathers* (1932), to his Academy Award-winning screenplay adaptation of *Around the World in Eighty Days* (1956, which also plays upon another Perelman talent, the comic travel book).

The bottom line, therefore, in differentiating between the varied antiheroic little men alter egos of Thurber, Perelman, and Cuppy could be seen as an extension of these character relationships with or (in Cuppy's case) without women. Thus, Thurber's print persona is essentially a grown-up Charlie Brown, years before Charles Schultz created the *Peanuts* character — forever victimized by the Lucys of the world. In contrast, with whomever Perelman parried, be it women or weasels, his wordsmithing was so laden with puns, parody, and attitude, he never seemed to be at a disadvantage. The Perelman persona is only antiheroic in the sense that he enjoyed spoofing whatever bothered him, for even the humorist's favorite self-deprecating axiom, "Before they made S. J. Perelman, they broke the mold," demonstrates a certain merry moxie which would carry him through.[14] So if Thurber is Mr. Milquetoast, Perelman is Mr. Smart Aleck.

Where does that leave Cuppy's little man? His antihero is in the final round of being the ultimate curmudgeon — the iconoclastic scholar ready to pull down the pillars of civilization. Unlike Sampson's mythical bringing down of the roof, Cuppy was a wisecracking *recluse/hermit* who questioned *all* human contact. Whereas Thurber was a misogynist, and Perelman was a saturation comedy parodist, Cuppy was a misanthrope. The author of *How to Become Extinct* was a study in cynicism and evolutionary suicide. One might comically describe him as a "tightly packed suitcase" who, in ironic reality, hated to travel. He just preferred to be left alone on either of the two islands he reluctantly shared with New Yorkers, the shack on Jones Beach, or the small Greenwich Village apartment in Manhattan.

Coming full circle back to Orwell's Cuppy-like Benjamin, the question remains: is the "unalterable law of life" hardship and disappointment? Thurber flirts with this verdict in his *The Last Flower: A Parable in Pictures* (1939), but ultimately, as E. B. White so eloquently notes in *The New Yorker*:

> Although [Thurber] is best known for "Walter Mitty" and *The Male Animal*, the book of his I like best is *The Last Flower*. In it you will find his faith in the renewal of life, his feelings for the beauty and fragility of life on earth.[15]

Robert Benchley, the writer that Cuppy's contemporaries placed a notch above all others.

Thurber's Chaplinesque anti-war "Last Flower," written subsequent to the start of World War II in Europe (November 1939), chronicles the collapse of civilization following the war which came *after World War XII*! Thurber ends his parable in pictures with the text: "This time the destruction was so complete ... that nothing at all was left in the world except one man and one woman and one flower." Accompanied by his delightfully minimalist drawings, which, like the art of Al Hirschfeld, do so much with a single curve, Thurber provides a modicum of hope. Yet, had Cuppy been so inclined to create a comparable apocalyptic parable, it would probably have ended with "neither a man nor a woman nor even a wombat surviving; and the single living thing would be a flower once popular in my youth — 'love-lies-bleeding,' which is not a perennial!" Thus, Cuppy's orchestration of how to become extinct would be complete.

So how does Benchley tie into a final peek at Cuppy's persona, via his comedy contemporaries? Briefly, Benchley represented God to these humorists, from books dedicated to him (such as Perelman's aforementioned *Crazy Like a Fox*), to Thurber's blanket hosanna: "One of the greatest fears of the humorist writer is that he has spent three weeks writing something done faster and better by Benchley in 1919."[16] If Thurber's alter ego was a milquetoast type, Perelman a smart aleck, and Cuppy a professorial curmudgeon/contrarian, Benchley was more the befuddled professorial every man.

While each of these humorists owe a huge comedy debt to Benchley, Cuppy is the most beholden. Yet, Cuppy still brought his own signature style to the material. Since Benchley did not follow the aforementioned first book club of 1929, à la Thurber, Perelman, and Cuppy, one might briefly demonstrate some final parallels between Cuppy and Benchley by perusing the latter humorist's *The Early Worm* (1927). This was Benchley's fourth book of the 1920s, and the closest in publishing proximity to *How to Be a Hermit*.

First, given Cuppy's day job as a mystery critic, one is struck by the fact that Benchley scatters black humor chronicles throughout *The Early Worm*— all beginning with the heading "Fascinating Crimes." Indeed, like Cuppy's later collection, *Murder Without Tears: An Anthology of Crime* (1946), Benchley's comic crime stories fluctuate between fact and fiction. Interestingly, given Cuppy's Hoosier background, which sometimes surfaces in both his humor books and anthologies, Benchley's first prominently placed such essay: "Fascinating Crimes: 1. The Odd Occurrence in the Life of Dr. Meethas," is a comic slant upon a true unsolved murder (October 14, 1879) set in Elkhart, Indiana! The most entertaining of these stories, however, was Benchley's absurdist, "Fascinating Crimes:111. The Missing Floor," which opens:

> It has often been pointed out that murderers are given to revisiting the scenes of their crimes. The case of [elevator operator and murder suspect] Edny Pastelle is the only one on record where the scene of the crime revisited the murderer.... When the [stuck elevator] car was finally dislodged, it was found to contain the body of [victim] Max Sorgossen. Furthermore, *the second floor, where the elevator should have stopped, was gone!*[17]

Second, Benchley the befuddled professorial type is also much in evidence in *The Early Worm*, as best demonstrated by the essay, "The World of Grandpa Benchley":

> This set me to thinking about atoms. I don't think that I have it straight even now ... just as I was getting accustomed to the idea that molecules *could* be divided into atoms, along comes somebody a few years ago and says that you can divide atoms into electrons.... [After that] I went out into the park and had a good cry.[18]

As much as Cuppy admired Benchley, if his contrarian professorial type had addressed the same subject, Cuppy would have been both much more scholarly precise about the details and undoubtedly would have proved the process problematic in general. Plus, Benchley's expert—"somebody a few years ago ... says ..."—would have been systematically shish kebobed. In short, Benchley generally kidded himself, while Cuppy's satirical Jihad was against society.

Third, both Benchley and Cuppy were reluctant critics, working at their craft out of financial necessity. Each made their reviewing chores more palatable by infusing their critiques with humor. Benchley amusingly addresses the topic in *The Early Worm* essay, "Storm Warnings for New York":

> I eke out barely enough money to buy gin for my children.... I don't like opening performances.... I would never go to see them if it were not for the fact that it is my life-work. Often I sit through them with my eyes shut.[19]

Obviously, both humorists exaggerated their dislike for reviewing. Still, if one reads their critiques today, it is because they now double as comic essays. In fact, if there is ever to be another posthumous Cuppy book, it would be a judicious collection of his reflection on often-forgettable fiction.

Fourth, neither Benchley not Cuppy held out much hope for humanity. Yet Benchley, as was consistent with his self-deprecating mask of iconoclasm, was often very gentle with his attacks on what H. L. Mencken and Cuppy would call the "booboisie" (bourgeoisie). An excellent example of this diplomacy occurs in Benchley's *Early Worm* essay, "The New Villainy":

> The hand of Freud reached out ... and we learned that whenever anyone is excessively religious, it is a sign that they are suffering from an inhibition which is likely some day to break loose and leave Broadway strewn with bits of broken bottles and confetti. The more they crave a good rip-snorting week-end at Atlantic City, registering under the wrong name. It is all very confusing.[20]

Fifth and final, Cuppy made a career of satirizing society by way of lower life forms. Benchley also enjoyed occasionally "lecturing" on the same subject. Yet, besides his aforementioned escape into befuddlement (versus Cuppy's ability to anchor his humor in hard facts) Benchley often preferred to mock, via absurdity, attacking significance to *any* kind of scholarship. Benchley's first *Early Worm* essay, "A Talk to Young Men," demonstrates this:

> [A rooster's] red crest is put there by Nature so that the hen can see the rooster coming in a crowd and can hop into a taxi or make a previous engagement if she wants to. A favorite dodge of a lot of hens when they see the red crest of the rooster making in their direction across the barnyard is to work up a sick headache.[21]

Benchley's chicken and rooster subtextual satire of the sexual relationship between men and women is a first cousin to Cuppy's later critter comedy. Yet, Benchley makes no attempt to layer his work with the scholarly subterfuge, which was the Cuppy signature.

This epilogue began with references to a watershed work, *Animal Farm*, which, published near the end of Cuppy's life, is emblematic of his work. The previous chapter opened with an examination of a suicide in another seminal literary work of the period, Arthur Miller's play *Death of a Salesman*, which speaks to the tragedy of Cuppy's own suicide. A final 1940s work of literature, also touching upon suicide, seems an apt way to close this book — both with regard to Cuppy, and the humorist he most admired, Robert Benchley. Thomas Heggen's multi-faceted opus *Mister Roberts*, first published as a novel in 1946, adapted as a play by Heggen and Joshua Logan in 1948, and an Oscar-nominated Best Picture in 1955, is the work in question.

The story is set upon an American cargo ship, the antiheroically named U.S.S. *Reluctant*, during the last months of World War II. Though a comedy, the ship's commander is of the same ilk as *Mutiny on the Bounty*'s Captain Bligh. A comic truce between commander and crew is only maintained by the title character, Mr. Roberts, who acts as the beloved executive officer of the *Reluctant*. Yet, unlike the name of this "bucket," he is anxious to get transferred to a battleship on the front lines of the Pacific theatre. Constantly stymied by his controlling captain, who benefits from the efficiency of Roberts's talents, the transfer only comes through when the crew risks court martial by submitting forged paperwork. This small victory turns sour when Roberts's new ship is struck by a Japanese kamikaze shortly after his arrival, and he is killed. Moreover, the senseless dark comedy of war — he wanted to see action — is further accented by the manner in which he died. Roberts was not manning some battle post battery but rather he was below deck drinking coffee when death arrived. Yet, a provocative last message from Roberts arrives in a letter he sent his replacement, back on the *Reluctant*, which reads, in part,

> I had to be here, I guess. But I'm thinking now of ... all the guys everywhere who sail from Tedium to Apathy and back again — with an occasional side trip to Monotony.... But I've discovered, Doc [his best friend], that the most terrible enemy of this war is the boredom that eventually becomes a faith and, therefore, a sort of suicide.[22]

I posit that the "Tedium to Apathy ... that eventually becomes ... a sort of suicide" is as apt a description/cause of Cuppy's suicide and Benchley's giving up on life as any explanation. Interestingly, though the play and film versions of *Mister Roberts* minimize any death wish feelings of the title character, the beginning of the quote suggests a Cuppy-like demise: "I had to be here, I guess." However, in the original novel there is no second-guessing the darker meaning. While the quoted passage from Roberts's letter does not appear in the book — only some general small talk about said letter — the following conversation between his closest friends from the *Reluctant* spell it out:

> Pulver spoke with sudden anguish: "Isn't that rough, Doc? You know how he [Roberts] batted his head to get off of here? You know how he wanted to get in the war? And then, as soon as he gets out there, he gets killed." His voice was almost pleading.
>
> The Doc nodded and chewed his lip. "That's funny," he said thoughtfully.
>
> "Funny?"
>
> The Doc looked up. "I don't mean funny, Frank," he said softly. He paused for a moment. "I mean that I think that's what he wanted."[23]

In Robert Match's review of the *Mister Roberts* novel, the newspaper critic might have been describing the humorist when he wrote, "Mr. Roberts' plight, the tragedy of the 'high-strung instrument in the low-strung role,' lies, like much of this book, somewhere between tears and laughter."[24]

Mr. Roberts died doing what Cuppy liked best — drinking coffee. Like Mr. Roberts, the war killed many people who never saw direct action. In fact, several Cuppy friends categorized the humorist this way, as Thomas Maeder observed in his "Afterword" to *The Decline and Fall of Practically Everybody*:

> When the war ended, he said he felt that he had died, as though one of the bombs had killed him.... He began to say he had written all he knew how to write, and that he was unable to do any more.[25]

That's as good a suicide note as any. Though Cuppy lived, after a fashion, for a short time following the war, death was just off stage. He had believed in neither superhumans (especially *not* Aristotle!), nor the supernatural. What he did believe in was the satirical questioning of all things human. When he could no longer maintain his own steeped-in-research brand of iconoclasm, he chose to end his life. Of course, being a very funny cynic, who is not to say that the last thoughts of this exceptionally frugal fellow were not unlike the closing to the sometimes Cuppy-like Woody Allen's *Love and Death* (1975), "The, the key here, I think, is to, to not think of death as an end but, but think of it more as a very effective way of, of cutting down on your expenses." Nonetheless, Cuppy's purpose in being the eternal dissenter about man's legacy, whether in his "animal" stories or his biting historical profiles, might be found in a final quote from Orwell (*1984*), "Who controls the past controls the future."[26] Regardless, with Cuppy's death, the world became a duller place.

Chapter Notes

Preface

1. Will Cuppy, *The Decline and Fall of Practically Everybody* (1950; rpt. Boston: Nonpareil Books, 1984), 42.
2. See the author's "*Mr. B" Or, Comforting Thoughts About the Bison* (Westport, CT: Greenwood Press, 1992); and *Film Classics Reclassified: A Shocking Spoof of Cinema* (Davenport, Iowa: Robin Vincent, 2001).
3. See the author's *Robert Wise: Shadowland* (Indianapolis: Indiana Historical Press, 2012).
4. The Erich Segal quote appears in Deborah Copaken Kogans's "Only Yesterday," *New York Times*, May 27, 2012, Book Review section, 27.
5. Max Eastman, *Enjoyment of Laughter* (New York: Simon & Schuster, 1936), 114.
6. Will Cuppy, Correspondence to Max Eastman, undated [1936], in Max Eastman Papers, Will Cuppy folder, Lilly Library, Indiana University, Bloomington, Indiana.

Chapter One

1. A.M. Sperber, *Murrow: His Life and Times* (New York: Freundlich Books, 1986), 470.
2. Stanley Kunitz and Howard Haycraft, eds., *Twentieth Century Authors* (New York: H.W. Wilson Co., 1942), 341.
3. Anthony Lane, "The Current Cinema: Devotions," *New Yorker*, August 29, 2011, 82.
4. Will Cuppy, *How to Tell Your Friends from the Apes* (1931; rpt. Boston: Nonpareil Books, 2005), 107.
5. Will Cuppy, *How to Become Extinct* (1941; rpt. Garden City, NY: Garden City Books, 1951), 31.
6. Ibid., 6.
7. Will Cuppy, *How to Attract the Wombat* (1949; rpt. Chicago: University of Chicago Press, 1983), 2.
8. Cuppy, *How to Tell Your Friends from the Apes*, xiv.
9. Charles Poore, "Books of the Times," *New York Times*, December 6, 1941, 15.
10. See the author's *The Marx Brothers: A Bio-Bibliography* (Westport, CT: Greenwood Press, 1987); and *Groucho & W.C. Fields: Huckster Comedians* (Jackson: University Press of Mississippi, 1994).
11. Thomas Maeder, afterword in *The Decline and Fall of Practically Everybody* by Will Cuppy (1950; rpt. Boston: Nonpareil Books, 1984), 232. (This special edition celebrated the centennial of Cuppy's birth, 1884–1984.)
12. Isabel Paterson Papers, Will Cuppy correspondence, Folder 1 (page 74, approximately letter 39), undated (circa mid-1920s), Herbert Hoover Presidential Library, West Branch, Iowa.
13. Ibid., Folder 1 (page 3, approximately letter 2), undated (circa 1923).
14. Ibid., Folder 1 (page 76, approximately letter 40), undated (circa 1924).
15. Robert N. Scott, ed., *War of the Rebellion: A Compilation of the Official Records of the Union and Confederate Armies* (Washington, D.C.: Government Printing Office, 1882), 248.
16. Ibid.
17. Alice Wayzata Chilcote, "The Cuppys of Whitley County — Abraham Cuppy & Sarah Collins Cuppy of South Whitley, Ind.," *Whitley County Roots* (the newsletter of the Whitley County Genealogical Society), Columbus City, Indiana, April 1999, 7.
18. Ibid.
19. Cuppy, *The Decline and Fall of Practically Everybody*, 62.
20. Ibid., 152.
21. Ibid., 42.
22. Paterson Papers, Will Cuppy correspondence, Folder 1 (page 42, approximately letter 15), undated (circa August 1924).

23. John Towner Frederick Papers, Will Cuppy correspondence, Box 32, Folder 3, biographical background letter, undated (circa 1941), Special Collections, University of Iowa, Iowa City, Iowa.
24. Burton Rascoe, *Before I Forget* (New York: Literary Guild of America, Inc., 1937), 179.
25. Frederick papers, Will Cuppy correspondence, Box 32, Folder 3, biographical background letter, undated (circa 1941).
26. "Death of Mrs. Cuppy," *Columbia City Post*, November 28, 1900.
27. Frederick Papers, Will Cuppy correspondence, Box 32 Folder 3, biographical background letter, undated (circa 1941).
28. Paterson Papers, Will Cuppy correspondence, Folder 2 (page 83, approximately letter 45), undated (circa 1929).
29. Ibid., Folder 1 (page 42, approximately letter 15), undated (circa August 1924).
30. Frederick Papers, Will Cuppy correspondence, Box 32, folder 2 (January 31, 1942).
31. Cuppy, *How to Become Extinct*, 64.
32. Will Cuppy, *How to Get from January to December* (1951; rpt. New York: Dell, 1962), 244.
33. Paterson Papers, Will Cuppy correspondence, Folder 1 (page 75, approximately letter 41, undated (circa 1927).
34. Cuppy, *How to Tell Your Friends from the Apes*, 8.
35. Paterson Papers, Will Cuppy correspondence, Folder 3 (page 10, letter 4), undated (circa 1926).
36. Ibid., Folder 3 (page 1, letter 1) undated (circa 1926).
37. Charles Bukowski, *Ham on Rye* (1984; rpt. New York: HarperCollins, 2002), 192.
38. Ibid., 166.
39. Mary Frances Lilly will, *Probate Order Book*, Circuit Court, DeKalb County, Indiana, December 12, 1927, p. 495. Recorded in *Will Record Book 7*, p. 484.
40. Wes D. Gehring, *Red Skelton: The Mask Behind the Mask* (Indianapolis: Indiana Historical Society Press, 2008).
41. "Will Cuppy, Critic and Author, Was 65," *New York Times*, September 20, 1949, 29.
42. See the author's *Leo McCarey: From Marx to McCarthy* (Lanham, MD: Scarecrow Press, 2005), 3.

Chapter Two

1. Will Cuppy, *Maroon Tales: University of Chicago Stories* (1909/1910; rpt. Nabu Public Domain Reprints, originally published by Chicago's Forbes & Company), 63.

2. John Towner Frederick Papers, Will Cuppy correspondence, Box 32, Folder 3, undated letter, page 4 (circa Christmas 1941), Special Collections, University of Iowa, Iowa City, Iowa.
3. Phone interviews with the Auburn Public Library reference person, the head librarian at DeKalb High School, and Joyce Heite of the Whitley County Genealogical Society, all September 2, 2011.
4. Burton Rascoe, *Before I Forget* (New York: Literary Guild of America, Inc., 1937), 176.
5. Ibid., 177.
6. John Martin Smith, *History of DeKalb County Indiana* (1987; rpt. Auburn, IN: Natmus, Inc., 1992).
7. Ibid.
8. Will Cuppy, *How to Become Extinct* (1941; rpt. Garden City, NY: Garden City Books, 1951), 163.
9. Cuppy, *Maroon Tales: University of Chicago Stories*, 289.
10. Will Cuppy, *The Decline and Fall of Practically Everybody* (1950; rpt. Boston: Nonpareil Books, 1984), 8.
11. Cuppy, *Maroon Tales: University of Chicago Stories*, 289–290.
12. Smith, *History of DeKalb County Indiana*.
13. Cuppy, *Maroon Tales: University of Chicago Stories*, 253.
14. Frederick Papers, Cuppy Correspondence, Box 32, Folder 3, July 17, 1942 letter.
15. Jane Addams Hull House Association site, http://www.hullhouse.org.
16. "James Weber Linn, Educator, 63, Dead," *New York Times*, July 17, 1939, 19.
17. "Robert M. Lovett, Educator, Is Dead," *New York Times*, February 9, 1956.
18. Cuppy, *Maroon Tales: University of Chicago Stories*, 291.
19. Smith, *History of DeKalb County Indiana*.
20. See the author's *American Dark Comedy: Beyond Satire* (Westport, CT: Greenwood Press, 1996).
21. Stephen Cox, *The Women and the Dynamo: Isabel Paterson and the Idea of America* (New Brunswick: Transaction, 2004), 334.
22. Robert Herrick, 70, "Aide Ickes, Dead," *New York Times*, December 24, 1938, 15.
23. Robert Herrick dust jacket profile, *The Web of Life* (1900; rpt. U.K: Dodo Press, 2011).
24. Will Cuppy, *How to Be a Hermit* (1929; rpt. New York: Liveright, 1987), 216.
25. Will Cuppy, *How to Tell Your Friends from the Apes* (1931; rpt. Boston: Nonpareil Books, 2005), 50.

26. Robert Herrick website, http://en.wiki pedia.org/wiki/Robert_Herrick_(novelist).
27. Will Cuppy, *How to Attract the Wombat* (1949; rpt. Chicago: University of Chicago Press, 1983), 97.
28. Cuppy, *Maroon Tales: University of Chicago Stories*, 284–285.
29. "Stagg Dies at 102; Dean of Coaches," *New York Times*, March 18, 1965, 1, 30.
30. Cuppy, *Maroon Tales: University of Chicago Stories*, 283.
31. James Thurber, *My Life and Hard Times* (1933; rpt. New York: Bantam Books, 1947), 120, 123.
32. Cuppy, *Maroon Tales: University of Chicago Stories*, 277.
33. Rascoe, *Before I Forget*, 177.
34. Stanley J. Kunitz, ed., *Authors Today and Yesterday* (New York: H.W. Wilson, 1933), 182.
35. Isabel Paterson Papers, Will Cuppy correspondence, Folder 3 (pages 73 and 74, approximately letter 33), undated (circa 1927), Herbert Hoover Presidential Library, West Branch, Iowa.
36. Fred Feldkamp, "Introduction," in Will Cuppy's *The Decline and Fall of Practically Everybody*, 2.
37. See the Will Cuppy Papers, Special Collections Research Center, University of Chicago Library, Chicago, Illinois.
38. Leonard Louis Levinson, *The Left Handed Dictionary* (New York: Collier Books, 1978), 82.
39. William Jacob Cuppy, *The Elizabethan Conception of Prose Style* (Chicago: University of Chicago Department of English, 1914), 42.
40. Cuppy, *How to Tell Your Friends from the Apes*, 36.
41. Cuppy, *The Decline and Fall of Practically Everybody*, 86.
42. Cuppy, *How to Attract the Wombat*, 10.
43. For example, see W.C. Sellar and R.J. Yeatman's *Garden Rubbish & Other Country Bumps* (New York: Farrar & Rinehart, 1937).
44. Cuppy, *How to Tell Your Friends from the Apes*, 17.
45. Cuppy, *How to Become Extinct*, 84.
46. Cuppy, *How to Tell Your Friends from the Apes*, 34.
47. Ibid., 46.
48. Cuppy, *How to Become Extinct*, 81.
49. Ibid., 112, 112–114.
50. Wes D. Gehring, *Film Classics Reclassified: A Shocking Spoof of Cinema* (Davenport, IA: Robin Vincent Publishing, 2001).
51. Roger Rosenblatt, "The Spooky Art," *New York Times*, July 10, 2011, Book Review section, 27.

Chapter Three

1. Will Cuppy, *How to Tell Your Friends from the Apes* (1931; rpt. Boston: Nonpareil Books, 2005), dedication.
2. Jed Perl, "Freedom of Expression," *New York Times*, July 10, 2011, Book Review section, 14.
3. Paul Murray Kendall, *The Art of Biography* (1965; rpt. W.W. Norton, 1985), 130.
4. Christopher Buckley, *Losing Mum and Pup* (New York: Twelve Hachette Book Group, 2009), 68.
5. Bill Russell (with Alan Steinberg), *Red and Me: My Coach, My Lifelong Friend* (New York: HarperCollins, 2009), 145.
6. Thomas Maeder, afterword in *The Decline and Fall of Practically Everybody* by Will Cuppy (1950; rpt. Boston: Nonpareil Books, 1984), 233.
7. Burton Rascoe, *Before I Forget* (New York: Literary Guild of America, 1937), 179.
8. Stephen Cox, *The Woman and the Dynamo: Isabel Paterson and the Idea of America* (New Brunswick, NJ: Transaction Publisher, 2004), 92.
9. Ibid., 93.
10. Isabel Paterson Papers, Will Cuppy correspondence, Folder 2 (page 4, letter 3), undated (circa 1927), Herbert Hoover Presidential Library, West Branch, Iowa.
11. Will Cuppy, *How to Be a Hermit* (1929; rpt. New York: Liveright, 1987), 174.
12. Ibid., 178.
13. Isabel Paterson, "Turns with a Bookworm," *New York Herald Tribune*, June 24, 1934.
14. Cox, *the Woman and the Dynamo: Isabel Paterson and the Idea of America*, 67.
15. Paterson Papers, Will Cuppy correspondence, Folder 1 (page 79, approximately letter 41), undated (circa 1925).
16. Gilbert Seldes, *The 7 Lively Arts* (1924; rpt New York: McCelland and Stewart Limited, 1957).
17. Paterson Papers, Will Cuppy correspondence, Folder 1 (page 6, approximately letter 3), undated (circa 1924).
18. Will Cuppy, "Mystery and Adventure," *New York Herald Tribune*, September 15, 1946, 7:19.
19. Paterson Papers, Will Cuppy correspondence, Folder 1 (page 6, approximately letter 3), undated (circa 1924).
20. Ibid., Folder 1 (page 31, approximately letter 13), undated (circa mid-1920s).
21. Robert Benchley, *After 1903—What?* (New York: Harper & Brothers, 1938), 42.
22. Hells Kitchen, Manhattan, http://en.wiki pedia.org/wiki/Hell's_Kitchen,_Manhattan.

23. Cox, *The Woman and the Dynamo: Isabel Paterson and the Idea of America*, 184.
24. Cuppy, *The Decline and Fall of Practically Everybody*, 154.
25. Paterson Papers, Will Cuppy correspondence, Folder 1, (p 67, approximately letter 35), undated (circa 1925).
26. Cox, *The Woman and the Dynamo: Isabel Paterson and the Idea of America*, 94.
27. Oscar Levant, *The Memoirs of an Amnesiac* (1965; rpt. New York: Bantam Books, 1966); Oscar Levant, *The Unimportance of Being Oscar* (1968; rpt. New York: Pocket Books, 1969).
28. Oscar Levant, *A Smattering of Ignorance* (Garden City, NY: Garden City, 1942), ix.
29. Cox, *The Woman and the Dynamo: Isabel Paterson and the Idea of America*, 94.
30. Ibid., 89.
31. Paterson Papers, Will Cuppy correspondence, Folder 1 (page 26, approximately letter 12), undated (circa 1925).
32. Ibid., Folder 1 (page 50, approximately letter 21), undated (circa 1925).
33. Frank Sullivan, "Will Cuppy: A Wry and Witty Humorist," *New York Herald Tribune*, November 20, 1949, Book Review section, 7.
34. Paterson Papers, Will Cuppy correspondence, Folder 3 (page 25, approximately letter 11), undated (circa 1929).
35. Stanley Kunitz, Howard Haycraft, and Wilbur Hadden, *Authors Today and Yesterday* (New York: H.W. Wilson Co., 1933), 183.
36. Paterson Papers, Will Cuppy correspondence, Folder 1 (page 9, approximately letter 4), undated (circa 1925).
37. Ibid., Folder 1 (page 10, approximately letter 5).
38. Isabel Paterson, "Turns with a Bookworm," *New York Herald Tribune*, September 24, 1939, Books section.
39. Several sources, including Cox's biography of Paterson.
40. Cuppy, *The Decline and Fall of Practically Everybody*, 18.
41. Ibid., 19.
42. Cox, *The Woman and the Dynamo: Isabel Paterson and the Idea of America*, 94.
43. Paterson Papers, Will Cuppy correspondence, Folder 1 (page 17, approximately letter 8), undated (circa 1925).
44. Ibid., Folder 2 (page 61, approximately letter 32), undated (circa 1928).
45. Ibid., Folder 3 (page 29, approximately letter 14), undated (circa 1929).
46. Harrison Kinney, *James Thurber: His Life and Times* (New York: Henry Holt, 1995), 457.
47. Ibid., 581.
48. Neil A. Grauer, *Remember Laughter: A Life of James Thurber* (Lincoln: University of Nebraska Press, 1995), 41.
49. Thomas Maeder, e-mail to the author, October 24, 2011.
50. Paterson Papers, Will Cuppy correspondence, Folder 2 (pages 1–2, letter 2), undated (circa 1927).
51. Charles Bukowski, *Ham on Rye* (1984; rpt. New York: HarperCollins, 2002), 210.
52. Gilbert Seldes, *The 7 Lively Arts* (1924; rpt. New York: McClelland and Stewart, 1957), 212.

Chapter Four

1. Will Cuppy, *How to be A Hermit* (1929; rpt. New York: Liveright, 1987), 22.
2. Henry David Thoreau, *Walden*, ed. Jeffrey S. Cramer (1854; rpt. New Haven, CT: Yale University Press, 2006), 19.
3. Ibid., 182–183.
4. Ralph Waldo Emerson, *Selected Writings*, ed. Brooks Atkinson (New York: Modern Library, 1950), 898.
5. Thoreau, *Walden*, 59.
6. Garrison Keillor, "Trailblazer," *New York Times*, October 23, 2011, Book Review section, 15.
7. Cuppy, *How to Be a Hermit*, 257.
8. See the author's *Screwball Comedy: A Genre of Madcap Romance* (Westport, CT: Greenwood Press, 1986), 28.
9. Cuppy, *How to Be a Hermit*, 155.
10. John Gerber, "New England and Crackerbarrel Philosophy" (lecture in *American Humor and Satire* class, University of Iowa, 1975).
11. Walter Blair, *Horse Sense in American Humor* (Chicago: University of Chicago Press, 1942), vii.
12. See the author's extensive writing on American comedy genres, particularly the aforementioned *Screwball Comedy: A Genre of Madcap Romance*, and *Populism and the Capra Legacy* (Westport, CT: Greenwood Press, 1995).
13. See the author's books on the subject: *Leo McCarey and the Comic Antihero in American Humor* (New York: Arno Press, 1980); *Laurel & Hardy: A Bio-Bibliography* (Westport, CT: Greenwood Press, 1990); and *Leo McCarey: From Marx to McCarthy* (Lanham, Maryland: Scarecrow Press, 2005).
14. Cuppy, *How to Be a Hermit*, 109, 115.
15. Robert Benchley, *Love Conquers All* (New York: Henry Holt, 1922), 298.
16. Cuppy, *How to Be a Hermit*, 20, 82, 27.
17. Ibid., 32

18. See the author's "*Mr. B" Or, Comforting Thoughts About the Bison: A Critical Biography of Robert Benchley* (Westport, CT: Greenwood Press, 1992).
19. Robert Benchley, *My Ten Years in a Quandary and How They Grew* (1936; rpt. Garden City, NY: Blue Ribbon Books, 1940), 28.
20. Will Rogers, *Letters of a Self-Made Diplomat to His President* (New York: Albert & Charles Boni, 1926), 234.
21. Cuppy, *How to Be a Hermit*, 107, 113.
22. Ibid., 55.
23. Ibid., 111.
24. Robert Benchley, *The Treasurer's Report and Other Aspects of Community Singing* (New York: Grosset & Dunlap, 1930), 220, 231; Robert Benchley, *From Bed to Worse, or Comforting Thoughts about the Bison* (New York: Harper & Brothers, 1934), 26–31.
25. Cuppy, *How to Be a Hermit*, 200.
26. Ibid., 238.
27. Ibid., 21.
28. Robert Benchley, *Pluck and Luck* (New York: Henry Holt, 1925), 217–223.
29. Benchley, *From Bed to Worse, or Comforting Thoughts about the Bison*, 255–259.
30. Will Cuppy Papers, Special Collections Research Center, University of Chicago Library, Box 102, folder 4, Chicago, Illinois.
31. Cuppy, *How to Be a Hermit*, 108.
32. "Mr. Cuppy's Life as a Part-time Hermit," *New York Times*, December 29, 1929, 4:15.
33. Isabel Paterson Papers, Will Cuppy correspondence, Folder 2 (page 44, approximately letter 22) undated (circa 1927), Herbert Hoover Presidential Library, West Branch, Iowa.
34. Ibid., Folder 2 (page 14, approximately letter 7), undated (circa 1927).
35. Ibid., Folder 3 (page 3, letter 2), undated (circa 1926).
36. Will Cuppy, *The Decline and Fall of Practically Everybody* (1950; rpt. Boston: Nonpareil Books, 1984), 56.
37. Paterson Papers, Will Cuppy correspondence, Folder 2 (page 58, approximately letter 31), undated (circa 1927), Herbert Hoover Presidential Library.
38. Ibid., Folder 2 (page 40, approximately letter 21), undated (circa 1927).
39. Ibid., Folder 3 (page 24, approximately letter 11), undated (circa 1926).
40. Ibid., Folder 1 (page 66, approximately letter 34), undated (circa 1926).
41. Thomas Maeder e-mail to the author, October 24, 2011.
42. Paterson Papers, Will Cuppy correspondence, Folder 1 (page 27, approximately letter 12) undated (circa 1925), Herbert Hoover Presidential Library.
43. Ibid., Folder 2 (page 53, approximately letter 28), undated (circa 1927).
44. Ibid.
45. Ibid., Folder 2 (page 7, approximately letter 4) undated (circa 1926).
46. Ibid., Folder 2 (page 25, approximately letter 14) undated (circa 1927).
47. James Thurber, "The Greatest Man in the World" (1931), *The Thurber Carnival* (New York: Dell, 1964), 154–160.
48. Dilly Tante, ed., "H.L. Mencken" entry, *Living Authors: A Book of Biographies* (New York: H.L. Wilson, 1931), 264–265.
49. Paterson Papers, Will Cuppy correspondence, Folder 1 (page 5, approximately letter 3) undated (circa 1924).
50. Ibid., Folder 1 (page 84, approximately letter 45), undated (circa 1925).
51. Ibid., Folder 2 (page 69, approximately letter 39), undated (circa 1927).
52. See the author's *W.C. Fields: A Bio-Bibliography* (Westport, CT: Greenwood Press, 1984); and *Groucho & W.C. Fields: Huckster Comedians* (Jackson: University Press of Mississippi, 1994).
53. Paterson Papers, Will Cuppy Correspondence, Folder 3 (page 2, letter 1) undated (circa 1925).
54. Ibid., Folder 2 (page 39, approximately letter 20) undated (circa 1927).
55. Jo Ranson, "Living from Can to Mouth," *Brooklyn Eagle*, November 24, 1929.
56. Ibid.
57. Will Cuppy, "The Hermit Looks at Bookshops," *Author's League Bulletin*, December 1929, 9.
58. Will Cuppy, "Little Brother of the Clam," *New York Herald Tribune*, September 29, 1929, 12:7.
59. Ibid.
60. Isabel Paterson, "Turns with a Bookworm," *New York Herald Tribune*, September 22, 1929, 12:23.
61. Ibid., September 29, 1929, 12:43.
62. Ibid., October 13, 1929, 12: 27.
63. Ibid., November 10, 1929, 12: 27.
64. Ibid., September 29, 1929, 12: 43.
65. Andy Borowitz, *The 50 Funniest American Writers* (New York: Library of America, 2011), 94–101.
66. Frank Sullivan, "Humorist Turns Critic, Reviewer," uncredited, circa late 1929, in the Will Cuppy Papers, Special Collections Research Center, University of Chicago Library, Box 108, scrapbook 1.
67. "Mr. Cuppy's Life as a Part-time Hermit."
68. Sam Kashner and Nancy Schoenberger, *A Talent for Genius: The Life and Times of Oscar Levant* (New York: Random House, 1994), 243–244.

Chapter Five

1. Will Cuppy, *How to Tell Your Friends from the Apes* (1931; rpt. Boston: Nonpareil Books, 2005), 29.
2. Ibid., 36.
3. Stanley Cavell, *The Senses of Walden* (New York: Viking Press, 1972), 5.
4. Cuppy, *How to Tell Your Friends from the Apes*, xiv.
5. Robert Moses, *Public Works: A Dangerous Trade* (New York: McGraw-Hill, 1970), 1.
6. Isabel Paterson Papers, Will Cuppy correspondence, Folder 3 (page 94, approximately letter 43), undated (circa 1929), Herbert Hoover Presidential Library, West Branch, Iowa.
7. Moses, *Public Works: A Dangerous Trade*, 104.
8. Robert Moses, "From the Bridge: More About Will Cuppy," *Newsday*, May 28, 1966, 4 w.
9. Ibid.
10. Will Cuppy, *How to Be a Hermit* (1929; rpt. New York: Liveright, 1987), 41.
11. Ibid., 42.
12. Andrew Delbanco, "The Reviewer," *New York Times*, November 13, 2011, Book Review section, 10.
13. Henry D. Thoreau, *Walden; and Resistance to Civil Government*, ed. William Rossi (New York: Norton & Company, 1992).
14. Moses, *Public Works: A Dangerous Trade*, 104.
15. Multiple sources, such as: Neil Lancotot's *Campy: The Two Lives of Roy Campanella* (New York: Simon & Schuster, 2011), 359, 361.
16. Will Cuppy, *How to Attract the Wombat* (1949; rpt. Chicago: University of Chicago Press, 1983), 3.
17. Frank Bruni, "The Director of 'Sideways' Sees His Life Go Forward," *New York Times*, November 13, 2011, Arts & Leisure section, 12.
18. Cuppy, *How to Tell Your Friends from the Apes*, 46.
19. See the author's *W.C. Fields: A Bio-Bibliography* (Westport, CT: Greenwood Press, 1984), 91.
20. Cuppy, *How to Tell Your Friends from the Apes*, 43.
21. Sandra Lieb, "Will Cuppy," in *Dictionary of Literary Biography*, Vol. 11, editor Stanley Trachtenberg (Detroit: Gale Research Co., 1982), 97.
22. Cuppy, *How to Tell Your Friends from the Apes*, 67.
23. Ibid., 60.
24. Ibid., 107.
25. Paterson Papers, Will Cuppy correspondence, Folder 2 (page 52, approximately letter 27) undated (circa 1929), Herbert Hoover Presidential Library.
26. Ibid., Folder 1 (page 53, approximately letter 24).
27. See the author's *Groucho & W.C. Fields: Huckster Comedians* (Jackson: University of Mississippi Press, 1994).
28. David Greenberg, "Standing Pat," *New York Times*, November 20, 2011, Book Review section, 9.
29. Dwight Gardner, "Bring It On," *New York Times*, October 23, 2011, Book Review section, 35.
30. Will Cuppy, "Little Brother of the Clam," *New York Herald Tribune*, September 29, 1929, 12:7.
31. Isabel Paterson, "Turns with a Bookworm," *New York Herald Tribune*, September 22, 1929, 12:23.
32. Will Cuppy, "Mystery and Adventure," *New York Herald Tribune*, October 6, 1929, 12:15.
33. Ibid., September 15, 1929, 12:26.
34. Ibid., November 10, 1929, 12:24.
35. Ibid., October 6, 1929.
36. Ibid., November 10, 1929.
37. P.G. Wodehouse, introduction to *How to Tell Your Friends from the Apes*, x.
38. P.G. Wodehouse, "Out-Topping Knowledge," *New York Herald Tribune*, November 29, 1931, 11:4.
39. Kenneth McLeigh, *Arts in the Twentieth Century* (1985; rpt. New York: Penguin Books, 1986), 199.

Chapter Six

1. Sam Kashner and Nancy Schoenberger, *A Talent For Genius: The Life and Times of Oscar Levant* (New York: Random House, 1994), 341.
2. Isabel Paterson Papers, Will Cuppy Correspondence, Folder 1 (page 11, approximately letter 5) undated (circa 1924), Herbert Hoover Presidential Library, West Branch, Iowa.
3. Ambrose Bierce, *The Devil's Dictionary* (1911; rpt. New York: Dover, 1958), 88.
4. Ambrose Bierce, *The Sardonic Humor of Ambrose Bierce*, ed. George Barkin (New York: Dover, 1963), 42.
5. Jean-Dominique Bauby, *The Diving Bell and the Butterfly*, trans. Jeremy Leggatt (1996; rpt. New York: Vintage Books, 1997).
6. See the author's *"Mr. B" Or Comforting Thoughts About the Bison: A Critical Biography of Robert Benchley* (Westport, CT: Greenwood Press, 1992).

7. Stephen Cox, *The Woman and the Dynamo: Isabel Paterson and the Idea of America* (New Brunswick, NJ: Transaction Publishers, 2004), 67.
8. Paterson Papers, Will Cuppy Correspondence, Folder 1 (page 15, approximately letter 7), undated (circa 1924), Herbert Hoover Presidential Library.
9. Bauby, *The Diving Bell and the Butterfly*, 82.
10. Ibid., 94.
11. Eric Weiner, "Americans Undecided About God?" *New York Times*, December 11, 2011, Sunday Review section, 5.
12. Isabel Paterson, "Turns with a Bookworm," *New York Herald Tribune*, October 11, 1931, 11:14.
13. "Benches," *Newsweek*, December 27, 1943, 10.
14. Will Cuppy, "Hither and Yon," *New York Herald Tribune*, January 17, 1926, 6:12.
15. Stanley J. Kunitz, ed., "Will Cuppy" entry in *Authors Today and Yesterday* (New York: H.W. Wilson Company, 1933), 183.
16. Isabel Paterson Papers, Paterson Letter to Will Cuppy, Folder 1 (pp. 117–118, letter 1), undated (late summer 1929).
17. Ibid., postcard to Will Cuppy, Folder 1 (p 116, postcard 2), undated (late summer 1929).
18. Paterson, "Turns with a Bookworm," *New York Herald Tribune*, September 15, 1929, 12:27.
19. Will Cuppy, "Kidding a Continent," *New York Herald Tribune*, September 6, 1931, 11:11.
20. Will Cuppy, "Certainly, I Play the Piano!," in *The Home Book of Laughter*, ed. May Lamberton Becker (New York: Dodd, Mead & Company, 1948), 32.
21. Bud Schulberg, *The Disenchanted* (New York: Random House, 1950), 119.
22. Charles J. Shields, *And So It Goes: Kurt Vonnegut: A Life* (New York: Henry Holt, 2011), 90.
23. Frank Sullivan Papers, Sullivan Letter to Will Cuppy on *New York World* stationery, Cuppy Folder, dated August 23, 1929, Manuscript Collection, Cornell University, Ithaca, New York.
24. Ibid., Sullivan Letter to Will Cuppy on *New Yorker* stationery, with the salutation, "Dear Cup," Cuppy Folder, undated (circa early 1930s).
25. Ibid.
26. Ibid.
27. David Derby, "Double Dare," *New Yorker*, December 12, 2011, 94.
28. Frank Sullivan Papers, Sullivan letter to Will Cuppy, Cuppy Folder, dated November 1, 1934.
29. Ibid.
30. Ibid., Sullivan letter to Will Cuppy, post-dated "1930?"
31. Ibid., Sullivan letter to Will Cuppy dated August 7, 1937.
32. Paterson, "Turns with a Bookworm," *New York Herald Tribune*, November 22, 1931, 11:19.
33. Ibid., December 6, 1931, 11:31.
34. Frank Sullivan Papers, Sullivan letter to Will Cuppy, Cuppy Folder, undated [1928].
35. Ibid., May 17, 1927.
36. Ibid.
37. Ibid., August 7, 1937.
38. Will Cuppy Papers, William Steig letter to Will Cuppy, Box 96: Folder 24 (William Steig correspondence), undated letter (1936), Special Collections, University of Chicago, Chicago, Illinois.
39. Sarah Boxer, "William Steig, 95, Cartoonist and Master of Damsels, Drunks and Satyrs, Dies," *New York Times*, October 6, 2003, 1: 39.
40. Will Cuppy Papers, William Steig letter to Will Cuppy, Box 96: Folder 24 (William Steig correspondence) May 31, 1935.
41. Ibid.
42. Ibid., undated letter (circa 1941).
43. William Saroyan, introduction to *The Lonely Ones*, by William Steig (1942; rpt. New York: Windmill Books, 1970), 6–7.
44. "William Steig," in *Current Biography 1944*, ed. Anna Rothe (New York: H.W. Wilson, 1945), 653.
45. Claudia J. Nahson, introduction to *The Art of William Steig* (New Haven, CT: Yale University Press, 2007), 5.
46. Jeanne Steig, "Clowning Around," in *The Art of William Steig*, 73, 75, 78.
47. Shields, *And So It Goes: Kurt Vonnegut: A Life*, 251.
48. Ibid., 158.
49. Jim Knipfel, *Quitting the Nairobi Trio* (2000; rpt. New York: Berkley Books, 2001), 277.

Chapter Seven

1. Jincy Willett, "Henry Alford on How to Behave," *New York Times*, January 8, 2012, Book Review section: 8.
2. See the author's *Screwball Comedy: A Genre of Madcap Romance* (Westport, CT: Greenwood Press, 1986), and *Romantic vs. Screwball Comedy: Charting the Difference* (Lanham, MD: Scarecrow Press, 2002).
3. Herb Stone, *I Married a Witch* review, *Rob Wagner's Script*, December 19, 1942, in *Selected Film Criticism, 1941–1950*, ed. Anthony

Slide (Metuchen, NJ: Scarecrow Press, 1983), 85.

4. Pagan Kennedy, "Rewiring Reality," *New York Times*, January 15, 2012, Book Review section: 8.

5. See Roger Kahn's *A Flame of Pure Fire: Jack Dempsey and the Roaring '20s* (New York: Harcourt, Brace, 1999).

6. See the author's *American Dark Comedy: Beyond Satire* (Westport, CT: Greenwood Press, 1996).

7. Isabel Paterson, *The Golden Vanity* (New York: William Morrow, 1934), Kindle version, Loc 370.

8. Ibid, Kindle version, Loc 1057.

9. For example, see Louis Kronenberger's, "'The Golden Vanity' and Other Recent Works of Fiction," *New York Times*, October 21, 1934, 5:6.

10. Ibid.

11. Paterson, *The Golden Vanity*, Kindle version, Loc 1229.

12. Frank Sullivan Papers, Sullivan Letter to Will Cuppy, Cuppy Folder, dated Friday [1929], Manuscript Collection, Cornell University, Ithaca, New York.

13. Paterson, *The Golden Vanity*, Kindle version, Loc 1661, 1684.

14. Ibid., Kindle version, Loc 480, 3823.

15. Frank Sullivan Papers, Sullivan Letter to Will Cuppy, Cuppy Folder, May 17, 1927, Manuscript Collection, Cornell University.

16. Paterson, *The Golden Vanity*, Kindle version, Loc 1084.

17. Ibid., Kindle version, Loc 1788.

18. Ibid., Kindle version, Loc 4076, 3943, 3949.

19. Frank Sullivan Papers, Sullivan Letter to Will Cuppy, Cuppy Folder, September 23, 1929.

20. Will Cuppy, "Bluebirds and What Not," *New York Herald Tribune*, December 8, 1929, 12:5.

21. Paterson, *The Golden Vanity*, Kindle version, Loc 3904.

22. Ibid., Kindle version, Loc 2902.

23. Isabel Paterson, "The Abbe Children, Who Are Never Bored," *New York Herald Tribune*, April 5, 1936, 7:3.

24. Paterson, *The Golden Vanity*, Kindle version, Loc 2006.

25. Will Cuppy, *How to Tell Your Friends from the Apes* (1931; rpt. Boston: Nonpareil Books, 2005), 18.

26. Will Cuppy, "Mystery and Adventure," *New York Herald Tribune*, April 12, 1936, 7:15.

27. Isabel Paterson, "Turns with a Bookworm," *New York Herald Tribune*, April 12, 1936, 7:19.

28. See the author's "*Mr. B" Or Comforting Thoughts About the Bison: A Critical Biography of Robert Benchley* (Westport, CT: Greenwood Press, 1992).

29. Will Cuppy, "Mystery and Adventure," *New York Herald Tribune*, April 5, 1936, 7:22.

30. Ibid., July 19, 1931, 11:13.

31. Ibid., August 16, 1931, 11:14; November 15, 1931, 11:24.

32. Ibid., November 3, 1929, 12:14.

33. Ibid., September 11, 1949, 7:18.

34. Ibid., April 12, 1936, 7:15.

35. Ibid.

36. Adam Kirsch, "In Praise of Style," *New York Times*, January 22, 2012, Book Review section: 13.

37. Will Cuppy, "Mystery and Adventure," *New York Herald Tribune*, May 10, 1936, 7:14.

38. Ibid., April 19, 1936, 7:16.

39. Ibid., November 15, 1931, 11:24.

40. Ibid., May 24, 1936, 7:16.

41. Ibid.

42. Ibid., May 3, 1936, 7:10.

43. Ibid., 7:16.

44. Ibid., April 19, 1936, 7:16.

45. See the author's *Parody as Film Genre: "Never Give a Saga an Even Break."* (Westport, CT: Greenwood Press, 1999).

46. Cuppy, "Mystery and Adventure," *New York Herald Tribune*, August 9, 1931, 11:10.

47. Ibid., May 17, 1936, 7:10.

48. Alexander Woollcott, "Capsule Criticism," in *The Cream of the Jesters*, ed. J.B. Mussey (1931; rpt New York: Tudor, 1937), 238.

49. Cuppy, "Mystery and Adventure," *New York Herald Tribune*, May 10, 1936, 7:14.

50. Ibid., September 6, 1931, 11:12; May 31, 1936, 7:10.

51. Ibid., August 23, 1931, 11:9.

52. Ibid., November 15, 1931, 11:24.

53. Ibid.

54. Will Cuppy Papers, William Steig letter to Will Cuppy, Box 96: Folder 24 (William Steig correspondence), March 1938, Special Collections, University of Chicago, Chicago, Illinois.

55. Norris W. Yates, *The American Humorist: Conscience of the Twentieth Century* (Ames: Iowa State University Press, 1964), 328.

56. Will Cuppy, "The Goldfish," in *A Treasury of Laughter*, ed. Louis Untermeyer (New York: Simon & Schuster, 1946), 198.

57. Louis Untermeyer, "Will Cuppy," in *A Treasury of Laughter*, 197.

58. Yates, *The American Humorist: Conscience of the Twentieth Century*, 329.

59. Will Cuppy, The Plesiosaur," *A Treasury of Laughter*, 201.

60. Ibid., "The Pterodactyl," 199.

61. Ibid., 200.

62. Ibid., 199.
63. Will Cuppy, "The Goldfish," 198.
64. Will Cuppy, "The Pterodactyl," 199.
65. Ibid., 200.
66. Will Cuppy, *How to Attract the Wombat* (1949; rpt. Chicago: University of Chicago Press, 1983), 2–3.
67. Will Cuppy papers, *New Yorker* letter to Will Cuppy, Box 96 (*New Yorker* correspondence), May 10, 1937, Special Collections, University of Chicago, Chicago, Illinois.
68. David Denby, "Lost Love," *New Yorker*, January 16, 2012, 80.
69. Will Cuppy, "Mystery and Adventure," *New York Herald Tribune*, September 16, 1934, 7:16.
70. Albert Guerard, "A Novel of the Mad Era of Normalcy: *The Golden Vanity*," *New York Herald Tribune*, October 21, 1934, 7:4.
71. Stanley J. Kunitz, ed., "Will Cuppy," in *Authors Today and Yesterday* (New York: H.W. Wilson, 1933), 184.
72. Will Cuppy Papers, Frank Sullivan letter to Will Cuppy, Box 96: Folder 24 (Frank Sullivan correspondence), May 16, 1933, Special Collections, University of Chicago, Chicago, Illinois.
73. Ibid., Cuppy letter to Pat Morgan (Henry Morgan's wife), Box 96 (general correspondence), undated (circa 1930s).
74. "Gardens, and All That," *New York Times*, April 18, 1937, 7:12.
75. Ibid.
76. W. C. Sellar and R. J. Yeatman *Garden Rubbish & Other Country Bumps* (New York: Farrar & Rinehart, 1937), 93.
77. Ibid., 87.
78. Ibid., 96.
79. See the author's "*Mr. B" Or Comforting Thoughts About the Bison: A Critical Biography of Robert Benchley*.
80. Dorothy Herriman, *S. J. Perelman: A Life* (1986; rpt. New York: Simon & Schuster, 1987), 285.
81. See the author's *Parody as Film Genre: "Never Give a Saga an Even Break"* (Westport, CT: Greenwood Press, 1999).
82. See Robert Benchley's *The Treasurer's Report and Other Aspects of Community Singing* (New York: Grosset & Dunlap, 1930).
83. Will Cuppy, "I'm Not the Budget Type," *Scribners*, December 1937, 19–21.
84. Isabel Paterson, "Turns with a Bookworm," *New York Herald Tribune*, February 16, 1936, Book section, in Will Cuppy Papers, Box 108: "IMP Comments," 1920s-1930s, Special Collections, University of Chicago, Chicago, Illinois.
85. Cyrus Fisher, "Radio Reviews: 'Just Relax,'" *The Forum*, October 1933, 254.

86. Amelia Earhart Papers, Will Cuppy Western Union Cablegram to Earhart, Correspondence folders, May 22, 1932, Purdue University, West Lafayette, Indiana.
87. Thomas Maeder, afterword in *The Decline and Fall of Practically Everybody* by Will Cuppy (1950; rpt. Boston: Nonpareil Books, 1984), 231–242.

Chapter Eight

1. Will Cuppy, introduction to *World's Great Detective Stories*, ed. Will Cuppy (New York: World Publishing Co., 1943), 10.
2. "Will Cuppy, Critic and Author, Was 65," *New York Times*, September 20, 1949, 29.
3. Will Cuppy, introduction to *Murder Without Tears*, ed. Will Cuppy (New York: Sheridan House, 1946), v-vi.
4. See the author's *Screwball Comedy: A Genre of Madcap Romance* (Westport, CT: Greenwood Press, 1986).
5. "Will Cuppy, Critic and Author, Was 65," *New York Times*, September 20, 1949, 29.
6. John Towner Frederick Papers, Will Cuppy correspondence, Box 32, Folder 3, undated letter, pages 1, 2, 3 (circa Christmas 1941), Special Collections, University of Iowa.
7. Ibid., 2.
8. William Faulkner, "A Rose for Emily," in *World's Great Mystery Stories*, ed. Will Cuppy (New York: World Publishing Co., 1943), 24.
9. Ibid.
10. Sandra Lieb, "Will Cuppy," in *Dictionary of Literary Biography*, ed. Stanley Trachtenberg (Detroit: Gale Research Co., 1982), 94–100.
11. Ambrose Bierce, "The Boarded Window," in *World's Great Mystery Stories*, ed. Will Cuppy (New York: World Publishing Company, 1943), 259.
12. Ibid.
13. See the author's *Film Classics Reclassified: A Shocking Spoof of Cinema* (Davenport, IA: Robin Vincent Publishing, 2001), 1.
14. Agatha Christie, "The Adventure of the Egyptian Tomb," in *World's Great Detective Stories*, 211.
15. Dashiell Hammett, "They Can Only Hang You Once," in *Murder Without Tears*, 550.
16. Dashiell Hammett, "A Man Called Spade," in *World's Great Detective Stories*, 53.
17. Ibid., 39.
18. Dorothy L. Sayers, "The Abominable History of the Man with Copper Fingers," in *World's Great Detective Stories*, 19.
19. Robert Kuhn McGregor and Ethan Lewis, *Conundrums for the Long Weekend: En-*

gland, *Dorothy L. Sayers and Lord Peter Wimsey* (Kent, OH: Kent State Press, 2000).
20. Dorothy L. Sayers, "In the Teeth of the Evidence," in *Murder Without Tears*, 469.
21. Ibid., 474.
22. Ibid., 475.
23. Mark Twain, "The Stolen White Elephant," in *World's Great Detective Stories*, 303.
24. Ibid., 314, 315.
25. Ibid., 301.
26. See the author's *Parody as Film Genre: "Never Give a Saga an Even Break"* (Westport, CT: Greenwood Press, 1999).
27. Stephen Leacock, "Who Do You Think Did It? or, The Mixed-Up Murder Mystery," in *World's Great Mystery Stories*, 282.
28. Ibid., 289.
29. Ibid., 281.
30. Stephan Leacock, "Maddened by Mystery or The Defective Detective," in *Murder Without Tears*, 553.
31. Ibid., 554.
32. Irvin S. Cobb, "A Bird in the Hand," in *World's Great Mystery Stories*, 119.
33. Ibid., 124.
34. Ibid., 134.
35. See the author's *American Dark Comedy: Beyond Satire* (Westport, CT: Greenwood Press, 1996).
36. F. Scott Fitzgerald, "A Short Trip Home," in *World's Great Mystery Stories*, 166.
37. Ibid., 175.
38. James Thurber, "A Sort of Genius," in *Murder Without Tears*, 102.
39. Neil A. Grauer, *Remember Laughter: A Life of James Thurber* (Lincoln: University of Nebraska Press. 1995), 48–49.
40. Edmund Pearson, "Rules for Murderesses," in *Murder Without Tears*, 11, 12.
41. Stewart H. Holbrook, "Belle of Indiana," in *Murder Without Tears*, 114.
42. Ibid., 115.
43. Ibid., 131.
44. H.G. Wells, "The Door in the Wall," in *World's Great Mystery Stories*, 210.
45. Will Cuppy, introduction to *World's Great Detective Stories*, 7, 8.
46. Patrick Healy, "Albee is Ready to Revisit His Past," *New York Times*, March 3, 2012, C-4.
47. Iris Barry, "William Steig's Loonies," *New York Herald Tribune*, January 17, 1943, 8:12.

Chapter Nine

1. Elsie Paterson, "She Had to Be a Writer," uncredited Sunday supplement newspaper piece, February 12, 1933, in the Will Cuppy Papers, Box 108: "IMP Comments," 1920s–1930s, Special Collections, University of Chicago, Chicago, Illinois.
2. Will Cuppy Papers, Box 108: "IMP Comments," 1920s–1930s [saved Paterson columns include the 1940s], Special Collections, University of Chicago, Chicago, Illinois.
3. Isabel Paterson, "Turns with a Bookworm," *New York Herald Tribune*, June 4, 1933, Book section, in Will Cuppy Papers, Box 108: "IMP Comments."
4. Ibid.
5. Ibid., November 29, 1936, Book section.
6. Ibid., 1938.
7. Ibid., March 5, 1939.
8. See also his very "puzzle"—focused review in "Mystery and Adventure," *New York Herald Tribune*, November 7, 1943, 6:30.
9. Isabel Paterson, "Turns with a Bookworm," *New York Herald Tribune*, December 17, 1939, Book section, in Will Cuppy Papers, Box 108: "IMP Comments."
10. Isabel Paterson, "Turns with a Bookworm," *New York Herald Tribune*, March 14, 1937, 10:26.
11. Brenda Wineapple, "The Missing Pages," *New York Times*, March 4, 2012, Book section: 19.
12. Robert K. Massie, "Parting Words," *New York Times*, March 4, 2012, Book section: 27.
13. Will Cuppy Papers, Box 108: "IMP Comments," Special Collections, University of Chicago, Chicago, Illinois.
14. Isabel Paterson, "Turns with a Bookworm," *New York Herald Tribune*, December 14, 1941.
15. Ibid., November 23, 1941, 9:34.
16. Ibid., March 23, 1941, Book section.
17. Ibid., December 10, 1944.
18. Ibid.
19. Ibid.
20. Ibid., February 25, 1945; January 2, 1947.
21. Ibid., December 5, 1948, 7:7.
22. Ibid., February 16, 1936, Book section 7:11.
23. Ibid., February 16, 1936, Book section.
24. John Tower Frederick Papers, Will Cuppy correspondence, Box 32, Folder 3, January 17, 1942, Special Collections, University of Iowa, Iowa City, Iowa.
25. Ibid., Christmas [1942].
26. Will Cuppy letter to Warren Bower, undated [circa 1942], in Will Cuppy Papers, Box 96, Radio correspondence folder, Special Collections, University of Chicago, Chicago, Illinois.
27. Dr. Raymond L. Ditmars, Review of

How to Become Extinct, by Will Cuppy, *Tomorrow*, February 1942, 54.
28. Will Cuppy letter to Warren Bower, undated [circa 1942], in Will Cuppy Papers, Box 96, Radio correspondence folder, Special Collections.
29. William Beebe, "Great Truths of Natural History: Even Aristotle Sometimes Guessed — but Cuppy? Ah Cuppy!," *New York Herald Tribune*, November 16, 1941, 9:4.
30. Ibid.
31. Charles Poore, "Books of the Times," *New York Times*, December 6, 1941, 15.
32. Ibid.
33. Edward Frank Allen, "Mr. Cuppy's Primer to Extinction," *New York Times*, December 14, 1944, 6:9.
34. Ibid.
35. For instance, see the John Towner Frederick Papers, Will Cuppy correspondence, Box 32, Folder 3, May 16, 1942, Special Collections, University of Iowa, Iowa City, Iowa.
36. Roger Pippett, "There's War on the List, Good Americana And Anthologies," *PM*, December 7, 1941, 57.
37. Ibid.
38. Stanley M. Rinehart, Jr. letter to Will Cuppy, October 24, 1944, in Will Cuppy Papers, Box 96, Correspondence folder, Special Collections.
39. Will Cuppy, *How to Attract the Wombat* (1949; rpt. Chicago: University of Chicago Press, 1983), 146.
40. Phillip Lopate, "The Enthusiast," *New York Times*, March 18, 2012, Book section: 21.
41. Fred Feldkamp, introduction to *How to Get from January to December*, by Will Cuppy (1951; rpt. New York: Dell, 1962), 5.
42. Will Cuppy, "The Wart Hog," *How to Attract the Wombat*, 29.
43. Will Cuppy, "Are Wombats People," *How to Attract the Wombat*, 1.
44. Will Cuppy, "How to Swat a Fly," *How to Attract the Wombat*, 92.
45. Will Cuppy, "The Kiwi," *How to Attract the Wombat*, 130.
46. Will Cuppy, "The Butterfly," *How to Attract the Wombat*, 106–107.
47. Will Cuppy, "The Poet and the Nautilus," *How to Attract the Wombat*, 55.
48. Will Cuppy, "How to Swat a Fly," *How to Attract the Wombat*, 91.
49. Will Cuppy, "Certainly, I Play the Piano" (1943), anthologized in *The Home Book of Laughter*, ed. May Lamberton Becker (New York: Dodd, Mead, 1948), 27–32.
50. Will Cuppy "The Octopus," *How to Attract the Wombat*, 82.
51. Will Cuppy, "More About Wombats," *How to Attract the Wombat*, 145.

52. Will Cuppy Papers, William Steig letter to Will Cuppy, Box 96: Folder 24 (William Steig correspondence), postmarked July 27, 1944, Special Collections, University of Chicago, Chicago, Illinois.
53. Ibid., postmarked August 7, 1944.
54. Ibid., postmarked July 29, 1944.
55. Ibid., August 7, 1944.
56. Ibid., postmarked January 3, 1945.
57. Ibid.
58. Ibid., postmarked September 26, 1949.
59. "Will Cuppy Dies At 65; Critic and Humorist," *New York Herald Tribune*, September 19, 1949, 12.
60. "Will Cuppy, 65, Dies; Humorist and Critic Was Educated Here," *Chicago Tribune*, September 20, 1949, 1:20.
61. Interview with Craig Buckles, M.D., March 13, 2012, St. John's Anderson Center, Anderson, Indiana.
62. "Will Cuppy," *Authors Today and Yesterday*, ed. Stanley J. Kunitz (New York: H.W. Wilson Co., 1933), 183.
63. Sandra Lieb, "Will Cuppy," *Dictionary of Literary Biography*, vol. 2 (Detroit, MI: Gale Research Co., 1982), 94–99; See also the University of Chicago's "Guide to the Will Cuppy Papers," Special Collections, University of Chicago, Chicago, Illinois, 3.
64. "Will Cuppy Dies At 65; Critic and Humorist."
65. "Will Cuppy, 65, Writer, Dies," *New York Sun*, September 19, 1949, 30; "Will Cuppy: Author Humorist, Critic," *New York Daily News*, September 20, 1949, 47.
66. "Will Cuppy, 65; Author and Critic," *New York Journal American*, September 19, 1949, 28.
67. "Will Cuppy, Critic and Author, Was 65," *New York Times*, September 20, 1949, 29.
68. "Will Cuppy Dies at 65; Critic and Humorist," *New York Herald Tribune*.
69. "The Phoenix Nest," *The Saturday Review of Literature*, October 15, 1949, 40.

Chapter Ten

1. Arthur Miller, *Death of a Salesman* (1949 rpt. New York: Penguin Books, 1998), Act 1:40.
2. Leland de la Durantraye, "Enchanted Hunter," *New York Times*, April 1, 2012, Book section: 17.
3. Arthur Miller, *Timebends: A Life* (New York: Grove Press, 1987), 127.
4. Charles Isherwood, "'Salesman' Comes Calling, Right on Time," *New York Times*, February 26, 2012, Arts section: 27.
5. Oscar Levant, *A Smattering of Ignorance*

(Garden City, NY: Garden City Publishing, 1942), ix.
6. Several sources, such as Sandra Lieb's "Will Cuppy," in *Dictionary of Literary Figures*, ed. Stanley Trachtenberg (Detroit, MI: Gale Research Co., 1982), 94–99.
7. See the author's *James Dean: Rebel With a Cause* (Indianapolis: Indiana Historical Society Press, 2005).
8. Frank Sullivan, "Will Cuppy: A Wry and Witty Humorist," *New York Herald Tribune*, November 20, 1949, Book section: 7.
9. Ibid.
10. Will Cuppy, *The Great Bustard and Other People* (New York: Murray Hill, 1944), 82.
11. See the author's *"Mr. B" Or Comforting Thoughts About the Bison: A Critical Biography of Robert Benchley* (Westport, CT, 1992), 77.
12. Frank Sullivan, introduction to *Chips Off the Old Benchley*, by Robert Benchley (New York: Harper & Brothers, 1949), xv–xvi.
13. Charles Poore, "Of Wombats and Such," *New York Times*, November 13, 1949, Book section: 8.
14. Will Cuppy, "Master of Sense and Sentences," *New York Herald Tribune*, March 5, 1939, 9:2.
15. Stanley Walker, "Will Cuppy's Last and Best Compendium," *New York Herald Tribune*, October 22, 1950, 7:4.
16. Lionel Oley, "Through History With Will Cuppy," *Saturday Review*, December 16, 1950, 16.
17. Charles Poore, "Books of the Times: Pinpointing of [Cuppy] Personalities," *New York Times*, October 5, 1950, 29.
18. C. B. Palmer, "A Footnote Covers Lady Godiva," *New York Times*, October 8, 1950, 7: 7.
19. Ibid.
20. For example, see also: "Everyone Is Covered (Even Godiva) by Cuppy," *Indianapolis News*, October 14, 1950, 2.
21. Richard Blakesley, "Will Cuppy's Last Laugh Is His Best," *Chicago Tribune*, October 18, 1950, 4: 4.
22. Ibid.
23. "Everyone Is Covered (Even Godiva) by Cuppy."
24. Ibid.
25. Ibid.; "A Footnote Covers Lady Godiva."
26. Of the author's many Chaplin works, see especially the chapter on *The Great Dictator* in *Forties Film Funnymen: The Decade's Great Comedians at Work in the Shadow of War* (Jefferson, NC: McFarland, 2010).
27. "Chaplin Strikes Back at New York Critics," *Los Angeles Times*, January 5, 1941.
28. Lotys Benning Steward, "'Innocents From Indiana' [Review]," *Indianapolis Star*, October 22, 1950, 6:14.
29. See the author's *American Dark Comedy: Beyond Satire* (Westport, CT: Greenwood Press, 1996); *Populism and the Capra Legacy* (Westport, CT: Greenwood Press, 1995); *Mr. Deeds Goes to Yankee Stadium: Baseball Films in the Capra Tradition* (Jefferson, NC: McFarland, 2004).
30. Will Cuppy, "November 7," in *How to Get from January to December*, ed. Fred Feldkamp (1951, rpt. New York: Dell, 1962), 216–217.
31. Ibid., "January 5," 11–12.
32. Ibid., "October 8," 197.
33. Ibid., "October 14," 200.
34. Ibid., "January 13," 16.
35. Ibid., "June 12," 117.
36. Ibid., "February 26," 44.
37. Charles Poore, "Books of the Times," *New York Times*, October 13, 1951, 15.
38. Cuppy, "April 9," in *How to Get from January to December*, 73.
39. Ibid, "August 29," 166.
40. Ibid., "March 9," 53.
41. Ibid., "February 24," 42–43.
42. Ibid., "June 9," 115.
43. Ibid., "April 17" and "June 7," 77, 113–114.
44. Ibid., "February 15," 38.
45. Ibid., "June 15," 118.
46. Ibid., "February 10," 34.
47. Ibid.
48. Will Cuppy Papers, Robert Benchley correspondence, September 17, 1935, Folder A–B, Box 96, Special Collections, University of Chicago Library, Chicago, Illinois.
49. Poore, "Books of the Times."
50. Richard Blakesley, "Cuppy Shows How to Grope Thru the Year," *Chicago Tribune*, October 14, 1951, Part 4: 5.
51. Herbert Kupferberg, "A Sort of Cuppy Calendar," *New York Herald Tribune*, October 14, 1951, 6: 21.
52. J. D. Salinger, "A Perfect Day for Bananafish," *New Yorker*, January 31, 1948.
53. Norris W. Yates, *The American Humorist: Conscience of the Twentieth Century* (1964, rpt. Ames: Iowa State Press, 1967), 330.
54. Alexandra Styron, *Reading My Father: A Memoir* (2011; rpt. New York: Scribners, 2012), 6.
55. Will Cuppy, Note to clipping service person, undated (circa mid-1940s), in the Will Cuppy Papers, Special Collections Research Center, University of Chicago Library, Box 111, *Saturday Evening Post* folder.

Afterword

1. George Orwell, *Animal Farm* (1945; rpt. New York: Signet Classic, 1996), 130.
2. Ibid., 133.
3. See the author's *Film Clowns of the Depression: Twelve Defining Comic Performances* (Jefferson, NC: McFarland, 2007), 144; See also, George Orwell's *1984* (1949; rpt. New York: Signet Classics, 1961).
4. Isabel Paterson, "Turns with a Bookworm," *New York Herald Tribune*, August 18, 1946, 7:11.
5. Ibid.
6. Orville Prescott, "Books of Times," *New York Times*, August 26, 1946, 21.
7. Will Cuppy, *How to Get from January to December* (1951; rpt. New York: Dell, 1962).
8. Norris W. Yates *The American Humorist* (1964; rpt. Ames: Iowa State University Press).
9. James Thurber, "The Secret Life of Walter Mitty," *New Yorker*, March 18, 1939 — first collected in his book *My World and Welcome to It* (New York: Harcourt, Brace and Company, 1942); James Thurber, "The Unicorn in the Garden," *New Yorker*, October 31, 1939 — first collected in his book *Fables for Our Time and Famous Poems Illustrated* (New York: Harper & Brothers, 1940).
10. S. J. Perelman, "Nothing but the Tooth," *Crazy Like a Fox* (1944; rpt. New York: Vintage Books, 1972.), 69.
11. S. J. Perelman, "Puppets of Passion," *Dawn Ginsbergh's Revenge* (New York: Horace Liveright, 1929), 12.
12. S. J. Perelman, What It Means to Be a Professional Beauty," *Dawn Ginberght's Revenge*, 98.
13. S. J. Perelman, "The Pitfalls of the Stage," *Dawn Ginbergh's Revenge*, 66.
14. Quoted frequently in Dorothy Herrman's *S. J. Perelman: A Life* (1986; rpt. New York: Simon & Schuster, Inc., 1987).
15. Quoted in the 1971 re-issuing of James Thurber's *The Last Flower: A Parable in Pictures* (1939; rpt. New York: Harper Colophon Books, 1971), originally appeared in an E. B. White *New Yorker* feature, November 11, 1939.
16. Burton Bernstein, *Thurber: A Biography* (1975; rpt. New York: Ballantine Books, 1976), 227.
17. Robert Benchley, "Fascinating Crimes: III. The Missing Floor," in *The Early Worm* (New York: Henry Holt, 1927), 115, 118.
18. Ibid., "The World of Grandpa Benchley," 205.
19. Ibid., "Storm Warnings for New York," 252, 254.
20. Ibid., "The New Villainy," 224, 226.
21. Ibid., "A Talk to Young Men," 5.
22. Thomas Heggen and Joshua Logan, *Mister Roberts: A Play* (New York: Random House, 1948), 159–160.
23. Thomas Heggen, *Mister Roberts* (Boston: Houghton Mifflin, 1946), 218.
24. Richard Match, "Between Tears and Laughter," *New York Herald Tribune*, August 25, 1946, 7:4.
25. Thomas Maeder, afterword in *The Decline and Fall of Practically Everybody*, by Will Cuppy (1950; rpt. Boston: Nonpareil Books, 1984), 241.
26. The George Orwell quote appears in Lloyd Grove's "Forget the Alamo," *New York Times*, June 10, 2012, Book Review section: 14.

Bibliography

Several special collections helped make this book possible, starting with the Cuppy Papers of the University of Chicago. Other archives noted below included correspondence between the humorist and his writing friends. The most significant was the Isabel Paterson Papers at the Herbert Hoover Presidential Library (West Branch, Iowa). Listings of particularly important letters are under "Books" and "Shorter Works." The Cuppy letters to Paterson under "Correspondence" below are often undated and vague about where they begin and end. Thus, there is much use of "circa" and "approximately" from letter numbers. Maybe this vagueness is appropriate for someone fond of satirizing history — Cuppy was not making it easy for future biographers.

Special Collections

"Amelia Earhart Papers." Purdue University, West Lafayetter, Indiana.
"Frank Sullivan Papers." Manuscript Collection, Cornell University, Ithaca, New York.
"Isabel Paterson Papers." Herbert Hoover Presidential Library, West Branch, Iowa.
"John Towner Frederick Papers." Special Collections, University of Iowa, Iowa City.
"Max Eastman Papers." Lilly Library, Indiana University, Bloomington.
"Will Cuppy File." Auburn Public Library, Auburn, Indiana.
"Will Cuppy Papers." Special Collections, University of Chicago.

Books

Bauby, Jean-Dominque. *The Diving Bell and the Butterfly*. Translated by Jeremy Leggatt. 1996. Reprint, New York: Vintage Books, 1997.
Becker, May Lamberton, ed. *The Home Book of Laughter*. New York: Dodd, Mead, 1948.
Benchley, Robert. *After 1903 — What?* New York: Harper & Brothers, 1938.
_____. *The Early Worm*. New York: Henry Holt, 1927.
_____. *From Bed to Worse, or Comforting Thoughts About the Bison*. New York: Harper & Brothers, 1934.
_____. *Love Conquers All*. New York: Holt, 1922.
_____. *My Ten Years in a Quandary, and How They Grew*. 1936. Reprint, Garden City, NY: Blue Ribbon Books, 1940.
_____. *Pluck and Luck*. New York: Henry Holt, 1925.
_____. *The Treasurer's Report and Other Aspects of Community Singing*. New York: Grosset & Dunlap, 1930.
Bernstein, Burton. *Thurber: A Biography*. 1975. Reprint, New York: Ballantine, 1976.
Bierce, Ambrose. *The Devil's Dictionary*. 1911. Reprint, New York: Dover, 1958.
_____. *The Sardonic Humor of Ambrose Bierce*. Edited by George Barkin. New York: Dover, 1963.
Blair, Walter. *Horse Sense in American Humor*. Chicago: University of Chicago Press, 1942.
Borowitz, Andy. *The 50 Funniest American Writers*. New York: Library of America, 2011.

Buckley, Christopher. *Losing Mum and Pup*. New York: Twelve Hachette Book Group, 2009.

Bukowski, Charles. *Ham on Rye*. 1984. Reprint, New York: HarperCollins, 2002.

Cavell, Stanley. *The Sense of Walden*. New York: Viking, 1972.

Cox, Stephen. *The Woman and the Dynamo: Isabel Paterson and the Idea of America*. New Brunswick: Transaction, 2004.

Cuppy, Will. *The Decline and Fall of Practically Everybody*. 1950. Reprint, Boston: Nonpareil, 1984.

———. "The Elizabethan Conception of Prose Style." Master's thesis, University of Chicago, 1914.

———. *The Great Bustard and Other People*. New York: Murray Hill, 1944.

———. *How to Attract the Wombat*. 1949. Reprint, Chicago: University of Chicago Press, 1983.

———. *How to Be a Hermit*. 1929. Reprint, New York: Liveright, 1987.

———. *How to Become Extinct*. 1941. Reprint, Garden City, NY: Garden City, 1951.

———. *How to Get from January to December*. 1951. Reprint, New York: Dell, 1962.

———. *How to Tell Your Friends from the Apes*. 1931. Reprint, Boston: Nonpareil, 2005.

———. *Maroon Tales: University of Chicago Stories*. 1909/1910. Reprint, Nabu Public Domain Reprints, undated.

Cuppy, Will, ed. *Murder Without Tears: An Anthology of Crime*. New York: Sheridan House, 1946.

Cuppy, Will, ed. *World's Great Detective Stories*. New York: World, 1943.

Cuppy, Will, ed. *World's Great Mystery Stories*. New York: World, 1943.

Eastman, Max. *Enjoyment of Laughter*. New York: Simon & Schuster, 1936.

Emerson, Ralph Waldo. *Selected Writings*. Edited by Brooks Atkinson. New York: Modern Library, 1950.

Gehring, Wes D. *American Dark Comedy: Beyond Satire*. Westport, CT: Greenwood Press, 1996.

———. *Film Classics Reclassified: A Shocking Spoof of Cinema*. Davenport, IA: Robin Vincent, 2001.

———. *Film Clowns of the Depression: Twelve Defining Comic Performances*. Jefferson, NC: McFarland, 2007.

———. *Forties Film Funnymen: The Decade's Great Comedians at Work in the Shadow of War*. Jefferson, NC: McFarland, 2010.

———. *Groucho & W.C. Fields: Huckster Comedians*. Jackson: University Press of Mississippi, 1994.

———. *James Dean: Rebel with a Cause*. Indianapolis: Indiana Historical Society Press, 2005.

———. *Laurel & Hardy: A Bio-Bibliography*. Westport, CT: Greenwood Press, 1990.

———. *Leo McCarey and the Comic Antihero in American Humor*. New York: Arno Press, 1980.

———. *Leo McCarey: From Marx to McCarthy*. Lanham, MD: Scarecrow Press, 2005.

———. *The Marx Brothers: A Bio-Bibliograhpy*. Westport, CT: Greenwood Press, 1987.

———. *"Mr. B" or, Comforting Thoughts About the Bison: A Critical Biography of Robert Benchley*. Westport, CT: Greenwood Press, 1992.

———. *Mr. Deeds Goes to Yankee Stadium: Baseball Films in the Capra Tradition*. Jefferson, NC: McFarland, 2004.

———. *Parody as Film Genre: "Never Give a Saga an Even Break."* Westport, CT: Greenwood Press, 1999.

———. *Populism and the Capra Legacy*. Westport, CT: Greenwood Press, 1995.

———. *Red Skelton: The Mask Behind the Mask*. Indianapolis: Indiana Historical Society Press, 2008.

———. *Robert Wise: Shadowland*. Indianapolis: Indiana Historical Society Press, 2012.

———. *Romantic vs. Screwball Comedy: Charting the Difference*. Lanham, MD: Scarecrow Press, 2002.

———. *Screwball Comedy: A Genre of Madcap Romance*. Westport, CT: Greenwood Press, 1986.

———. *W.C. Fields: A Bio-Bibliography*. Westport, CT: Greenwood Press, 1984.

Grauer, Neil A. *Remember Laughter: A Life of James Thurber*. Lincoln: University of Nebraska Press, 1995.

Heggen, Thomas. *Mister Roberts*. Boston: Houghton Mifflin, 1946.

Heggen, Thomas, and Joshua Logan. *Mister Roberts: A Play*. New York: Random House, 1948.

Herrick, Robert. *The Web of Life.* 1900. Reprint, U.K.: Dodo Press, 2011.

Herriman, Dorothy. *S.J. Perelman: A Life.* 1986. Reprint, New York: Simon & Schuster, 1987.

Kahn, Roger. *A Flame of Pure Fire: Jack Dempsey and the Roaring '20s.* New York: Harcourt Brace, 1999.

Kashner, Sam, and Nancy Schoenberger. *A Talent for Genius: The Life and Times of Oscar Levant.* New York: Random House, 1994.

Kendall, Paul Murray. *The Art of Biography.* 1965. Reprint, W.W. Norton, 1985.

Kinney, Harrison. *James Thurber: His Life and Times.* New York: Henry Holt, 1995.

Knipfel, Jim. *Quitting the Nairobi Trio.* 2000. Reprint, New York: Berkley Books, 2001.

Kunitz, Stanley, Howard Haycraft, and Wilbur Hadden. *Authors Today and Yesterday.* New York: H.W. Wilson, 1933.

Kunitz, Stanley, Howard Haycraft, eds. *Twentieth Century Authors.* New York: H. W. Wilson, 1942.

Lancotot, Neil. *CAMPY: The Two Lives of Roy Campanella.* New York: Simon & Schuster, 2011.

Levant, Oscar. *The Memoirs of an Amnesiac.* 1965. Reprint, New York: Bantam, 1966.

———. *A Smattering of Ignorance.* Garden City, NY: Garden City, 1942.

———. *The Unimportance of Being Oscar.* 1968. Reprint, New York: Pocket Books, 1969.

Levinson, Leonard Louis. *The Left Handed Dictionary.* New York: Colliers Books, 1978.

McGregor, Robert Kuhn, and Ethan Lewis. *Conundrums for the Long Weekend: England, Dorothy L. Sayers and Lord Peter Wimsey.* Kent, OH: Kent State Press, 2000.

McLeisch, Kenneth. *Arts in the Twentieth Century.* 1985. Reprint, New York: Penguin Books, 1986.

Miller, Arthur. *Death of a Salesman.* 1949. Reprint, New York: Penguin Books, 1998.

———. *Timebends: A Life.* New York: Grove Press, 1987.

Moses, Robert. *Public Works: A Dangerous Trade.* New York: McGraw-Hill, 1970.

Orwell, George. *Animal Farm.* 1945. Reprint, New York: Signet Classic, 1996.

———. *1984.* 1949. Reprint, New York: Harcourt, Brace, 1961.

Paterson, Isabel. *The Golden Vanity.* New York: William Morrow, 1934, Kindle Version, Loc 370.

Perelman, S. J. *Crazy Like a Fox.* 1944. Reprint, New York: Vintage Books, 1972.

———. *Dawn Ginsbergh's Revenge.* New York: Horace Liveright, 1929.

Rascoe, Burton. *Before I Forget.* New York: Literary Guild of America, 1937.

Rogers, Will. *Letters of a Self-Made Diplomat to His President.* New York: Albert & Charles Boni, 1926.

Russell, Bill, and Alan Steinberg. *Red and Me: My Coach, My Lifelong Friend.* New York: HarperCollins, 2009.

Schulberg, Bud. *The Disenchanted.* New York: Random House, 1950.

Scott, Robert N., ed. *War of the Rebellion: A Compilation of the Official Records of the Union and Confederate Armies.* Washington, D.C.: Government Printing Office, 1882.

Seldes, Gilbert. *The 7 Lively Arts.* 1924. Reprint, New York: McClelland & Stewart, 1957.

Sellar, W.C., and R.J. Yeatman. *Garden Rubbish & Other Country Bumps.* New York: Farrar & Rinehart, 1937.

Shields, Charles J. *And So It Goes: Kurt Vonnegut: A Life.* New York: Henry Holt, 2011.

Smith, John Martin. *History of DeKalb County Indiana.* 1987. Reprint, Auburn, IN: Natmus, 1992.

Sperber, A. M. *Murrow: His Life and Times.* New York: Freundlich, Books, 1986.

Styron, Alexandra. *Reading My Father: A Memoir.* 2011. Reprint, New York: Scribner, 2012.

Thoreau, Henry David. *Walden.* 1854. Reprint, New Haven, CT: Yale University Press, 2006.

———. *Walden; and Resistance to Civil Government.* Edited by William Rossi. New York: Norton, 1992.

Thurber, James. *Fables for Our Time and Famous Poems Illustrated.* New York: Harper & Brothers, 1940.

Thurber, James, and E. B. White. *Is Sex Necessary?* 1929. Reprint, New York: Harper & Brothers, 1957.

———. *The Last Flower: A Parable in*

Pictures. 1939. Reprint, New York: Harper Colophon Books, 1971.
____. *My Life and Hard Times*. 1933. Reprint, New York: Bantam Books, 1947.
____. *My World and Welcome to It*. New York: Harcourt, Brace, 1942.
Yates, Norris W. *The American Humorist: Conscience of the Twentieth Century*. Ames, IA: Iowa State University Press, 1964.

Shorter Works

Allen, Edward Frank. "Mr. Cuppy's Primer to Extinction." *New York Times*. December 14, 1941: Section 6:9.
Beebe, William. "Great Truths of Natural History: Even Aristotle Sometimes Guessed—but Cuppy? Ah Cuppy!" *New York Herald Tribune*. November 16, 1941: Section 9:4.
"Benches." *Newsweek*, December 27, 1943, 10.
Benchley, Robert. "Fascinating Crimes: III. The Missing Floor." In *The Early Worm*. New York: Henry Holt, 1927.
____. "The New Villainy." In *The Early Worm*. New York: Henry Holt, 1927.
____. "Storm Warnings for New York." In *The Early Worm*. New York: Henry Holt, 1927.
____. "A Talk to Young Men." In *The Early Worm*. New York: Henry Holt, 1927.Bierce, Ambrose. "The Boarded Window." In *World's Great Mystery Stories*. Edited by Will Cuppy. New York: World Publishing, 1943.
Blakesley, Richard. "Cuppy Shows How to Grope Thru the Year." *Chicago Tribune*, October 14, 1951: Part 4:5.
____. "Will Cuppy's Last Laugh Is His Best." *Chicago Tribune*, October 18, 1950: Section 4:4.
Boxer, Sarah. "William Steig, 95, Cartoonist and Master of Damsels, Drunks and Satyrs, Dies." *New York Times*, October 6, 2003.
Bruni, Frank. "The Director of 'Sideways' Sees His Life Go Forward." *New York Times*, November 13, 2011, Arts & Leisure section: 12.
"Chaplin Strikes Back at New York Critics." *Los Angeles Times*, January 5, 1941.
Chilcote, Alice Wayzata. "The Cuppys of Whitley County—Abraham Cuppy & Sarah Collins Cuppy of South Whitley, Ind." *Whitley County Roots*, April 1999.
Christie, Agatha. "The Adventure of the Egyptian Tomb." In *World's Great Detective Stories*. Edited by Will Cuppy. New York: World Publishing, 1943.
Cobb, Irwin S. "A Bird in the Hand." In *World's Great Mystery Stories*. Edited by Will Cuppy. New York: World Publishing, 1943.
Cuppy, Will. "April 9." In *How to Get from January to December*. 1951. Reprint, New York: Dell, 1962.
____. "April 17." In *How to Get from January to December*. 1951. Reprint, New York: Dell, 1962.
____. "Are Wombats People?" In *How to Attract the Wombat*. 1949. Reprint, Chicago: University of Chicago Press, 1983.
____. "August 29." In *How to Get from January to December*. 1951. Reprint, New York: Dell, 1962.
____. "Bluebirds and What Not." *New York Herald Tribune*, December 8, 1929, Section 12:5.
____. "The Butterfly." In *How to Attract the Wombat*. 1949. Reprint, Chicago: University of Chicago Press, 1983.
____. "Certainly, I Play the Piano!" In *The Home Book of Laughter*. Edited by May Lamberton Becker. New York: Dodd, Mead, 1948.
____. "February 10." In *How to Get from January to December*. 1951. Reprint, New York: Dell, 1962.
____. "February 15." In *How to Get from January to December*. 1951. Reprint, New York: Dell Publishing, 1962.
____. "February 24." In *How to Get from January to December*. 1951. Reprint, New York: Dell, 1962.
____. "February 26." In *How to Get from January to December*. 1951. Reprint, New York: Dell, 1962.
____. "The Goldfish." In *A Treasury of Laughter*. Edited by Louis Untermeyer. New York: Simon & Schuster, 1946.
____. "The Hermit Looks at Bookshops." *Author's League Bulletin*, December 29, 1929: 9.
____. "Hither and Yon." *New York Herald Tribune*, January 17, 1926: Section 6:12.
____. "How to Swat a Fly." In *How to*

[Cuppy, Will, *continued*] *Attract the Wombat*. 1949. Reprint, Chicago: University of Chicago Press, 1983.

———. "I'm Not the Budget Type." *Scribners*, December 1937: 19–21.

———, "Introduction." In *Murder Without Tears*. Edited by Will Cuppy. New York: Sheridan House, 1946.

———. "Introduction." In *World's Greatest Detective Stories*. Edited by Will Cuppy. New York: World Publishing, 1943.

———. "January 5." In *How to Get from January to December*. 1951. Reprint, New York: Dell, 1962.

———. "July 28." In *How to Get from January to December*. 1951. Reprint, New York: Dell, 1962.

———. "June 9." In *How to Get from January to December*. 1951. Reprint, New York: Dell, 1962.

———. "June 7." In *How to Get from January to December*. 1951. Reprint, New York: Dell, 1962.

———. "June 12." In *How to Get from January to December*. 1951. Reprint, New York: Dell, 1962.

———. "June 15." In *How to Get from January to December*. 1951. Reprint, New York: Dell, 1962.

———. "Kidding a Continent." *New York Herald Tribune*, September 6, 1931: Section 11:11.

———. "The Kiwi." In *How to Attract the Wombat*. 1949. Reprint, Chicago: University of Chicago Press, 1983.

———. "Little Brother of the Clams." *New York Herald Tribune*, September 29, 1929: Section 12:7.

———. "March 9." In *How to Get from January to December*. 1951. Reprint, New York: Dell, 1962.

———. "Master of Sense and Sentences." *New York Herald Tribune*, March 5, 1939: Section 9:2.

———. "More About Wombats." In *How to Attract Wombats*. 1949. Reprint, Chicago: University of Chicago Press, 1983.

———. "Mysteries and Adventure." *New York Herald Tribune*, April 12, 1936: Section 7:15.

———. "Mystery and Adventure." *New York Herald Tribune*, April 5, 1936: Section 7:22.

———. "Mystery and Adventure." *New York Herald Tribune*, April 19, 1936: Section 7:16.

———. "Mystery and Adventure." *New York Herald Tribune*, August 9, 1931: Section 11:10.

———. "Mystery and Adventure." *New York Herald Tribune*, August 16, 1931: Section 11:14.

———. "Mystery and Adventure." *New York Herald Tribune*, August 23, 1931: Section 11:9.

———. "Mystery and Adventure." *New York Herald Tribune*, July 19, 1931: Section 11:13.

———. "Mystery and Adventure." *New York Herald Tribune*, May 17, 1936: Section 7:10.

———. "Mystery and Adventure." *New York Herald Tribune*, May 10, 1936: Section 7:14.

———. "Mystery and Adventure." *New York Herald Tribune*, May 31, 1936: Section, 7:10.

———. "Mystery and Adventure." *New York Herald Tribune*, May 3, 1936: Section 7:16.

———. "Mystery and Adventure." *New York Herald Tribune*, May 24, 1936: Section 7:16.

———. "Mystery and Adventure." *New York Herald Tribune*, November 15, 1931: Section 11:24.

———. "Mystery and Adventure." *New York Herald Tribune*, November 7, 1943: Section 6:30.

———. "Mystery and Adventure." *New York Herald Tribune*, November 10, 1929: Section 12:24.

———. "Mystery and Adventure." *New York Herald Tribune*, October 6, 1929: Section 12:15.

———. "Mystery and Adventure." *New York Herald Tribune*, September 11, 1949: Section 7:18.

———. "Mystery and Adventure." *New York Herald Tribune*, September 15, 1929: Section 12:26.

———. "Mystery and Adventure." *New York Herald Tribune*, September 6, 1931: Section 11:12.

———. "Mystery and Adventure." *New York Herald Tribune*, September 15, 1946: Section 7:19.

———. "Mystery and Adventure." *New York*

Herald Tribune, September 16, 1934: Section 7:16.
_____. "November 7." In *How to Get from January to December*. 1951. Reprint, New York: Dell, 1962.
_____. "October 8." In *How to Get from January to December*. 1951. Reprint, New York: Dell, 1962.
_____. "October 14." In *How to Get from January to December*. 1951. Reprint, New York: Dell, 1962.
_____. "The Octopus." In *How to Attract the Wombat*. 1949. Reprint, Chicago: University of Chicago Press, 1983.
_____. "The Plesiosaur." In *A Treasury of Laughter*. Edited by Louis Untermeyer. New York: Simon & Schuster, 1946.
_____. "The Poet and the Nautilus." In *How to Attract the Wombat*. 1949. Reprint, Chicago: University of Chicago Press, 1983.
_____. "The Pterodactyl." In *A Treasury of Laughter*. Edited by Louis Untermeyer. New York: Simon & Schuster, 1946.
_____. Radio transcript for the New York Municipal Broadcasting System. January 18, 1942. In Will Cuppy Papers, In Will Cuppy Papers, Box 102, Folder 4. Special Collections, University of Chicago Library.
_____. "September 8." In *How to Get from January to December*. 1951. Reprint, New York: Dell, 1962.
_____. "The Wart Hog." In *How to Attract the Wombat*. 1949. Reprint, Chicago: University of Chicago Press, 1983.
_____. "Ye Housewife's Almanack." Appeared on a monthly basis in the *South Whitley Tribune* (Indiana newspaper), circa 1934. The duration of said column, and its possible limited circulation in other newspapers, is unclear.
"Death of Mrs. Cuppy." *Columbia City Post*, November 28, 1900.
Delbanco, Andrew. "The Reviewer." *New York Times*, November 13, 2011: Book Review section: 10.
Denby, David, "Double Dave." *New Yorker*, December 12, 2011.
_____. "Lost Love." *New Yorker*, January 16, 2012.
Ditmars, Dr. Raymond L. Review of *How to Become Extinct*, by Will Cuppy. *Tomorrow*, February 1942.

Durantraye, Leland de la. "Enchanted Hunter." *New York Times*, April 1, 2012: Book Section: 17.
Evans, Ernestine. "Having Fun with the Comrades." *New York Herald Tribune*, August 25, 1946: Section 7:4.
"Everyone Is Covered (Even Godiva) by Cuppy." *Indianapolis News*, October 14, 1950:2.
Faulkner, William. "A Rose for Emily." In *World's Great Mystery Stories*. Edited by Will Cuppy. New York: World Publishing, 1943.
Fisher, Cyrus. "Radio Reviews: 'Just Try to Relax.'" *The Forum*, October 1933: 254.
Fitzgerald, F. Scott. "A Short Trip Home." In *World's Great Mystery Stories*. Edited by Will Cuppy. New York: World Publishing, 1943.
Feldkamp, Fred. "Introduction." In *How to Get from January to December*, by Will Cuppy. 1951. Reprint, New York: Dell, 1962.
_____. "Introduction." In *The Decline and Fall of Practically Everybody*, by Will Cuppy. 1950. Reprint, Boston: Nonpareil Books, 1984.
"Former Resident [Anna Cuppy Clark] Dies." *South Whitley Tribune*, April 11, 1940.
"Gardens and All That." *New York Times*, April 18, 1937: Section 7:12.
Gardner, Dwight. "Bring It On." *New York Times*, October 23, 2011: Book Review section: 35.
Gehring, Wes D. "The Comic Anti-Hero in American Fiction: Its First Full Articulation." *Thalia: A Journal of Studies in Literary Humor* (Winter 1979–1980).
_____. "A Cuppyful of Laughter—and Sorrow." *USA Today Magazine*, September 2011.
_____. "Death and Laughter." *USA Today Magazine*, September 2005.
_____. E-mail interview with Thomas Maeder, October 24, 2011.
_____. "'Inside Benchley': The Early Diaries." *Studies in American Humor*, Vol. 7, 1989 [1992].
_____. Interview with Craig Buckles, M. D, St. John's Anderson Center, Anderson, Indiana, March, 13, 2012.
_____. Phone Interview with Joyce Heite

of the Whitley County Genealogical Society, September 2, 2011.

⸺. Phone Interview with several librarians at DeKalb High School, September 2, 2011.

⸺. "Television's Other Groucho." *HUMOR: International Journal of Humor Research* (1992) 5:3.

⸺. "The Yankee Figure in American Comedy Fiction." *Thalia: A Journal of Studies in Literary Humor* (Winter 1978–1979).

Gerber, John. (Spring 1975). "New England and Crackerbarrel Philosophy." *American Humor and Satire*. Lecture conducted from University of Iowa, Iowa City.

Greenberg, David. "Standing Pat." *New York Times*, November 20, 2011: Book Review section: 9.

Grove, Lloyd. "Forget the Alamo." *New York Times*, June 10, 2012: Book Review section: 14.

Guerard, Albert. "A Novel of the Mad Era of Normalcy: *The Golden Vanity*." *New York Herald Tribune*, October 21, 1934: Section 7:3.

Hammett, Dashiell. "They Can Only Hang You Once." In *Murder Without Tears*. Edited by Will Cuppy. New York: Sheridan House, 1946.

Hells, Kitchen, Manhattan, http://enwikipedia.org/wiki/Hells__Kitchen,__Manhanttan.

Holbrook, Stewart H. "Belle of Indiana." In *Murder Without Tears*. Edited by Will Cuppy. New York: Sheridan House, 1946.

Isherwood, Charles. "'Salesman' Comes Calling, Right on Time." *New York Times*, February 26, 2012: Arts section: 27.

"Jack Ralson Cuppy [obituary]." *Columbia City Post and Mail*, June 15, 1878.

"James Weber Linn, Educator, 63, Dead." *New York Times*, July 17, 1939:19.

Jane Addams Hull House Association site, http://www.hullhouse.org.

Keillor, Garrison. "Trailblazer." *New York Times*, October 23, 2011: Book Review section: 15.

Kennedy, Pagan. "Rewiring Reality." *New York Times*, January 15, 2012: Book Review section: 8.

Kirsch, Adam. "In Praise of Style." *New York Times*, January 22, 2012: Book Review section: 13.

Kogan, Deborah Copaken. "Only Yesterday." *New York Times*, May 27, 2012: Book Review section: 27.

Kronenberger, Louis. "'The Golden Vanity' and Other Recent Works of Fiction." *New York Times*, October 21, 1934: Section 5:6.

Kunitz, Stanley J., ed. "Will Cuppy." In *Authors Today and Yesterday*. New York: H.W. Wilson Company, 1933.

Kupferberg, Herbert. "A Sort of Cuppy Calender." *New York Herald Tribune*, October 14, 1951: Section 6:21.

Lane, Anthony. "The Current Cinema: Devotions." *New Yorker*, August 29, 2011.

Leacock, Stephen. "Maddened by Mystery or the Defective Detective." In *Murder Without Tears*. Edited by Will Cuppy. New York: Sheridan House, 1946.

⸺. "Who Do You Think Did It? or, The Mix-Up Murder Mystery." In *World's Great Mystery Stories*. Edited by Will Cuppy. New York: World Publishing, 1943.

Lieb, Sandra. "Will Cuppy." In *Dictionary of Literary Biography*, Vol. ll. Edited by Stanley Trachtenberg. Detroit: Gale Research, 1982.

Lilly, Mary Frances. Last will and testament. *Probate Order Book. Will Record v.7*. Circuit Court, DeKalb County, Indiana. December 12, 1927: 484.

Lopate, Phillip. "The Enthusiast." *New York Times*. March 18, 2012: Book section: 21.

Maeder, Thomas. "Afterword." In *The Decline and Fall of Practically Everybody*, by Will Cuppy. 1950. Reprint, Boston: Nonpareil Books, 1984.

Massie, Robert K. "Parting Words." *New York Times*, March 4, 2012: Book section: 27.

Match, Richard. "Between Tears and Laughter." *New York Herald Tribune*, August 25, 1946: Section 7:4.

"Mr. Cuppy's Life as a Part-time Hermit." *New York Times*, December 29, 1929: Section 4:15.

Moses, Robert. "From the Bridge: More About Will Cuppy." *Newsday*, May 28, 1966.

Nahson, Claudia J. "Introduction." In *The Art of William Steig*. New Haven: Yale University Press, 2007.

Olay, Lionel. "Through History with Will Cuppy." *Saturday Review*, December 16, 1950.

Palmer, C.B. "A Footnote Covers Lady Godiva." *New York Times*, October 8, 1950: Section 7:7.

Paterson, Elsie. "She Had to Be a Writer." Unaccredited Sunday supplement newspaper piece. February 12, 1933. In Will Cuppy Papers, Box 108, "IMP Comments," 1920s–1930s folder, Special Collections, University of Chicago.

Paterson, Isabel. "The Abbe Children, Who Are Never Bored." *New York Herald Tribune*, April 5, 1936: Section 7:3.

____. "Turns with a Bookworm." *New York Herald Tribune*, April 12, 1936, Section 7:19.

____. "Turns with a Bookworm." *New York Herald Tribune*, August 18, 1946: Section 7:11.

____. "Turns with a Bookworm." *New York Herald Tribune*, August 25, 1946: Section 7.

____. "Turns with a Bookworm." *New York Herald Tribune*, December 5, 1948: Section 7:7.

____. "Turns with a Bookworm." *New York Herald Tribune*, December 14, 1944: Section 9:23.

____. "Turns with a Bookworm." *New York Herald Tribune*, December 17, 1939: Book Section. In Will Cuppy Papers, Box 108, "IMP Comments" folder. University of Chicago.

____. "Turns with a Bookworm." *New York Herald Tribune*, December 6, 1931: Section 11:31.

____. "Turns with a Bookworm." *New York Herald Tribune*, December 10, 1944: Book Section. In Will Cuppy Papers, Box 108, "IMP Comments" folder. University of Chicago.

____. "Turns with a Bookworm." *New York Herald Tribune*, February 16, 1936: Book Section. In Will Cuppy Papers, Box 108, "IMP Comments" folder. University of Chicago.

____. "Turns with a Bookworm." *New York Herald Tribune*, January 9, 1949: Section 7:11.

____. "Turns with a Bookworm." *New York Herald Tribune*, January 2, 1947: Book Section. In Will Cuppy Papers, Box 108, "IMP Comments" folder. University of Chicago.

____. "Turns with a Bookworm." *New York Herald Tribune*, June 24, 1934.

____. "Turns with a Bookworm." *New York Herald Tribune*, March 5, 1939: Book Section. In Will Cuppy Papers, Box 108, "IMP Comments" folder. University of Chicago.

____. "Turns with a Bookworm." *New York Herald Tribune*, March 14, 1937: Section 10:26.

____. "Turns with a Bookworm." *New York Herald Tribune*, March 23, 1941: Book Section. In Will Cuppy Papers, Box 108, "IMP Comments" folder. University of Chicago.

____. "Turns with a Bookworm." *New York Herald Tribune*, 1938: Book Section. In Will Cuppy Papers, Box 108, "IMP Comments" folder. University of Chicago.

____. "Turns with a Bookworm." *New York Herald Tribune*, November 10, 1929, Section 12:27.

____. "Turns with a Bookworm." *New York Herald Tribune*, November 29, 1936. In Will Cuppy Papers, Box 108, "IMP Comments" folder. University of Chicago.

____. "Turns with a Bookworm." *New York Herald Tribune*, November 23, 1941: Section 9:34.

____. "Turns with a Bookworm." *New York Herald Tribune*, November 22, 1931: Section 11:19.

____. "Turns with a Bookworm." *New York Herald Tribune*, October 11, 1931: Section 11:14.

____. "Turns with a Bookworm." *New York Herald Tribune*, October 13, 1929: Section 12:27.

____. "Turns with a Bookworm." *New York Herald Tribune*, September 15, 1929: Section 12:27.

____. "Turns with a Bookworm." *New York Herald Tribune*, September 24, 1939: Book Review section.

____. "Turns with a Bookworm." *New York Herald Tribune*, September 29, 1929: Section 12:43.

———. "Turns with a Bookworm." *New York Herald Tribune*, September 22, 1929: Section 12:23.
Pearson, Edmund. "Rules for Murderesses." In *Murder Without Tears*. Edited by Will Cuppy. New York: Sheridan House, 1946.
Perl, Jed. "Freedom of Expression." *New York Times*, July 10, 2011: Book Review section: 14.
"The Phoenix Nest." *The Saturday Review of Literature*, October 15, 1949.
Pippet, Roger. "There's a War on the List, Good Americana and Anthologies." *PM*. December 7, 1941.
Perelman, "Nothing but the Tooth." In *Crazy Like a Fox*. 1944. Reprint, New York: Vintage Books, 1972.
———. "The Pitfalls of the Stage." In *Dawn Ginsbergh's Revenge*. New York: Horace Liveright, 1929.
———. "Puppets of Passion." In *Dawn Ginsbergh's Revenge*. New York: Horace Liveright, 1929.
———. "What It Means to Be a Professional Bounty." In *Dawn Ginsbergh's Revenge*, New York: Horace Liveright, 1929.
Prescott, Orville. "Books of Times." *New York Times*, August 26, 1946: 21.
Poore, Charles. "Books of the Times." *New York Herald Tribune*, December 6, 1941: 15.
———. "Of Wombats and Such." *New York Times*, November 13, 1949: Book section: 8.
———. "Books of the Times: Pinpointing of [Cuppy] Personalities." *New York Times*, October 5, 1950: 29.
———. "Books of the Times." *New York Times*, October 13, 1951: 15.
Ranson, Jo. "Living From Can to Mouth." *Brooklyn Eagle*, November 24, 1929.
"Robert Herrick, 70, Aid of Ickes, Dead." *New York Times*, December 24, 1938: 15.
Robert Herrick websit, http://en.wiki pedia.org/wiki/Robert__Herrick__(novelist).
"Robert M. Lovett, Educator, Is Dead." *New York Times*, February 9, 1956.
Rosenblatt, Roger, "The Spooky Art." *New York Times*, July 10, 2011: Book Review section: 27.
Salinger. J. D. "A Perfect Day for Bananafish." *New Yorker*, January 31, 1948.
Saroyan, William. "Introduction." In *The Lonely Ones*, by William Steig. 1942. Reprint, New York: Windmill Books, 1970.
Sayers, Dorothy L. "The Abominable History of the Man With Copper Fingers." In *World's Great Detective Stories*. Edited by Will Cuppy. New York: World Publishing, 1943.
———. "In the Teeth of the Evidence." In *Murder Without Tears*. Edited by Will Cuppy. New York: Sheridan House, 1946.
"Stagg Dies at 102; Dean of Coaches." *New York Times*, March 18, 1965: 1, 30.
Steig, Jeanne. "Clowning Around." In *The Art of William Steig*. New Haven, CT: Yale University Press, 2007.
Stewart, Latys Benning. "Innocents from Indiana." *Indianapolis Star*, October 22, 1950: Section 6:14.
Stone, Herb. *I Married a Witch* review, *Rob Wagner's Script*, December 19, 1942. In *Selected Film Criticism, 1941–1950*. Edited by Anthony Slide. Metuchen, NJ: Scarecrow Press, 1983.
Sullivan, Frank. "Humorist Turns Critic, Reviewer." Uncredited. Circa late 1929. In Will Cuppy Papers, Box 108, Scrapbook 1. Special Collections, University of Chicago Library.
———. "Introduction." In *Chips off the Old Benchley*, by Robert Benchley. New York: Harper & Brothers, 1949.
———. "Will Cuppy: A Wry and Witty Humorist." *New York Herald Tribune*, November 20, 1949, Book Review section: 7.
Tante, Dilly, ed. "H. L. Mencken." In *Living Authors: A Book of Biographies*. New York: H. L. Wilson, 1931.
"Thos. J. Cuppy Dies After Hard Fight." *Auburn Courier*, December 19, 1912.
Thurber, James. "A Sort of Genius." In *Murder Without Tears*. Edited by Will Cuppy. New York: Sheridan House, 1946.
———. "The Greatest Man in the World." In *The Thurber Carnival*. New York: Dell, 1964.
———. "The Secret Life of Walter Mitty." *New Yorker*, March 18, 1939.
———. "The Unicorn in the Garden." *New Yorker*, October 31, 1939.
Untermeyer, Louis, ed. "Will Cuppy." In

A Treasury of Laughter. New York: Simon & Schuster, 1946.
Twain, Mark. "The Stolen White Elephant." In *World's Great Detective Stories.* Edited by Will Cuppy. New York: World Publishing, 1943.
Walker, Stanley, "Will Cuppy's Last and Best Compendium." *New York Herald Tribune,* October 22, 1950: Section 7:4.
Weiner, Eric. "Americans Undecided About God?" *New York Times,* December 11, 2011: Book Review section: 5.
Wells, H. G. "The Door in the Wall." In *World's Great Mystery Stories.* Edited by Will Cuppy. New York: World Publishing, 1943.
"Will Cuppy: Author, Humorist, Critic." *New York Daily News,* September 20, 1949: 47.
"Will Cuppy." In *Authors Today and Yesterday.* Edited by Stanley J. Kunitz. New York: H.W. Wilson, 1933.
"Will Cuppy, Critic and Author, Was 65." *New York Times,* September 20, 1949: 29.
"Will Cuppy, 65, Writer, Dies." *New York Sun,* September 1949: 30.
Willett, Jincy. "Mr. Manners." *New York Times,* January 8, 2012: Book Review section: 8.
"William Steig." In *Current Biography 1944.* Edited by Anna Rothe. New York: H. W. Wilson, 1945.
Wineapple, Brenda. "The Missing Pages." *New York Times.* March 14, 2012: Book Section: 19.
Wodehouse, P. G. "Introduction." In *How to Tell Your Friends from the Apes,* by Will Cuppy. 1931. Reprint, Boston: Nonpareil Books, 2005.
Woolcott, Alexander. "Capsule Criticism." In *The Cream of the Jesters.* Edited by J. B. Mussey. 1931. Reprint, New York: Tudor Publishing, 1937.

Correspondence

Benchley, Robert. Correspondence to Will Cuppy, September 17, 1935, Folder A-B, Box 96, Special Collections, University of Chicago.
Cuppy, Will. An autographed note to a Mr. Anderson. In *How to Become Extinct.* Garden City, NY: Garden City Books, 1941.
_____. Correspondence to Isabel Paterson Papers. Circa 1923. In Isabel Paterson Papers, Folder 1, page 3, approximately letter 2, Herbert Hoover Presidential Library. West Branch, Iowa.
_____. Correspondence to Isabel Paterson. Circa 1924. In Isabel Paterson Papers, Folder 1, page 5, approximately letter 3. Herbert Hoover Presidential, Library. West Branch, Iowa.
_____. Correspondence to Isabel Paterson. Circa 1924. In Isabel Paterson Papers, Folder 1, page 11, approximately letter 5. Herbert Hoover Presidential Library. West Branch, Iowa.
_____. Correspondence to Isabel Paterson. Circa 1924. In Isabel Paterson Papers, Folder 1, page 15, approximately letter 7. Herbert Hoover Presidential Library. West Branch, Iowa.
_____. Correspondence to Isabel Paterson. Circa August 1924. In Isabel Paterson Papers, Folder 1, page 42, approximately letter 15. Herbert Hoover Presidential Library. West Branch, Iowa.
_____. Correspondence to Isabel Paterson. Circa 1924. In Isabel Paterson Papers, Folder 1, page 76, approximately letter 40. Herbert Hoover Presidential Library. West Branch, Iowa.
_____. Correspondence to Isabel Paterson. Mid-1920s. In Isabel Paterson Papers, Folder 1, page 31, letter 13. Herbert Hoover Presidential Library. West Branch, Iowa.
_____. Correspondence to Isabel Paterson. Mid-1920s. In Isabel Paterson Papers, Folder1, page 74, approximately letter 39. Herbert Hoover Presidential Library. West Branch, Iowa.
_____. Correspondence to Isabel Paterson. Circa 1925. In Isabel Paterson Papers, Folder 1, page 9, approximately letter 4. Herbert Hoover Presidential Library. West Branch, Iowa.
_____. Correspondence to Isabel Paterson. Circa 1925. In Isabel Paterson Papers, Folder 1, page 10, approximately letter 5. Herbert Hoover Presidential Library. West Branch, Iowa.
_____. Correspondence to Isabel Paterson. Circa 1925. In Isabel Paterson Papers, Folder 1, page 17, approximately letter 8. Herbert Hoover Presidential Library. West Branch, Iowa.

———. Correspondence to Isabel Paterson. Circa 1925. In Isabel Paterson, Folder 1, page 26, approximately letter 12. Herbert Hoover Presidential Library. West Branch, Iowa.

———. Correspondence to Isabel Paterson. Circa 1925. In Isabel Paterson Papers, Folder 1, page 50, approximately letter 21. Herbert Hoover Presidential Library. West Branch, Iowa.

———. Correspondence to Isabel Paterson. Circa 1925. In Isabel Paterson Papers, Folder 1, page 67, approximately letter 35. Herbert Hoover Presidential Library. West Branch, Iowa.

———. Correspondence to Isabel Paterson. Circa 1925. In Isabel Paterson Papers, Folder 1, page 79, approximately letter 44. Herbert Hoover Presidential Library. West Branch, Iowa.

———. Correspondence to Isabel Paterson. Circa 1925. In Isabel Paterson Papers, Folder 1, page 84, approximately letter 45. Herbert Hoover Presidential Library. West Branch, Iowa.

———. Correspondence to Isabel Paterson. Circa 1925. In Isabel Paterson Papers, Folder 3, page 2, letter 1. Herbert Hoover Presidential Library. West Branch, Iowa.

———. Correspondence to Isabel Paterson. Circa 1926. In Isabel Paterson Papers, Folder 1, page 66, approximately letter 34. Herbert Hoover Presidential Library. West Branch, Iowa.

———. Correspondence to Isabel Paterson. Circa 1926. In Isabel Paterson Papers, Folder 2, page 7, approximately letter 4. Herbert Hoover Presidential Library. West Branch, Iowa.

———. Correspondence to Isabel Paterson. Circa 1926. In Isabel Paterson Papers, Folder 3, page 1, letter 1. Herbert Hoover Presidential Library. West Branch, Iowa.

———. Correspondence to Isabel Paterson. Circa 1926. In Isabel Paterson Papers, Folder 3, page 3, letter 2. Herbert Hoover Presidential Library. West Branch, Iowa.

———. Correspondence to Isabel Paterson. Circa 1926. In Isabel Paterson Papers, Folder 3, page 10, letter 4. Herbert Hoover Presidential Library. West Branch, Iowa.

———. Correspondence to Isabel Paterson. Circa 1926. In Isabel Paterson Papers, Folder 3, page 24, approximately letter 11. Herbert Hoover Presidential Library. West Branch, Iowa.

———. Correspondence to Isabel Paterson. Circa 1927. In Isabel Paterson Papers, Folder 1, page 75, approximately letter 41. Herbert Hoover Presidential Library. West Branch, Iowa.

———. Correspondence to Isabel Paterson. Circa 1927. In Isabel Paterson Papers, Folder 2, page 1–2, letter 2. Herbert Hoover Presidential Library. West Branch, Iowa.

———. Correspondence to Isabel Paterson. Circa 1927. In Isabel Paterson Papers, Folder 2, page 4, letter 3. Herbert Hoover Presidential Library. West Branch, Iowa.

———. Correspondence to Isabel Paterson. Circa 1927. In Isabel Paterson Papers, Folder 2, page 14, approximately letter 7. Herbert Hoover Presidential Library. West Branch, Iowa.

———. Correspondence to Isabel Paterson. Circa 1927. In Isabel Paterson Papers, Folder 2, page 20, letter 11. Herbert Hoover Presidential Library. West Branch, Iowa.

———. Correspondence to Isabel Paterson. Circa 1927. In Isabel Paterson Papers, Folder 2, page 25, approximately letter 14. Herbert Hoover Presidential Library. West Branch, Iowa.

———. Correspondence to Isabel Paterson. Circa 1927. In Isabel Paterson Papers, Folder 2, page 39, approximately letter 20. Herbert Hoover Presidential Library. West Branch, Iowa.

———. Correspondence to Isabel Paterson. Circa 1927. In Isabel Paterson Papers, Folder 2, page 40, approximately letter 21. Herbert Hoover Presidential Library. West Branch, Iowa.

———. Correspondence to Isabel Paterson. Circa 1927. In Isabel Paterson Papers, Folder 2, page 44, approximately letter 22. Herbert Hoover Presidential Library. West Branch, Iowa.

———. Correspondence to Isabel Paterson. Circa 1927. In Isabel Paterson Papers, Folder 2, page 53, approximately letter 28. Herbert Hoover Presidential Library. West Branch, Iowa.

———. Correspondence to Isabel Paterson.

Circa 1927. In Isabel Paterson Papers, Folder 2, page 58, approximately letter 31. Herbert Hoover Presidential Library. West Branch, Iowa.

———. Correspondence to Isabel Paterson. Circa 1927. In Isabel Paterson Papers, Folder 2, page 69, approximately letter 39. Herbert Hoover Presidential Library. West Branch, Iowa.

———. Correspondence to Isabel Paterson. Circa 1927. In Isabel Paterson Papers, Folder 3, pages 73–74, approximately letter 33. Herbert Hoover Presidential Library. West Branch, Iowa.

———. Correspondence to Isabel Paterson. Circa 1929. In Isabel Paterson Papers, Folder 2, page 52, approximately letter 24. Herbert Hoover Presidential Library. West Branch, Iowa.

———. Correspondence to Isabel Paterson. Circa 1929. In Isabel Paterson Papers, Folder 2, page 83, approximately letter 45. Herbert Hoover Presidential Library. West Branch, Iowa.

———. Correspondence to Isabel Paterson. Circa 1929. In Isabel Paterson Papers, Folder 3, page 25, approximately letter 11. Herbert Hoover Presidential Library. West Branch, Iowa.

———. Correspondence to Isabel Paterson. Circa 1929. In Isabel Paterson Papers, Folder 3, page 29, approximately letter 14. Herbert Hoover Presidential Library. West Branch, Iowa.

———. Correspondence to Isabel Paterson. Circa 1929. In Isabel Paterson Papers, Folder 3, page 94, approximately letter 43. Herbert Hoover Presidential Library. West Branch, Iowa.

———. Correspondence to Pat Morgan (Henry Morgan's wife). Circa 1930s. In Will Cuppy Papers, Box 96, General correspondence folder. Special Collections, University of Chicago.

———. Correspondence to Max Eastman. Circa 1936. In Max Eastman Papers, Will Cuppy folder. Lily Library. Indiana University, Bloomington.

———. Correspondence to John Towner Frederick. Circa 1941. In John Towner Frederick Papers. Box 32, Folder 3. Special Collections, University of Iowa, Iowa City.

———. Correspondence to John Towner Frederick. Circa Christmas 1941. In the John Towner Frederick Papers. Box 32, Folder 3. Special Collections, University of Iowa, Iowa City.

———. Correspondence to Warren Bower. Circa 1942. In Will Cuppy Papers, Box 96, Radio correspondence folder. Special Collections. University of Chicago.

———. Correspondence to John Towner Frederick. January 17, 1942. In John Towner Frederick Papers. Box 32, Folder 3. Special Collections, University of Iowa, Iowa City.

———. Correspondence to John Towner Frederick. January 31, 1942. In John Towner Frederick Papers. Box 32, Folder 2. Special Collections, University of Iowa, Iowa City.

———. Correspondence to John Towner Frederick. May 16, 1942. In John Towner Frederick Papers. Box 32, Folder 3. Special Collections, University of Iowa, Iowa City.

———. Correspondence to John Towner Frederick. July 17, 1942. In John Towner Frederick Papers. Box 32, Folder 3. Special Collections, University of Iowa. Iowa City.

———. Correspondence to Max Eastman. December 27, 1943. In Max Eastman Papers, Will Cuppy folder. Lily Library. Indiana University, Bloomington.

———. Correspondence to Max Eastman. Undated [1936]. In Max Eastman Papers, Will Cuppy folder. Lily Library. Indiana University, Bloomington.

———. Note to clipping service person. Mid-1940s. In Will Cuppy Papers, Box 111, *Saturday Evening Post* folder. Special Collections Research Center, University of Chicago.

———. Western Union Cablegram to Amelia Earhart. May 22, 1932. In Amelia Earhart Papers, Correspondence folders. Purdue University. West Lafayette, Indiana.

Gibbs, Wolcott. Correspondence to Will Cuppy. May 10, 1937. In Will Cuppy Papers, Box 96. *New Yorker* correspondence folder. Special Collections, University of Chicago.

Paterson, Isabel. Correspondence to Will Cuppy. Late summer 1929. In Isabel Paterson Papers, Folder 1, pages 117–118, letter 1. Herbert Hoover Presidential Library. West Branch, Iowa.

———. Correspondence to Will Cuppy. Late summer 1929. In Isabel Paterson Papers, Folder 1, page 116, postcard 2. Herbert Hoover Presidential Library. West Branch, Iowa.

Rinehart, Stanley M. Correspondence to Will Cuppy. October 24, 1944. In Will Cuppy Papers, Box 96, General correspondence folder. Special Collections, University of Chicago.

Steig, William. Correspondence to Will Cuppy. May 31, 1935. In Will Cuppy Papers, Box 96, Folder 24. Special Collections, University of Chicago.

———. Correspondence to Will Cuppy. Circa 1936. In Will Cuppy Papers, Box 96, Folder 24. Special Collections, University of Chicago.

———. Correspondence to Will Cuppy. March, 1938. In Will Cuppy Papers, Box 96, Folder 24. Special Collections, University of Chicago.

———. Correspondence to Will Cuppy. Circa 1941. In Will Cuppy Papers, Box 96, Folder 24. Special Collections, University of Chicago.

———. Correspondence to Will Cuppy. July 27, 1944. In Will Cuppy Papers, Box 96, Folder 24. Special Collections, University of Chicago.

———. Correspondence to Will Cuppy. July 29, 1944. In Will Cuppy Papers, Box 96, Folder 24. Special Collections, University of Chicago.

———. Correspondence to Will Cuppy. August 7, 1944. In Will Cuppy Papers, Box 96, Folder 24. Special Collections, University of Chicago.

———. Correspondence to Will Cuppy. January 3, 1945. In Will Cuppy Papers, Box 96, Folder 24. Special Collections, University of Chicago.

———. Correspondence to Will Cuppy. September 26, 1949. In Will Cuppy Papers, Box 96, Folder 24. Special Collections, University of Chicago.

Sullivan, Frank. Correspondence to Will Cuppy. May 17, 1927. In Frank Sullivan Papers, Will Cuppy Folder. Manuscript Collection, Cornell University. Ithaca, New York.

———. Correspondence to Will Cuppy. Circa 1928. In Frank Sullivan Papers, Will Cuppy Folder. Manuscript Collection, Cornell University, Ithaca, New York.

———. Correspondence to Will Cuppy. Circa 1929. In Frank Sullivan Papers, Will Cuppy Folder. Manuscript Collection, Cornell University. Ithaca, New York.

———. Correspondence to Will Cuppy on *New York World* stationery. August 23, 1929. In Frank Sullivan Papers, Will Cuppy Folder. Manuscript Collection, Cornell University. Ithaca, New York.

———. Correspondence to Will Cuppy. September 23, 1929. In Frank Sullivan Papers, Will Cuppy Folder. Manuscript Collection, Cornell University. Ithaca, New York.

———. Correspondence to Will Cuppy. Post-dated "1930?" In Frank Sullivan Papers, Will Cuppy Folder, Manuscript Collection, Cornell University. Ithaca, New York.

———. Correspondence to Will Cuppy on *New Yorker* stationery, with the salutation, "Dear Cup." Early 1930s. In Frank Sullivan Papers, Will Cuppy Folder. Manuscript Collections, Cornell University. Ithaca, New York.

———. Correspondence to Will Cuppy on *New York World* stationery. Early 1930s. In Frank Sullivan Papers, Will Cuppy Folder. Manuscript Collection, Cornell University. Ithaca, New York.

———. Correspondence to Will Cuppy. May 16, 1933. In Will Cuppy Papers, Box 96, Folder 24, Frank Sullivan correspondence folder. Special Collections, University of Chicago.

———. Correspondence to Will Cuppy. November 1, 1934. In Frank Sullivan Papers, Will Cuppy Folder. Manuscript Collection, Cornell University. Ithaca, New York.

———. Correspondence to Will Cuppy. August 7, 1937. In Frank Sullivan Papers, Will Cuppy Folder. Manuscript Collection, Cornell University. Ithaca, New York.

Index

Numbers in **_bold italics_** indicate pages with photographs.

Adams, Franklin P. 91
Addams, Jane 27
Albee, Edward 138–139
Algonquin Round Table 90–91
Allen, Edward Frank 149
Allen, Woody 92, 101, 161, 173, 176, 183
American Splender 148
Animal Farm 174–176, 178, 181
Aristotle 36, 42, 112, 148, 152, 170, 183
Armour, Richard 5, 37
Audubon, John James 76
Author Today and Yesterday 48

Bankhead, Tallulah 114
Barrymore, John 34
Bauby, Jean-Dominque, "locked-in syndrome and" 90, 91–92
Becker, Mary Lamberton 19–20
Beebe, William 147–148, 152
Benchley, Marjorie (daughter-in-law) 161
Benchley, Nathaniel (son) 161–162
Benchley, Robert 41, ***44***, ***93***, 99, ***162***, ***178***; as Cuppy's favorite humorist 6, 42, 57; movies and 92, ***93***, 120–121; parallels between Cuppy and 43, 58–62, 110, 120–121, 161–162, 171, 173, 176–181; writing retirement of 92–93, 161
Bierce, Ambrose 89–90, 127–128, 129, 134, 137
The Big Sleep 124
Blair, Waiter 57
Bogart, Humphrey 124, 160
Bronx Zoo 39
Brooklyn Dodgers 80, 83
Brown, Joe E. 1
Buckley, Christopher 39

Bukowski, Charles 5–6, 20–21, 51
Burnett, W.R. 114

Carlin, George 160
Catch-22 14
Cavell, Stanley 76
Cedar, Joseph 6–7
Christie, Agatha 127, 128, 137
Cobb, Irvin S. 131, 132–134, ***133***, 137
Conan Doyle, Sir Arthur 127, 131–132
Connelly, Marc 91
Conrad, Joseph 160
Coolidge, Calvin 77
Coward, Noël 103, 105
Cuppy, Anna (sister) 17, 18, 19, 23, ***24***, 108
Cuppy, Frances Stahl (mother) 12, 13, 16, 17, 18, 19, 21, 23, 47, 168
Cuppy, Jack (brother) 18, 23
Cuppy, Martha (aunt) 15, 18, 108
Cuppy, Sarah Collins (grandma) 9, 10, 14–15, 16, 17, 18, 21, 22, 23, 29, 108, 138
Cuppy, Thomas Jefferson (father) 12, 13–14, 15, 16, 23, 47, 95, 108, 152, 159
Cuppy, Will ***22***, ***24***, ***76***, ***126***; alter ego 126, 145; anthologies and 114–115, 123–139, 150; antihero and 57–68, 79, 152, 161, 176, 177–178; birth 9, 163; coast guard and 53, 54, 57, 68–69, 71, 77, 78, 79, 126; column 41, 42, 53–54, 71, 86–87, 90, 92, 109, 110–115, 116, 123, 125, 155; comedy theory and 7, 41, 42, 53–54, 71, 86–87, 90, 92, 109, 110–115, 116, 123, 125; death of 123, 125, 154–157, 158–173, 183; film noir and 124–125, 128; footnotes and 34–35, 76–77,

211

81, 119–120, 131, 136–137, 140, 151, 152, 161, 165; *Golden Vanity* and 19, 48, 105–110, 115, 119, 137; Hate Cuppy movement and 23–24, 25, 58, 75, 103, 122, 126, 150, 155, 163; health and/or hypochondria and 16, 25, 46, 48–49, 117, 155, 161–162; Indiana and 2, 9–22, 34, 83, 89, 95, 136, 138, 165, 166–169; *Just Relax* radio program and 46, 102, 118; music and 18, 19, 20, 22, 86, 137, 142, 148–149; mystery and 37, 41, 53, 87, 111, 114, 124, 125, 129, 130, 131, 138, 171; research and 1, 2, 5, 7, 10, 15, 34, 91–92, 108, 150–151, 155, 163, 164, 183; sea shack of 20, 39, 45, 53–54, 58, 59, 61, 65, 69, 78, 79, 80, 109, 154, 176, 178; sexuality of 49–50, 64, 108–109, 176; speaking engagements by 120–121; suicide and 2, 46, 50, 62–63, 64, 68, 82, 86, 89, 90, 91, 92, 117, 118, 141, 143, 150, 135, 160, 165, 172, 182, 185; unfinished play of 18–19, 26, 32, 39, 47, 48, 53, 54, 64, 105, 107, 150, 161, 163; *see also* Benchley, Robert; Paterson, Isabel
Cuppy, William H. (uncle) 14, 15, 18

Darwin, Charles 36, 112, 126, 149
Day, Clarence 58
Dean, James 1, 160
Death of a Salesman 158, 159–160, 172, 181
The Decline and Fall of Practically Everybody 2, 5, 99, 117, 119, 121, 145, 150, 158, 182; best selling 163; biting style returns with 152–153; masterpiece implications of 14, 32, 152, 153; quotes from 14, 32, 152, 153; review of 163–166
Demprey, Jack 103–104
Dickens, Charles 78
Disney, Walt 81
Ditmars, Raymond 147, 148, 149
The Diving Bell and the Butterfly 90
Duck Soup ***84***, 85, 96

Earhart, Amelia 122
Eastman, Max 7
"The Elizabethan Conception of a Prose Style" 34
Emerson, Ralph Waldo 54, 55
Enjoyment of Laughter 7

Faulkner, William 127, 128, 129
Feldkamp, Fred 32, 34, 117, 145, 151, 163, 164, 165, 168, 171

Feldman, Marty 49
Fields, W.C. 1, 2, 3, 69, ***70***, 81
Film Classics Reclassified: A Shocking Spoof of Cinema 37
Fitzgerald, F. Scott 95, 110, 127, 135, 158
Footnote 6–7
Ford, Corey 94
Ford, John 68, 132
Franklin, Benjamin 57, 168, 171
Frederick, John Towner 16, 19, 23, 27, 29, 125, 146

Gable, Clark ***104***, 160
Garden Rubbish, and Other Country Bumps 119–120
Gibbs, Wolcott 117
"The Goldfish" 115–116
Goldman, William 103
The Great Bustard and Other People 145, 150
The Great Dictator 166, ***167***
Greenwich Village apartment 45, 82–83, 97, 118, 150, 155, 178
Griffith, Andy 57, 133

Ham on Rye 21
Hammett, Dashiell 124–125, 127, 128–129, 137
Harding, Warren G. 13, 56
Harrison, Henry 168
Hawks, Howard 103
Heart of Darkness 160
Heggen, Thomas 181–183
"Hell's Kitchen" 43–44
Hemingway, Ernest 83, 108, 153
Henry, O. 127
Herrick, Robert 27, 29–30
Herriman, George 51, 57
Hirschfeld, Al 179
Hitchcock, Alfred 128
Holbrook, Steward H. 136–137
Honeycutt, Ann 50
Horse Feathers ***11***, 85, 177
How to Attract the Wombat 2, 10, 158, 160, 163; insight to Cuppy from 150–154, 162; introduction to 117, 150; reviews 160–161, 162–163
How to Be a Hermit 2, 5, 9, 23, 25, 29, 89, 94, 96, 179; contrasting *How to Tell Your Friends from the Apes* with 80–88; parallels between *Apes* and 75–77; quotes from 30, 40–41, 58, 79; reviews 69–73, 147; *Walden* and 39, 53, 54–56, 62, 76, 79, 112; writing 53–74
How to Become Extinct 1, 2, 5, 23, 80, 81, 117, 143, ***144***, 156, 166, 175, 178; quotes

from 10, 36, 105–106, 110, 112, 149; radio PR for 62; reviews 12, 143, 146, 147, 148–149, 150
How to Get from January to December 2, 151, 158, 166–173, 176
How to Tell Your Friends from the Apes iv, 2, 6, 9, 89, 92, 96, 117, 135, 143, 145, 147; contrasting *How to Be a Hermit* with 80–88; parallels between *Hermit* and 75–77; quotes from 11, 20, 30, 35, 36, 38, 75, 76, 81, 105, 109; review 88
Hull House 28
Huxley, Aldous 40, 127

It Happened One Night 103, **104**

Jane Addams Hull House 27
Jones Beach Park 75, 77–79, 82
Just Relax (NBC radio) 46, 102, 118, 122

Kafka, Franz 14, 129
Kaufman, George S. 91
Keaton, Buster 176
Keillor, Garrison 55
Kendall, Paul Murray 38
Kimbrough, Emily 166
Knipfel, Jim 6, 102
Kovacs, Ernie 102
Krazy Kat 42, 51, 52, 56, 57, 58, 62, 175

LaCava, Gregory 103
LaGuardia, Fiorella 156–157
Lane, Anthony 9–10
Lardner, Ring 91, 172
Laurel & Hardy 1, 2, 3, 22, 58, **59**
Leacock, Stephen 131–132, 134–135, 137
Lennon, John 119
Letters of a Self-Made Diplomat to His President 60, 66
Levant, Oscar 5, 46, **73**–74, 89, 160
Lieb, Sandra 81
Lindbergh, Charles 67–68
Linn, James Weber 27, 28, 29, 30
Little Caesar 114
Long, Emily 39
Long, Michael David v
Lovett, Richard Morss 27–29

MacArthur, Charles 91
Maeder, Thomas 12, 39, 50, 64, 122, 163, 182
The Maltese Falcon 124
The Maroon Tales 29, 23–32, 37, 47, 75, 80
Marx, Groucho 1, 2, **11**, **84**; parallels between Cuppy and 11–12, 48, 83–85, 96, 103
Marx Bros. 1, 2, 11–12, 83–**84**, 85, 91, 96, 177
McCarey, Leo 22, 59, 103
McCartney, Paul 119
McKenna, Edward 72
McQueen, Steve 1
Mencken, H.L. 68, 111–1112, 180
Miller, Arthur 158, 159–160, 172, 181
Mr. Roberts 181–183
Morgan, Henry 118–119
Moses, Robert 77, 78–80, 82
Murder My Sweet 124
Murder Without Tears 123–139, 150, 179
Murrow, Edward R. 9

New York Public Library 39
New York Yankees 80, **170**

Orwell, George 6, 174–176, 178, 183

Palmer, C.B. 164, 165
Parker, Dorothy 41, 77, 91, 110
Paterson, Isabel 12–13, 16, **17**, **42**, 82, 96, 99, 100, 101, 102, **106**, 125, **146**, 163; connection between Cuppy and 40–52, 62–74, 94; Cuppy dedications to 38; *Golden Vanity* 19, 48, 105–110, 115, 118, 137; libertarianism and 28, 29, 46, 99, 109, 110, 143, 175; travel and 94, 95; "Turns with a Bookworm" and 40, 47, 92, 98, 110, 118, 121–122, 140–146, 175; vaudeville-like pattern between Cuppy and 40, 41, 43, 80, 106, 142, 176
Payne, Alexander 80
Pekar, Harvey Lawrence 158
Perelman, S.J. 9, 58, 83, 176–177
"The Pleisiosaur" 115–116
PM 149–150
Poe, Edgar Allan 135, 137
Poore, Charles 148–149, 169, 171
"The Pterodactyl" 115–116

Quitting the Nairobi Trio 6, 102

Radner, Gilda 63
Rand, Ayn 46, 143, 145, 146
Rascoe, Burton 16–**17**, 24–25, **26**, 32, 39–40, 51, 72, 86, 92
Remarque, Erich 96
Renoir, Jean 67–68
Road to Utopia 120
Robinson Crusoe 70–71
Rogers, Will 57, 58, 60, **66**–67, 132, **133**, 169

Rooney, Andy 77
Roosevelt, Franklin D. 28, 45, 85, 99
Rosenblatt, Roger 37
Ross, Harold 91, 117
Russell, Bill 39
Ruth, Babe *170*

Salinger, J.D. 172
Saroyan, William 100
Sayers, Dorothy L. 112, 113, 129–130
Schulberg, Bud 95, 96–98
Schultz, Charles 177
Segal, Erich 6
Seldes, Gilbert 42, 51–52
Seller, W.C. 119–120
Shapiro, Sidney 77, 78
Sinclair, Upton 30
Skelton, Red 1, 41
Slaughter-House Five 14
Smith, Thorne 97
Socrates 106
Stagg, Amos Alonzo 31–*33*, *35*
Steig, William 16, 93, 99–101, 115, 139, 153, 163, 164
Stein, Gertrude 41, 144, 153
Stewart, Donald 91
Sturges, Preston 103
Styron, William 172–173
Sullivan, Frank 48, 58, 73, 96–99, 101, 106, 107, 160–161, 162
Sweeney Todd 135

Swift, Jonathan 127, 174

The Thin Man 124
Thoreau, Henry David 39, 53, 54–56, 62, 75–76, 79, 112, 122
Thurber, James 9, 31–32, 50–51, 58, 67, 75, 85, 97, 108, 136, 137, 176–179
A Treasure of Laughter 115–116
Tunney, Gene 103–104, 140–141
Twain, Mark 22, 78, 130–131, 134

Untermeyer, Louis 115

Vonnegut, Kurt 96, 101–102

Walden 39, 53, 54–56, 62, 76, 79, 112
Wells, H.G. 137–138
White, E.B. 50, 163, 176, 178
Wilde, Oscar 103
Wilder, Thorton 142–143
Williams, Gluyas 99
Wise, Robert 1, 6
Wodehouse, P.G. 87–88, 129
Wolfe, Thomas 165
Woollcott, Alexander 86, 91, 114
World's Great Detective Stories 123–139, 150

Yates, Norris W. 115, 172, 176
Yeatman, R.J. 119

www.ingramcontent.com/pod-product-compliance
Lightning Source LLC
Chambersburg PA
CBHW032054300426
44116CB00007B/742